LABOR: *Free and Slave*

LABOR:

Free

AND

Slave

WORKINGMEN
AND THE ANTI-SLAVERY MOVEMENT
IN THE UNITED STATES

by

BERNARD MANDEL, *Ph.D.*

ASSOCIATED AUTHORS NEW YORK

The appearance of this book would have been impossible without the help of dozens of technicians and booklovers, who believe in the ASSOCIATED AUTHORS' *aim of getting into print worthwhile books that otherwise might not be published.* ASSOCIATED AUTHORS *would like to record here its gratitude for this invaluable assistance.*

Manufactured in the United States of America
by The Haddon Craftsmen, Inc.

To
My Parents

———

CONTENTS

Chapter

I. THE LABOR AND ABOLITION MOVEMENTS 11
The Birth of the Labor Movement
The Anti-Slavery Movement

II. IN THE LION'S DEN 28
Slavery and the Southern Workers
Anti-Slavery and the Southern Workers
Divide and Rule

III. NORTHERN LABOR CONSIDERS SLAVERY 61
Slavery and the Northern Workers, 1830-1845
Bread and Butter
Our Fair Escutcheon
"Chattel Slaves and Wage Slaves"
Lords of the Lash and Lords of the Loom

IV. THE SLAVE-POWER AND THE MUDSILLS 111
Land of the Free
The Slave-Power Conspiracy
Re-forming the Lines
Free Soil and Free Labor

V. "THE UPRISING OF A GREAT PEOPLE" 170
The Secession Crisis
Labor, Emancipation and the Civil War

VI. FRATERNITY IN FREEDOM 202
References 217
Acknowledgments 245
Index 247

LABOR: *Free and Slave*

CHAPTER I

THE LABOR AND
ABOLITION MOVEMENTS

The Birth of the Labor Movement

In the first half of the nineteenth century, the United States and Europe took gigantic strides forward in the transition from an agrarian to an industrial economy. Getting a late start on England, the industrial revolution in America was faced with many handicaps. The agrarian tradition of Jeffersonian democracy had impressed upon the American people a deep repugnance for industrialism and urban concentration. These, it was feared, would bring in their wake the disruption of widespread land ownership and the substitution of a propertyless proletariat for the "sturdy yeomen" population, thus threatening the economic basis of Jeffersonian democracy, to say nothing of the rule of the Southern planters.

Furthermore, the owners of capital hesitated long before making the decision to divert their funds from the lucrative fields of commerce and land speculation to the less familiar and more doubtfully profitable domains of manufacturing. And who would man these enterprises? Skilled labor was scarce, and the vast virgin valleys and plains to the West appeared to many as a great magnet to draw much of the potential laboring class from the East, and to leave the remainder in a position to demand impossible rewards for their work. Then, the stupendous, sprawling spaces of the young country, with its scattered small-scale farm units unconnected except by long, arduous and expensive routes

11

on rivers, seas and primitive roads, presented a serious impediment to the development of a national market and an integrated economic life. In any event, could an infant industry compete against British manufactures, which more than once threatened destruction to the early American factories? Finally, the development of industrial enterprise was thwarted by the institution of slavery, which placed limits on the growth of a unified national economy, kept its own section backward, and prevented the use of the central government for the erection of tariff barriers, the construction of internal improvements, the establishment of a national banking system, and similar measures for the protection and fostering of capital.

Gradually, however, and with accelerating tempo, most of these obstructions were overcome. The Napoleonic wars, the Embargo and the War of 1812 provided an opportunity for American businessmen to capture the home market and released a considerable amount of capital from the depressed carrying trade. Even Jefferson agreed in 1816 that manufacturing must become a national enterprise, for the sake of economic independence if nothing else. A fecund population and a swelling tide of immigrants provided hands for new textile establishments, forges and foundries, flour mills, shoe shops, paper mills and other enterprises, and increased the market for their products.[1] The country was knit together by a network of roads, canals and finally railroads, binding the Western and Southern markets to the manufacturing areas and furnishing a means for the amazing growth of the Middle West, inundated by floods of native and foreign immigrants.

Assisted by favorable corporation acts and internal improvements from state legislatures, industry was already exhibiting the tendencies toward concentration and centralization that were to be so marked after the Civil War. The total value of manufactures reached nearly two billion dollars on an investment of one billion by 1860, and American manufacturing advanced to fourth place in the world by the time of the Civil War.

One of the most important factors in the fashioning of this economic structure was the army of workers—men, women and children—recruited from the fields and towns of three continents. In the ante-bellum period it was common to use such terms as laborers and workingmen quite loosely, and they were often meant to include independent farmers and small businessmen. But it is necessary to define and describe more precisely what is now understood as the working class, namely, those whose principal income is derived from wages.

The pre-war census reports, as well as other sources of statistical information on the economic structure and the laboring population, are quite inadequate and often inexact, but they permit a number of reasonably accurate observations, particularly when evaluated with the help of detailed studies of various industries and regions. A fairly reliable picture of the composition and characteristics of the working class emerges from these data.[2]

In 1850, there were 1,288,000 mechanics, artisans and skilled laborers in the United States. We are not told what percentage of these were wage-earners, how many were self-employed or engaged in domestic manufactures, and what number were employers, but a closer view of the various crafts included in this category supplies helpful information. By the nature of their trades, mariners and railroaders were almost exclusively wage-earners; the former held fourth place among this class of workers, numbering 71,000, but the latter occupation, still in its infancy, came sixteenth with 5,000. At the other extreme were the blacksmiths, the third largest group with 100,000 craftsmen. The average number of blacksmiths per establishment, throughout the ante-bellum period and in all parts of the country, was two, and it may be taken as virtually certain that this was not only the average but the actual number for the great majority of such shops. If account is taken of the many one-man smithies and family or partnership enterprises, it is clear that only a small percentage of the blacksmiths were wage earners. In the other crafts the proportion of wage-earners ranged variously between these two extremes. Most numerous were the 185,000 carpenters, and it would seem that some three-fourths of them were employees. In the next largest group, about 150,000 shoemakers, nearly 90% were employed either by merchant capitalists or by manufacturers. On the whole it would appear reasonable to estimate that at least half of the mechanics, artisans and skilled laborers were wage-earners.

The rest of the wage-earning population is easier to identify. In 1850 there were only 11,000 "factory hands" reported,[3] and farm laborers were not included in the census. But there were 910,000 unskilled workers, 77,000 miners, and several hundred thousand servants, apprentices and laundresses. In all, then, the working class in 1850, not counting the families of workers, constituted about 10% of the whole population, or nearly 12% of the free population. (See Table.)

THE WORKING CLASS, 1850-1870

(All numbers given in thousands)

	1840	1850	1860				1870
			Total	North	South	% in N.	
No. of wage-earners		1700	3533	2734	799	77	7000
% of free pop.		−12%	13%	15%	10%		20%
No. of factory hands		11	87	79	8	90	428
No. of mechanics &c. (wage-earners)		600	865	690	175	80	1400
% of working class		35%	24%	25%	22%		20%
No. empl. in manuf'g	790	945	1311	1120	191	85	2054
% of free pop.	+5%	−5%	+5%	6%	+2%		+5%
% of working class		56%	37%	41%	24%		29%

By 1860, the wage-earning class numbered some 3,500,000,[4] but its relative size in the population had not materially increased.

However, the decade 1850-60 marked a very striking increase in the number of factory operatives to 87,000, of railroaders from 5,000 to 36,000, and of miners to 147,000, which gives evidence of the rapidly growing industrial economy and the rise of the manufacturing class. The distribution of industry is indicated by the fact that the wage-earning class in the South constituted less than 10% of the free population, whereas it was 15% of the Northern population and over 21% of the population of Massachusetts. The stimulus of the Civil War on industry is apparent from the fact that by 1870 the wage-earning population had increased to nearly 20% of the total, numbering over 7,000,000 in a population of 38,000,000. The number of factory workers had reached 428,000, nearly a 500% increase in one decade; and railroading had become the fourth largest occupation among skilled laborers, with 154,000 employees, a gain of over 400% since 1860.

When we turn to an examination of the manufacturing population, we find a steady increase from 790,000 in 1840 to over 2,000,-000 in 1870, and an equal number were employed in mining, transportation and trade in the latter year. Of the number in manufacturing in these years, 76-85% were in the Northern states, and 15-25% in New England alone. However, in spite of the increasing numbers of persons employed, manufacturing no more than held its own with respect to the growth of other branches of the economy, for the percentage of the total population engaged in manufactures hovered about the 5% mark from 1840 to 1870. The proportion of the Northern population employed in manufacturing likewise remained static at 6%; but while the figure for the South declined from 4% to 2% of the free population, it increased in the New England states from 8% to 11%.

In 1840, New England and the Southern states had an equal number of persons employed in manufactures (186,000 in each section), but by 1870 the former had outdistanced the latter, 527,-000 to 316,000. During the same period about 2% of the Western population was engaged in manufactures, and 7% of the Middle

Eastern states. Naturally, manufacturing was more concentrated in the cities: in the 102 largest cities in the country, over 11% of the population was in manufacturing, and in some cities like Philadelphia and Cincinnati the percentage reached above 17%.

The various industries and regions were, of course, unequally affected by mechanization, concentration, and the trend toward factory organization.[5] For example, carpentering, which employed the largest number of workers of any trade, averaged five laborers per establishment in Ohio and ten in Mississippi in 1860, with little change in the ensuing decade, although there was a 42% increase in the number of persons employed in the craft. Nor was there any substantial increase in the annual average product per worker. Blacksmithing presented similar features: the average number of workers per establishment remained at 2, while the total number in the craft more than trebled between 1860 and 1870, and the average annual product per worker remained fairly steady at $600 to $700 in various parts of the country. In these two trades, then, there was little concentration, centralization, or mechanization.

In some of the other leading industries, however, there was not only growth but marked trends toward concentration and mechanization. The textile industry was the second largest with reference to size of the labor force, which increased from 96,000 in 1840 to 132,000 in 1850 to 156,000 in 1860. In the same years the average number of workers per establishment grew from 18 to 70 and the average annual product per worker from $600 to $1000. The cotton mills were the largest in the textile field, and in fact among all industries: in 1860 the Northern establishments averaged 140 workers, and in Massachusetts 250, while a few employed as many as 1000 operatives. The boot and shoe industry presented characteristics which were common to a number of other leading manufactures. The number of workers in the industry increased from 105,000 to 136,000 between 1850 and 1870, while the capital invested nearly quadrupled ($13 million to $49

million), the annual product was more than trebled ($54 million
to $182 million), and the annual average product per worker rose
from $500 to $1300. This rapid growth of productivity reflected the
introduction of machinery and factory methods of organization,
which began in the 1840's,[6] but the average number of workers
per establishment actually decreased during these two decades
from 10 to less than 6. This was a result of the large number of
new enterprises which were started on a small scale even while
others were growing in size, thus reducing the average. Similar
phenomena are noted in the clothing, iron, carriage, and tobacco
industries. The data for these industries, as well as for carpentering and blacksmithing, give some indication of the number of
people, undoubtedly skilled laborers for the most part, who were
establishing new enterprises and thus becoming small businessmen, even while the total size of the wage-earning class was
increasing. In all branches of industry, 129,000 new establishments
were begun between 1850 and 1870.

The conditions of labor in the first half of the nineteenth century impelled the workers to remedial action. One of the most
persistent complaints of labor throughout this period, and one of
the most common causes of strikes, was the length of the working
day, which averaged twelve to fourteen hours for nearly all
workers in the ante-bellum period. Many of those engaged in
manufacturing performed their work in poorly lighted, unventi-
lated buildings, under a regime of severe discipline. The wages
for this work were often barely sufficient for survival, even when
the entire family was employed, and even part of this pittance
was sometimes filched by means of scrip payments and irregularities permitted by the absence of lien laws. In 1851, when wages
were relatively high for the pre-war period, Horace Greeley
published a weekly budget for a working-class family of five
which, including only the most essential items, carefully planned
and frugally expended, required $10.37. But in that same year
Pennsylvania coal miners were getting $6.96 a week; New York

carpenters $12.00; foremen in a Massachusetts cotton mill $12.00
and blacksmiths in a New York machine shop but $9.78.[7]

As a result, many workers were forced to crowd into wretche
hovels, and the slum made its appearance as a regular part o
the American city. Furthermore, the vicissitudes of illness, injur
age and business depressions imposed a tremendous burden o
insecurity and destitution. Among the skilled laborers, thes
conditions were somewhat mitigated, but it was precisely amon
them that the early unions were formed. David J. Saposs ha
concluded that the only motive of this group for organizing wa
to protect their status and their standards as skilled mechanic
It was precisely those who had the best chance of becoming bus
nessmen who formed the first unions: printers, shoemakers, tai
ors, carpenters and so forth. On the other hand there was littl
or no organization among the unskilled workers and factor
operatives. This is explained by the general rise in their wage
while the wages of the skilled mechanics were kept down by th
merchant capitalists, remaining stationary or even declining. "
was the desire to resist this pressure upon their standards of li
that actuated the skilled workers to band themselves together."

But the complaint was universal among all strata of the toilin
population that low wages, long hours and irregularity of en
ployment were reducing them to the edge of poverty. Facto
workers and unskilled laborers, although they did not organiz
like the skilled craftsmen, did conduct strikes, and nearly all c
them were on the issues of wages and hours.

As early as the last decade of the eighteenth century, skille
journeymen in various cities organized the first trade unions i
this country, working mainly for higher wages, shorter hou
and job security. In the 1820's a widespread movement for th
ten-hour day sprang up, out of which arose the first city-wic
federation of labor organizations, the Mechanics' Union
Trade Associations of Philadelphia, and later the New Englar
Association of Farmers, Mechanics, and Other Workingme
These organizations heralded the birth of the modern lab

movement. Seth Luther, leader of the New England workers, animated the young labor movement with the spirit of struggle in defense of its rights which were, he said, "not only endangered, but some of them already wrested from us by the powerful and inhuman grasp of monopolized wealth."[9] By 1860 a number of crafts had organized nation-wide unions, and there had even been an effort to form a national federation of trade unions. Most of these organizations did not last very long, being swept away by recurring economic crises, crippled by the courts, and diverted by reformist leaders. But at times they reached dimensions that were not surpassed, proportionately, until nearly a century later. In the middle 1830's the *Workingmen's Advocate* estimated that at least two thirds of the workers in the largest cities were members of unions,[10] and *The National Laborer* estimated the total union membership in 1836 at 300,000.[11] If this figure was approximately accurate, it would mean that about 20% of the working class was organized, and about 60% of the mechanics and skilled laborers. In 1854, when unionism reached another peak, total membership was estimated at 200,000 which would have been 7% of all workers and 25% of skilled laborers.[12] These unions won many improvements for their members, and taught them the value, indeed the necessity, of cooperative action to raise their living standards.

At the same time, many working people were arriving at the conclusion that if the ideals of the American Revolution were to be achieved, they would have to organize for political action as well. Various political parties and associations were formed to work for the establishment of public schools, the abolition of imprisonment for debt, abolition of contract convict labor, opposition to monopolies, land reform and the extension of democracy. Many outstanding achievements were secured by these movements during their short life. For the most part, however, in the thirty years before the Civil War, American labor tried to achieve its redemption through the major political parties.

A large number of workers were also attracted to various reform

movements, the most important of which were the Utopian social
ist schemes and the land reform movement. America had been a
fertile field for communitarian experiments since the seventeenth
century, but most of them had been of a religious character, and
usually their communal aspects were a result of expediency rather
than principle. But the early nineteenth century brought forth a
number of plans for the regeneration of society through the for
mation of cooperative societies which, by example and radiation
should eventually encompass all of society. These experiments or
iginated for the most part in Europe and were either brought to
America by their founders, like Robert Owen, Frances Wright
Wilhelm Weitling, Etienne Cabet and Victor Considerant, o
propagated in this country by converts, as Horace Greeley pro
claimed the virtues of Fourierism through the *Tribune*. In some
cases, they were native products, most notably the Transcendenta
communities at Fruitlands and Brook Farm. While such utopia
never actually involved a significant number of workers, th
propagation of their ideas and the influence of their leaders playe
an important part in developing an anti-capitalist orientatio
among the workers.

Also, most of the Utopian programs were connected with lan
reform, which won the support of large sections of the labor move
ment. The American people had always been dazzled by th
prospects of unlimited land, "with room enough for our descend
ants to the thousandth and thousandth generation." When th
consequences of an encroaching industrialism revealed themselve
it was natural for the workers, as well as the farmers and th
lower middle class, to look to unoccupied land for their salvatio
from loss of status, degradation of living standards and depressio
into the ranks of a permanent proletariat. But in spite of th
employers' fear that the West would drain off their workin
force, and in spite of constant liberalization of the land laws fror
1787 to 1841, it was apparent to those who actually proposed t
emigrate that the injunction to go West was not so easily accom

olished. There were numerous difficulties, above all, the pro-
hibitive cost of the initial investment. The land reformers, led by
George Henry Evans, proclaimed that the workers were in thrall
to the capitalists who engrossed the land, and demanded that the
right to the soil be recognized by the free grant of inalienable
homesteads to all actual settlers. This movement, while achieving
partial victory only with the passage of the Homestead Act of
1862, was instrumental in molding the social philosophy of many
wage-earners, in determining their attitude toward the Southern
politicians who resisted land reform, and in helping to pave the
way for the Free Soil and Republican parties.

Finally, there was a small element in the late ante-bellum labor
movement, largely of German origin, which accepted the principles of scientific socialism as enunciated by Marx and Engels in
the *Communist Manifesto* of 1848. This group attempted to influence the working class to adopt a policy of militant, united struggle for economic improvements and to organize politically for
the achievement of a workers' government and a socialist system.

While the American labor movement in some respects developed along the same lines as in Europe, there were also some striking differences. Although class lines were well established by the
1850's, they had not yet become fixed, and the individuals within
each class were constantly changing. There was still considerable
opportunity to rise out of the laboring class and to become a small
farmer, shopkeeper or manufacturer, because of the rapid expansion of the American economy. Consequently, it can hardly
be said that the working class had achieved an independent position: class-conscious as it was in so far as economic struggles
were concerned, it still followed in the train of the middle class
politically and ideologically. The revolutionary working-class
movement of 1848 in Europe had no counterpart in the United
States.

Two other factors were also responsible for this circumstance.
The American laboring class was probably the most heterogene-

ous in the world, being separated into native and foreign-born
constituents, and the latter sub-divided into a dozen or more
nationalities. Language barriers, national and religious prejudices
and economic stratification along nationality lines, reinforced by
the divisive policy of employers and politicians, were obstacles
to mutual understanding and to united economic and political
organization.

But the most decisive factor in disfiguring the American labor
movement was the existence in the Southern states of the institu
tion of chattel slavery.

The Anti-Slavery Movement

Not only the workers but all segments of the American people
were profoundly affected by the existence and dynamics of the
slave system, developing in juxtaposition to the emerging capi
talist economy of the North. The overthrow of slavery was accom
plished by certain of these groups against the resistance of others
and the role of each was determined by its position in the comple
relationship of social and economic forces that operated in nine
teenth century America. The anti-slavery movement, therefore
can be understood and evaluated only by analyzing these socio
economic factors, their effect on the material conditions and ide
ology of the various classes, and the resulting actions of these
people.

The only elements with a direct material stake in the preserva
tion of slavery were the slaveholders themselves and their depend
ents and associates. This latter group consisted of Northern mer
chants, bankers and cotton manufacturers who had business ties
with the South, and Democratic politicians with party connec
tions; the Southern politicians, lawyers, ministers and teacher
whose positions were dependent on the sufferance of the planters
overseers, police and others who constituted the apparatus o

pression; and those who had aspirations to enter the slavehold-
ng class. Every other stratum of the American population was at
ast a potential anti-slavery force.

Unquestionably the most persistent, thorough and effective
nti-slavery force in the nation was the slaves themselves. For
aree hundred years they resisted bondage and exploitation by
very means that ingenuity and courage could devise.[13] They fre-
uently took advantage of their masters' concern for the "operat-
ng efficiency" of their human machines by feigning illness, and
ousands of slaves assured their permanent incapacity by muti-
ating themselves, hacking off the fingers and hands that produced
rofit for their owners and unending drudgery for themselves.
[any slaves took their own lives rather than doling them
ut piecemeal, and mothers destroyed their babies at birth rather
aan sacrificing them to the auction block and the lash. A com-
on complaint of the slaveholders was the ceaseless, undetectable
nd varied forms of sabotage by which the slaves snatched pre-
ous minutes of their lives and silently registered their protest
gainst bondage: an imperceptible slowing up of their work, the
estruction of tools, implements and crops, the burning of barns
nd houses, the theft of property. Even the religion which was
iven to them by their masters in order to teach them humility,
ocility and obedience, was ingeniously turned into a means of
pressing their yearning for freedom. Their religious songs
ere full of double meanings; they sang about the children of
rael in Egypt and their liberator Moses, but what thoughts and
pes must have filled their hearts as they chanted the pregnant
frain, "Let my people go"? In their silent prayers, they appealed
their Lord in Heaven to save them from the oppression of their
rds on earth. Many, through hope and prayer, began their
est for a way of escape.

Perhaps the most effective form of resistance to slavery was
ght. Tens of thousands of men, women and children made the
ash for freedom, hiding in swamps and forests by day, moving

by night toward the North Star, with patrols and bloodhound
on their heels. Many were aided by the engineers of the Unde
ground Railroad—white and Negro men and women who guide
the fugitives, harbored them and passed them from station t
station. These conspirators against slavery rescued some sevent
five thousand slaves, and the boldest of them, like Harriet Tul
man, herself a fugitive, went into the South to snatch the slave
from the plantations under the very nose of the masters and ove
seers. Thousands of other slaves fought for their liberation b
rising in revolt. A few of the most extensive of these revolts an
their leaders are well known—Nat Turner, Gabriel, Denmar
Vesey—but there were hundreds of smaller risings and attempte
rebellions, enough of them to require the conversion of the Sout
into an armed camp and to cause slaveholders to sleep wit
revolvers under their pillows. In the 1850's the resistance of th
slaves mounted, and during the Civil War many seized th
opportunity to overthrow their oppressors as soldiers in the Unic
armies of liberation.

The vast majority of Southern nonslaveholding whites—farn
ers, mechanics and "poor whites"—also had a material interest i
the demise of slavery, which subjected them to a crushing an
demoralizing economic competition, saddled them with pover
and ignorance, and deprived them of their democratic right
Although many of the most alert and ambitious of them em
grated from the South, and although the rest were restricted i
the exercise of political rights and were confused, frightened an
divided by a devastating torrent of racial prejudice, the slavocra
was nevertheless in constant fear of the "great upbearing of ou
masses."[14]

The Northern anti-slavery movement, on the other hand, w
clearly capitalistic in its ideology and leadership. The ascendan
which that class had achieved in the American Revolution w
not complete, being shared with the Southern planters. As lor
as there was a fairly equal balance between the sections, as lor

there were no decisive points of conflict in national policy, as
ong as slavery appeared to be "in the course of ultimate extinc-
on," and especially until the time when industrial capitalism
ad reached maturity and had drawn the entire economy of the
Forth within its orbit, the capitalist class was willing to abide
is marriage of convenience. But with the progress of industrial-
m, the domain of capital surpassed the slave states in size, popu-
tion, wealth, energy and culture, and the capitalist class was no
onger content with its role of partner. In fact, it had become
rtually a junior partner, as the Northern allies of the planters
ad permitted the latter to fasten their control over the executive
ad judicial branches of the federal government. It was even in
anger of becoming a silent partner when, in the face of threat-
ing crisis, the South demanded additional security for its
culiar institution, including the suppression of free speech
roughout the nation and in Congress, censorship of the mails,
rict enforcement of the fugitive slave law, conquest of new
nds for the expansion of slavery, and unlimited freedom for
avery in the national territories. Gaining one position after an-
her by the threat of secession, the slavocracy had reached the
int where the North must either abdicate or make a stand
ainst the "aggressions of the slave power." The contest for
ntrol of the national goverment began with the struggle for
e territories.

People do not often speak publicly of ambition for mastery,
rticularly when the support of others is needed to gain it, and
was easy to place the moral issues in the foreground—and
oral issues were certainly involved. So the air and the press
ere filled with talk about the conflict between free labor and
ondage, humanity and barbarism, democracy and aristocracy,
ogress and decadence, virtue and sin. To many people these
emed to be the main points of contention, and to some they
ere everything. The abolitionists appealed to the conscience of
e world, reminding it of the Sermon on the Mount and the

Declaration of Independence. They won many converts, and made
many more uneasy with their embarrassing demands on the
application of Christian principles and democratic professions to
the solution of the irrepressible conflict. But many merchants and
politicians did not like this kind of talk, or the freeing of fugitive
slaves by mass action. That was not the way to do things. Southern
customers would cancel their orders, party associates would
withdraw their support, the South might even secede; besides
this unhealthy disrespect for property rights and legality could
become a dangerous business. Freedom must be defended, they
agreed, but defended legally and peacefully.

The farmers, the large majority of the Northern population,
had no organization of their own, nor did they have an independent position on the major political and social questions of the
day, being dominated by the lower middle class viewpoint and
bound to the industrial East by economic ties. But their strong
attachment to democracy, and their special concern for the exclusion of slavery from the territories—which they looked upon as a
domain reserved for their enjoyment and a guarantee of the
future prosperity—gave a tremendous fillip to the anti-slavery
movement, the struggle for non-extension, and the organization
of the Free Soil and Republican parties. The agrarian Northwest,
in fact, was a decisive force in the electoral victory of 1860 and
the successful conclusion of the war.

Finally, we return to the special subject of our study, the laboring class, whose interests demanded the abolition of slavery and
the overthrow of the slave power as a condition for its future
advancement. The growth of a vigorous labor movement in the
North was impeded by the restrictions placed on industrial progress by the slave system; the formation of a united national movement was virtually impossible while the Southern workers were
few in number and unable to organize effectively; and the "labor
question" could never be resolved so long as the nation was torn
by the slavery controversy and part of the republic was deformed

y an antiquated social system. Furthermore, the advancement
f labor was jeopardized by the slaveholders' attack on civil liber-
ies and the threat to extend slavery to the territories. It was plain
o many that "American slavery . . . must be uprooted and over-
hrown before that elevation sought by the laboring classes, can
e effected."[15] The majority of the workers, however, probably
id not attain such a clear understanding of the issue at least until
he time of the Civil War. Still in its infancy and tied to the lead-
ng strings of the middle class, the labor movement was unable to
lay a decisive independent role in the political life of the nation.
ut it did exercise some influence on the course of events, getting
 good education in the process, and emerging from the Civil
Var in a better position to work for the advancement of labor,
hich then included four million ex-slaves. This is the story that is
old in the following pages.

CHAPTER II

IN THE LION'S DEN

_____

Slavery and the Southern Workers

The blighting effects of slavery were much greater on the Southern workers than on wage-earners in the North. If the Northern labor movement was in its infancy, that of the South was hardly more than an embryo. The bulk of the labor force was the slaves, who in 1850 numbered three and a half million, more than four times the number of white workers in the Southern states. The number of factory workers was infinitesimal before the Civil War, and only 24 per cent of the free laborers were employed in manufacturing in 1860, as compared with 41 per cent in the North. Because the available wealth was invested in land and slaves rather than in industry, a relatively high percentage of the Southern workers were farm laborers. Among the mechanics and artisans, only a handful of trade unions was formed because of the small number of such workers (175,000 in 1860) their dispersion, and the opposition of employers and slaveholders. Furthermore, many could find no steady employment at all; they were occupied seasonally or when they could pick up a job or grubbed out a meager existence in the wastelands. A Southern political economist had observed as early as 1820 that the propertyless white class in the South was in "a deplorable state of degradation" because of slavery. The workingmen, he stated, were reduced to the level of the slaves and regarded as an inferior order of beings.[1]

Cassius M. Clay, cousin of Senator Henry Clay and one of the leading Southern abolitionists, constantly drove home the lesson at a mechanic in the South could not make a go of it because the local market was continually evaporating through the process of engrossing the land, driving out the small farmers, and replacing them with slaves, who were not very good customers. The mechanic could not sell his products in the open market because of the undeveloped transportation facilities and his inability to compete with Northern manufacturers; nor could he find employment elsewhere, for all trades were in the same condition. There was nothing left for him and his children but to move away or die. The tendency of slavery, Clay concluded, was "to destroy every free white laborer, or reduce him to the physical necessity and mental subservience of the black slave! The state loses all her middle class; effeminate aristocracy ensues on the one hand, and abject slavery on the other. *This is barbarism!*"[2] Repeatedly the complaint was made that slavery was reducing the working population to a state of physical debility, moral decay and hopeless idleness, which must inevitably lead them to complete degradation or desperate revolt.[3] A policy of industrialization as the only means to avoid these results was often urged by manufacturers like William Gregg and political leaders like Governor Hammond of South Carolina, but their pleas met with slight response.[4]

It was generally recognized that the economic backwardness of the area was inherent in the slave system, and one of the most frequently recurring themes in the literature was the lament over Southern stagnation as compared with Northern progress. During the Virginia convention of 1831-32, Thomas Marshall made a speech on the abolition of slavery which was frequently quoted by anti-slavery men in both the North and South for many years to come. Stating that he had no objection to slavery on moral grounds or because it was bad for the slaves, he averred that it was ruinous to the whites, drove out the yeomen and craftsmen, deprived the workmen of employment, made labor disreputable, and crushed incentive. He noted the impoverishment of Virginia, a state which, if cultivated by free labor, would sustain a dense

population of honorable laborers, and the " 'busy hum of me
would tell that all were happy, and that all were free."[5]

This was the dream of the Southern middle-class farmers ar
manufacturers and those who aspired to that station: to develc
an industrial society with "busy men" working for them. Th
complaint was often expressed that white workers, under the i
fluence of slavery, adopted the careless habits of the slaves ar
were even more indifferent than the slaves to the interests
their employers,[6] whereas the laboring class of the free states w
"incomparably more industrious, more thriving, more c
derly. . . . "[7] There was a still greater advantage to free lab
for employers: it did more work, with greater skill and less wast
and some thought that it was cheaper than slave labor because
received the same subsistence as slave labor and did not have
be maintained in illness and old age.[8] Many slaveholders reco
nized these facts but were unwilling to encourage a policy th
would strengthen the industrial classes, especially if that cou
be done only by abolishing slavery. But the incipient Southe
capitalist class was restless over the "stand-still" policy of slaver
which "dampened the spirit of enterprise"; it desired to emula
the motto of the rising Northern bourgeoisie: "Forward, alwa
forward."[9]

The institution of slavery was an instrument for the oppressi
not only of the bondsmen, but also of the wage-earners. The Ne
port, Kentucky, *Watchman* perceived this fact when it observe
although with some exaggeration, that the "wealthy men encou
age slavery more for the purpose of making profits out of t
white men, who work hard to be decent livers, than they do f
the profits received from the black slave."[10]

The most frequent and direct contact between the Southe
workers and the slaves was in the labor market, where they m
as competitors, if a situation in which one party had all the disa

ntages might fairly be called competition. Since the number of
nite laborers was generally small outside a few towns, the price
 wage labor was determined by the price of slave labor, which
as less than the minimum necessary to maintain the worker and
s family (for the slave did not have that responsibility). Conse-
uently, the wages of the workmen constantly tended to fall to
e level of the price commanded for the hire of slaves, and prob-
ly reached that point most of the time.[11] C. M. Clay aptly
mpared this situation with the competition offered by convict
oor, against which the mechanics had petitioned the legislature
 Kentucky, and concluded that only emancipation of the slaves
ould prevent them from continuing to underbid the free work-
gmen.[12]

Not only did the laborers have to meet the price of slave labor,
it they also had to produce as much as slaves to hold their own
 the struggle for existence, and consequently had to deliver a
ng day's labor. The ten-hour movement never achieved the
mensions that it did in the North, and had little possibility of
ccess in those circumstances. When the journeymen bricklayers
 Louisville were struggling for the ten-hour system, they met
 insuperable obstacle in the fact that they were replaceable by
aves, so they had to work as many hours as the slaves or abandon
eir trade. The stonecutters were able to win the ten-hour day
cause no slaves were employed in that occupation. But when
e carpenters and painters called a strike for shorter hours, it
as broken by the employment of slaves on their jobs; some strik-
s went back to work on the old terms, and others, disgusted
d demoralized, emigrated from the state. Thus "slavery tri-
mphed over freemen."[13]

Even when they reduced their standards to those of the slaves,
e mechanics of "Egyptland" could not always win jobs from
em, and found it increasingly difficult to do so as the years
ore on, for there were many reasons why the slave was given
eferential employment. In the self-sufficient economy of the

plantations there was no place for hired labor. The master had
find employment for his slaves throughout the year, for an id
slave was an unprofitable and a dangerous one, and there we
generally some who were physically incapable of the gruelli
field tasks. Such men were often trained as skilled craftsme
carpenters, blacksmiths, wheelwrights, bricklayers. General M
rion had called attention to this situation long before when
noted that "the people of Carolina form two classes—the rich a
the poor. The poor are generally very poor, because, *not bei*
necessary to the rich, who have slaves to do all their work, th
get no employment from them."[14]

This situation was not confined to the plantation but ove
flowed into the neighboring towns. It was quite common for t
masters to hire out their mechanic chattels when they were n
needed "at home," and they could afford to do so at very lc
rates. In some cases they were almost exclusively employed el
where, even being allowed to contract for their own hire, as you
Frederick Douglass did on the Baltimore waterfront, to the pe
of the white men's jobs and his own skin. The "wages," of cour
went to the owner of the laborer, not to the laborer. This pract
became a specialized business, as some men with capital boug
up gangs of slaves, qualified them as craftsmen, and let them o
to farmers, inn-keepers, and others who found it cheaper to j
than to buy slaves.[15] Another device by which slave artisans we
acquired at the expense of free labor was illustrated by the sto
of a Long Island carpenter who had moved to the South a
was asked for an estimate on a job. His prospective employ
demurred at the price, "and remarked that *he could do better*
buy a carpenter, let him do the work and sell him again when
was done. The free carpenter, being a man of sense, packed
his tools and returned to New York, where a rich man cannot b
a carpenter and sell him again. . . . "[16]

Even the State of Louisiana, not content with being the inst
ment for the rule of the slavocracy, became a slaveholder itself a

ngaged in the business of displacing day laborers with slaves.
The planters in the legislature concluded that the latter were
heaper than the former for relatively skilled labor as well as for
ield work, and the Senate Committee made the following esti-
nate of their relative cost for the construction of levees, canals
nd roads:

FREE LABOR

300 whites, at $30 per month	$108,000
Provisions	18,000
6 superintendents, at $1,000	6,000
	132,000

SLAVE LABOR

300 slaves, valued at $1,000 each ($300,000)	
Interest on investment, at 5%	15,000
Provisions and clothes	16,500
Loss by death	15,000
6 superintendents	6,000
Food for superintendents	360
	52,860
Balance in favor of slave labor	79,140

Consequently, in 1853, Louisiana abandoned the system of hir-
g free labor and purchased one hundred slaves. When they
ere sold in 1860 (those not included in "loss by death"), the
ate had made a considerable profit, the planters had benefited
y the improvements, the slaves were richer by so many worn
odies and broken bones, and an equivalent number of workers
d to search elsewhere for employment at slave-labor stand-
ds.[17]

The employment of the white workers in factories was consid-
ed by some to be the last refuge of hope for their salvation, but
en that possibility was threatened by the same curse of crushing
mpetition that drove them from other fields. One writer referred

to slave labor as "the best and cheapest factory labor in th
world,"[18] and his judgment was vindicated by the calculation
and experiences of numerous practical businessmen. At th
Saluda cotton mills near Columbia, South Carolina, the supe
intendent employed 128 slave operatives, most of whom we
discarded from the fields as not sufficiently strong to work ther
After two years of experimentation, he concluded that the diffe
ence in labor costs was over 30 per cent in favor of slave labo
In some cases, the rising cost of slaves in the 1850's forced en
ployers to give up slave labor in their factories in favor of fr
white labor,[19] but the most common experience throughout th
South was that slave labor was considerably cheaper than fr
labor.[20] One planter observed that a slave could be supported f
$20 a year, whereas a free laborer required $100 for food an
clothing alone, besides the "irregularities" incident to all labo
such as illness, rent, "useless mouths" of children to be fed, occ
sional relaxation, and dissipations. Laborers living in such "style
he said, could not hope to compete with slaves for employment.

Throughout the 1840's and '50's there was a growing tenden
to replace white workers with slave labor in many branches
employment. The principal reason for this was, as has been in
cated, the cheaper cost of the latter. Slaves were also common
preferred because their employment assured a steady labor for
without the hazards of "fluctuations," for they could neith
quit nor strike nor organize unions. As the London *Times* e
pressed it, "The real foundation of slavery in the Southern stat
lies in the power of obtaining labor at will at a rate which cann
be controlled by any combination of labourers." When a sug
planter experimented with the employment of a hundred Iri
and German laborers who went on strike in the middle of t
grinding season at a loss to him of $10,000, the lesson was not l
upon his confreres. The New Orleans *Crescent* commented su
cinctly that " 'the dragon of democracy,' the productive labori
element, having its teeth drawn, [is] robbed of its ability to

harm by being in a state of bondage."[22] Moreover, slaves could be subjected to a degree of control and discipline that free men would not tolerate. A number of people expressed to Olmsted the thought that, as a Virginia planter put it, "You never could depend on white men, and you couldn't *drive* them any; they wouldn't stand it. Slaves were the only reliable laborers—you could command them and make them do what was right." He believed that for this reason white workers could never compete with the slaves.[23]

There were several other inducements to the preferential employment of slaves. It seems to have gradually become more fashionable and respectable in Southern society to prefer slaves as a badge of "belonging" to the upper crust. It was also felt that the employment of white men in duties that were ordinarily performed by the slaves was humiliating not only to the employee but to his employer as well.[24] Besides, the slaveowner was able to use the weight of prestige, social influence and political power to get jobs for his "hands," and could make it easier by offering accommodating terms for their hire.[25] There was one exception to the rule: on dangerous jobs, the slaveholder wanted protection from the premature liquidation of his investment. One planter explained the employment of Irishmen on a dangerous job with the remark that "It's dangerous work, and a negro's life is too valuable to be risked at it. If a negro dies, it's a considerable loss, you know." And in unloading cotton bales, the slaves often worked on deck while Irishmen stopped the bales as they slid into the wharf. "The n—s are worth too much to be risked here; if the Paddies are knocked overboard, or get their backs broke, nobody loses anything."[26] These Irish workmen were literally "fall guys" for the slaveowners!

Little wonder that complaints were increasingly voiced against the encroachment of slave labor upon domains that had formerly been reserved by wage-earners. A Virginian wrote despairingly that, whereas young men could once find ready employment on the farms, they could no longer secure it at half the wages, because "Slavery is doing the labor on the rich lands of the Valley, and the sturdy young free white man must now learn a trade . . . or leave the country and his friends." And in Mississippi it was observed that white mechanics, unable to provide their families with the necessities of life, had to stand by while the available jobs were given to slaves.[27] A Montgomery, Alabama, mechanic commented bitterly on the competition of slave labor, which, "like the encroachments of Pharaoh's plagues, . . . has extended its conquest throughout the land, and consumes all the sources of the poor man's living. It has hunted the ingenious mechanic from town to town and from shop to shop. . . . " He asserted that the mechanics had often held secret meetings to discuss the problem. Some of them even suggested incendiarism and open rebellion, which betrayed the "extreme opposition that is now rising in every sensible mechanic's mind against the damnable pest which brings poverty to each of their homes."[28]

White laborers also came into competition with free Negro mechanics, whose wages were lower than the average and who were victims of a vicious fear and prejudice. While the oppressed status of the free Negroes increased the difficulties of the white workers, they themselves were sufferers from a triple band of exploitation which made their condition little better than that of the slaves, if any. They were subjected not only to the usual exploitation of the working men, increased by the competition with slave labor, but in addition were victimized by the hatred which fell to them as belonging to an oppressed race. When the wages of white carpenters were $1.56 a day, Negroes received no more than $1.25, because of the determination of the employer to mark the distinction between the status of the white and Negro artisan.[29] Furthermore, the free Negroes were discriminated against in the granting of employment, and in the 1840's and '50 they were virtually driven from many of the fields they had occupied previously.[30]

In addition to economic exploitation and social pressures, the free Negroes were also feared as a constant source of disturbance to the slaves, and their very presence, especially if they prospered in their trades, was considered a dangerous influence on the slaves. As a result of these circumstances, the free Negro population was subjected to a campaign designed to drive them out of the South, by restrictions on their movement and employment, heavy taxes, and prohibitions on their immigration. Thus the Negro working men were placed in a status between that of the white workers and the slaves, suffering from the competition of both, while the division between the three groups made it possible to increase the exploitation of all of them.[31]

The unequal competition between slavery and free labor not only tended to reduce the material standards of the latter to the level of the former, but, as a result, inevitably degraded it to the same social level. Performing work that was associated with slavery, on virtually the same terms as the slave, the free man suffered a loss of dignity and respect even in his own eyes. Manual labor in itself became a badge of servility, branding its executor with the stain of the auction block and stigmatizing him with the loss of caste. This was the unanimous observation both of the enemies of slavery who viewed it as one of the most damning accusations against the system, and of upholders of the institution who recoiled from its contaminating influence on the "master race." Scarcely one of the hundreds of Northern and European travelers in the South failed to take note of this phenomenon, like the Englishman who remarked:

When a person is accustomed from early youth to see every description of work performed by slaves, and by slaves of a different color from himself, he imbibes an opinion which is not to be wondered at, that labor is derogatory to a free white man. When he is taught in addition to this, to consider the blacks as an inferior race to the whites, he acquires not only the greatest reluctance to work, but habits of indolence from which he seldom recovers.[32]

Many slaveholders corroborated this assertion, William Byrd having stated as early as 1736 that slavery made the whites proud and disdainful of work because doing work that was usually performed by slaves made them look like slaves.[33] It was a constant complaint of the poor whites themselves,[34] and received a sharp indictment from Helper. He stated that in the South no kind of labor was either free or respectable, and that every workingman was treated like a "loathsome beast, and shunned with the utmost disdain." Any man who owned no slaves was a slave himself, and "would be deemed intolerably presumptuous, if he dared to open his mouth, even so wide as to give faint utterance to a three lettered monosyllable, like yea or nay, in the presence of an august knight of the whip and the lash."[35]

As a result of this contempt for labor, the workers lost self respect, immigrants shunned the Southern states, and Northern workers were repelled, quickly returning to their homes.[36] The employers, too, tended to look upon the wage-earners as their thralls, entitled to no more rights or consideration than their Negro co-workers, and tried to quell their protests as they would those of the slaves. When the white deck hands on the Mississippi steamboats, who were exploited worse than "the lowest African on the plantation of the most cruel master," resorted to a strike, the owners got the legislature to outlaw stoppages on the ships and wharves, and the strike leaders were arrested for "tampering with the crew. Roger Shugg points out that labor, both free and slave, suffered from the feudal outlook of the slaveholders and could not easily organize for self-defense. Consequently, the free worker was in danger of losing his freedom and being pulled into the orbit of slavery.[37]

That the slaveholders, born to command and trained to ride

their saddled underlings, assumed the usual aristocratic disdain
for the "lower order," whether Negro or white, was the most
natural thing in the world. And there was no mistaking it. While
it was often thinly disguised by a patronizing attitude, especially
around election time, people felt it, and saw it, and heard it. And,
from time to time, it came straight from the horse's mouth, proclaimed boldly by the masters themselves or their political and
journalistic spokesmen. These professions of the master-class
ideology were broadcast through the country by the enemies of
slavery, reprinted in a hundred newspapers, publicized in pamphlets, repeated a thousand times over by politicians and abolitionists, so that no one could be unaware of them. Some of the
favorites were these:

Free Society! we sicken of the name. What is it but a conglomeration of
greasy mechanics, filthy operatives, small fisted farmers and moon struck
theorists? All the Northern, and especially the New England States are
devoid of society fitted for well-bred gentlemen. The prevailing class one
meets with is that of mechanics struggling to be genteel, and small farmers
who do their own drudgery; and yet who are hardly fit for association with
gentleman's body servant. This is your free society which the Northern
hordes are endeavoring to extend into Kansas.[88]

We have got to hating everything with the prefix *free*—from free negroes
down and up, through the whole category of abominations, demagogueries,
lusts, philosophies, fanaticisms, and follies, free farms, free labor, free
——s, free society, free will, free thinking, free love, free wives, free
children, and free schools, all belonging to the same breed of damnable
isms whose mother is Sin and whose daddy is the Devil. . . . [89]

On the murder of an Irish hotel waiter by a Southern Congressman:

Any provocation that may have been given for the assault upon him [the
Southerner] . . . was at the most a provocation of words, and such a
provocation as a servant should not have a right to resent; and, if white
men accept the offices of menials, it should be expected that they will do

so with an apprehension of their relation to society, and the disposition quietly to encounter both the responsibilities and the liabilities which the relation imposes.[40]

The ruling oligarchy of the Southern states, according to its view, governed by divine right, for "nature puts the ruling elements uppermost, and the masses below and subject to those elements."[41] B. Watkins Leigh asked his colleagues in the Virginia state convention "whether they believe that those who depend on their daily labor for their daily subsistence, can, or do enter into political affairs?" and supplied the answer which was on all their lips: "They never do, never will, never can."[42] Why this must be so was explained by F. W. Pickens of South Carolina in the House of Representatives. He asserted that an elect and chosen few were made the "peculiar receptacles of the favors and blessings of an all-wise and all-pervading Providence." All societies were divided into capitalists and laborers, and the former must own the latter, either collectively through the government, as in the North, or individually in a state of servitude, as in the South. "If laborers ever obtain the political power of a country," he concluded, "it is in fact in a state of revolution, which must end in substantially transferring property to themselves . . . unless those who have it shall appeal to the sword and a standing army to protect it."[43] Calhoun recognized with equal clarity that the prevalence of democracy "would destroy our system and destroy the South."[44] Edmund Ruffin described the character of the Southern governments even more frankly, stating that they excluded from the suffrage "all of the lowest and most degraded classes, who, *whether slaves or free, white or black* . . . are and must be incapable of understanding or caring to preserve the principle or the benefits of free government." He predicted that if the propertyless classes were given the ballot, they would use it to plunder the property of the rich.[45]

Plainly the landed aristocracy intended to keep a tight control over their government in order to preserve their privileged position against the rising tide of slave revolts as well as the popular resistance of those they deigned to call the "mean whites." The methods by which they strove to hold power were many and varied in the different states, but commonly consisted of property qualifications for voting and office-holding, unequal representation, *viva voce* voting, demagogy, the prestige of wealth and social standing, the ignorance and division of the people, control of the churches, restriction of freedom of speech and the press, and terrorism. The working men of all the Southern states, in alliance with the backcountry farmers, waged a long and difficult struggle for democratic constitutional reforms and won a number of significant victories.[46] While these gains were of considerable aid in the fight for economic improvement, they did not seriously threaten the reign of the slavocracy. The ruling class of the South learned from experience that it could maintain the substance of despotism while yielding the forms of democracy. As General Downs, a leader of the Louisiana Democratic party, commented, there was no danger from the poor classes because property and money would always exercise an efficient control over them, and it was not necessary to deny them the suffrage.[47]

One of the major victories of the Northern labor movement in the ante-bellum years was the establishment of free public schools. In the South also this was a recurrent demand of the workers, but here it met the fierce resistance of the governing class. Many Southern leaders could see little value, and possibly much danger, in universal education. Chancellor Harper of South Carolina thought that a man destined to a life of labor would better be reared in ignorance and apathy and trained to endure his station in life. "If there are sordid, servile, and laborious offices to be performed," he asked, "is it not better that there should be sordid, servile, and laborious beings to fill them?"[48] The Richmond *Examiner* likewise feared that an educated people would not long remain servile, but would be a danger to "all conservatism of thought and all stability in general affairs." Free education, it stated, was "charged to the brim with incendiarisms, heresies, and all the explosive elements which uproot and rend and desolate society."[49] The nature of the plantation system, the scattered population, and the poverty of the South were forbidding obstacles in the way of public education, but an important reason for the failure to achieve this reform was the intransigence of the oligarchy and the weakness of the working class.[50]

On the issue of unequal taxation, however, significant successes were achieved, particularly in North Carolina. The complaint of the workers was that, whereas their tools and implements were taxed ten dollars per thousand, the tax on slaves was only fifty cents, and that was imposed only on those between the ages of twelve and fifty. A Raleigh worker voiced the grievance of his class in a letter to the Greensborough *Patriot,* complaining that his wages were subject to taxation, but the income of the employers and slaveowners escaped.[51]

In 1858 Moses A. Bledsoe, a Democratic state senator, introduced a bill into the legislature to equalize the tax burden by imposing an ad valorem tax on all property, including land and slaves. Defeated and read out of the party, he found support in the newly organized Raleigh Workingmen's Association, which declared its purpose to be "to insist upon that political equality and that participation in public affairs to which they as free men are entitled." The slaveholders took alarm, not only because of the increased cost to them of the proposed tax, but because they saw an impending split in the Democratic party based on a division between themselves and the non-slaveholders and involving indirectly the slavery question, a division which could become a serious challenge to the political supremacy of the aristocracy and to their Institution. Although the immediate issue was lost in the crisis of 1860-61, the organization of the workers politically had produced deep repercussions. Kenneth Rayner wrote in December

1860 that he had found great support in favor of "Union at any and all hazards," and that the non-slaveowners did not care to fight to protect rich men's slaves. He ascribed this sentiment partly to the recent agitation on ad valorem taxation, which had infused among the people the idea that there was an antagonism between poor people and slaveowners. "We shall, I fear, have to reap a harvest of trouble from the seeds of mischief then sown."[52] These struggles, which were echoed in other states as well, were harbingers of a maturing class conflict and served to strengthen and expand the consciousness and organization of the workers.

Anti-Slavery and the Southern Workers

In the face of the economic, social and political oppression described in the preceding section, a large number of Southern workers gave up the unequal struggle for survival in the slave states where, as one emigrant said, "there is no chance for the poor white man among slaves—he can not get work, and he is treated like a dog."[53] The furtive flight of fugitives on the Underground Railroad was paralleled by a denser traffic of thousands of white workers likewise seeking freedom from an unbearable burden of exploitation and tyranny. The *Kentucky News* gave a vivid description of this exodus and its effects, stating that society was divided into classes, with embittered prejudices and opposing interests. "The slaveholder despises the slave, the slave despises the poor white man, (except where each sees that the system makes them both slaves alike to the same master,) the poor white man regards both as his natural enemies." As a consequence, reported the writer, all parts of Kentucky held deserted farm houses falling into decay. He saw long processions of white farmers emigrating to the Northwest, alongside processions of slaves, "handcuffed and fettered, with tearful eyes and sorrowful countenances." Meanwhile, the schools and mechanical arts were neglected, and labor was falling into contempt. "Our country towns languish and decay. Enterprise is checked, manufactures perish. The young man of energy and enterprise finds nothing to do."[54]

* * *

In the summer of 1830, a group of workers in Wheeling were discussing their problems. They were hard pressed to earn a decent living for their families and provide an education for their children. They agreed that the country was in the hands of a gang of degenerate aristocrats bent only on its own pleasures, and giving no thought to the heartaches and misery of the workers. Something ought to be done about it, and since they couldn't expect anything from the politicians they would have to figure something out for themselves. Probably the only way out is to leave this God-forsaken place—get some land in the West—start over again. Why not go together, get some farmers in on it to raise the crops, while we'll take care of the building and manufacturing. Ideas sprang from unknown sources, a plan began to take shape. It sounds good. Come over to my place tonight, and we can work this out.

A dense smog hung in the heat of the crowded little room but it was not the weather that produced the flush on the men's faces; it was the fevered visions of the promised land, the agitated excitement of planning a new life. They had been thinking this over all day, and now they shot out their schemes without restraint. Some of the women folk had a few ideas too. It was getting a little complicated now, too many different plans, too many people talking at once. Somebody better write these things down—the printer had a gift for fancy words, let him do it. Provided with a sheet of paper and a pencil, he began to write, and the words came easily: " ... for bettering our condition and circumstance: not only in providing for the Temporal wants of ourselves and families; but for the moral and intellectual cultivation of the rising generation; and handing down to our posterity, the fair inheritance bequeathed to us, and purchased by the blood and toil of our fathers unimpaired by the cunning, intrigue and sophistry of aristocrats. . . . tyranny . . . oppression . . . misrule. . . ." All farmers and laborers are invited to join us.

He put down some of the ideas they had mentioned. These were discussed, refined and elaborated; some of the men were carried away by self-intoxication; a little grandiosity might be forgiven— it was not every day that a constitution for a new society was created. Then it was all written down for the world to see. A company would be formed, and shares would be sold for $50—no more than two per adult, one for a child. Land would be purchased from the government, a whole county in Illinois, at $1.25 an acre, one-fifth down. A city would be built for 10,000 families— on the plan of Philadelphia, thought one man who had been there —and the farms would be all around it. Everything would be owned in common, and the profits used for the benefit of all. They could sell the surplus products of the farms, workshops and forests at 25 per cent profit, which would be deposited in a cooperative bank and used to pay off the land, build schools, libraries, lyceums and reading rooms. There would be a cooperative warehouse and a mutual insurance company. There would have to be a few rules too: no liquor, gambling, whorehouses, lotteries, banks, horse-racing, cock-fighting or bear-baiting. Everything was figured out; the age-old dreams of mankind for freedom, security and opportunity were finally bearing fruit—"a splendid undertaking to emancipate ourselves and our fellow-workingmen, from the slavery, the bondage and thralldom of oppression and misrule, of narrow-minded aristocrats, and short-sighted politicians." The meeting was over, work would begin tomorrow.

In the cool light of morning the constitution-makers wondered if the plan would really work. People were wary about buying in; ten thousand families didn't want to leave, nor one thousand, nor hundred. Things will get better, they were told; you can't change human nature; smarter people have tried to remake the world and failed; that's life; what's the use? The plan was gradually forgotten, and the working men's utopia did not dawn. Nobody knew just what happened to the sheet of brown wrapping paper on which the plan had been drafted, or to the men and women who designed it; but many understood the thoughts that poured through their minds and the feelings that pulsed through their hearts on that hot summer night.[55]

* * *

For those who were unable or unwilling to choose exile, there was no effective alternative but resistance to exploitation and oppression. Not understanding the true cause of their problem, they at first directed their force not against their rulers or the slave system, but against the slaves themselves, much as the English workers earlier had vented their wrath against the invasions of capital by smashing the machines that seemed to be the root of their poverty and unemployment. It was natural for the workers to turn their attention first to the competition they suffered from slave labor, and attempt to exclude it by economic or political action.

One of the outstanding examples of the former method was the strike at the Tredegar iron works at Richmond, Virginia, an event which received wide publicity in both the North and South. After 1843 most of the unskilled jobs at the rolling mill were filled by slaves supervised by skilled white mechanics, the management having made a successful experiment along those lines because of the relatively high wages of white labor. In 1847 the plant was expanded, necessitating a sudden doubling of the number of operatives. Consequently, some of the slaves were placed in more responsible positions and a number of white puddlers and rollers assigned to teach newly hired slaves. Fearing that their jobs would be usurped once the training period was completed, the workers held a meeting and pledged "not to go to work unless the negroes be removed from the Puddling Furnaces at the new mill—likewise from the squeezer and Rolls at the old mill." The president of the iron works, Joseph Anderson, refused to bargain or to recognize the right to strike. Accepting the strike action as "quitting my employment," he advertised for Negro operatives and broke the strike.[56] In this action he had the complete support of the propertied classes, for they recognized that in spite of its limited objectives, the strike was, as Anderson said, "a direct attack on slave property." The Richmond *Times and Compiler* seconded this view: "The principle is advocated for the first time, we believe, in a slaveholding state, that the employer may be prevented from making use of slave labor. This principle strikes at the root of all the rights and privileges of the master and, if acknowledged, or permitted to gain a foothold, will soon wholly destroy the value of slave property."[57]

The *National Anti-Slavery Standard* correctly defined the issue as "a struggle between Slave-labor, and Free-Labor—between the slaveholder, who lives upon the toil of others, and the laboring man, who only asks a fair field and no favors; and the latter, of course, went to the wall."[58]

As the intensity of competition with slave labor grew, more and more workers came to agree with the artisan who said he was "only better than the slave because he is entitled to vote and must give that sometimes for promise of a job," and in some cases they resorted to desperate action.[59] A mechanics' association was formed in Wilmington, North Carolina, as early as 1795, and among other things discussed ways of protecting the skilled trades from encroachment by slave labor.[60] In 1857 the framework of a new building that had been erected by slaves was burned to the ground, and a placard was left threatening similar action against other buildings so constructed.[61] This house-warming party received applause and the flattery of imitation elsewhere, but the local authorities were horrified, denouncing the perpetrators as abolitionists, plug uglies and dead rabbits. The mechanics held a meeting in which they repelled these accusations but repeated their indignation that the laws prohibiting the hiring and contracting of slave labor were flouted by the slaveowners with impunity.[62]

While these demonstrations had the merit of dramatically calling attention to the problem, they could not have much more than a nuisance value, and the workers turned to political action for redress of their grievances. Throughout the Southern states, and for many years, laborers held meetings at which they endorsed resolutions and drew up petitions addressed to the city councils, state legislatures, and even the Navy Department. In one case at least the slaveholders themselves were moved to join in the campaign because of the unprecedented emigration of laborers from their vicinity, and one pro-slavery newspaper supported it because it feared that the continuation of this situation would place a severe strain on the loyalty of the laborers to the "institution."[63] These memorials described the ruinous effects of the competition and demanded laws prohibiting the apprenticing of Negroes to the skilled trades, restricting the movement of slave and free Negroes looking for jobs, forbidding free Negroes from teaching their trades to any but their own sons, excluding slaves and free Negroes from any mechanical occupations, and placing a poll tax on free Negroes.[64]

Once again the workers had to face a storm of reaction from the intransigent autocracy. This movement was feared, and justly as the first blow in the struggle for democracy. L. W. Spratt of Charleston wrote that if this campaign succeeded the worker would question the right of masters to employ their slaves as they wished, and would use their votes to that end. " . . . they may acquire the power to determine municipal elections; they will inexorably use it; and thus the town of Charleston, at the very heart of slavery, may become a fortress of democratic power against it."[65] When the mechanics of Concord, North Carolina held a meeting to protest against the underbidding of their contracts by the owners of slave mechanics, the leader was driven out of town.[66] A laborer in Columbia, South Carolina, was tarred and feathered and expelled from the city for suggesting that slaves be confined to the plantations.[67] In 1860 Robert Tharin, an Alabama lawyer, set up a paper called the *Non-Slaveholder,* which he hoped to make an organ of the workingmen in the campaign against competitive slave employment in industry and the handicrafts; he was run out of the state before the appearance of the first issue.[68]

Consequently, this movement also failed to achieve any significant success. With the solitary exception of a Georgia law passed in 1845, which included slaves in its provisions, every law relating to the employment of Negroes was confined in its application to free Negroes: restrictions on their movement and employment, poll taxes, prohibition of manumission, exclusion of immigration of free Negroes. The kind of law the workers wanted most was defeated by the objection that they interfered with the rights of slaveholders. And the legislation that was passed was designed more from fear of the abolitionist and revolutionary activities of the Negro freemen and to deflect the discontent of the workers than from any desire to protect them. Furthermore, whenever these laws conflicted with the interests of the slaveholders and employers, the influence of the latter was great enough to have them ignored.[69] Nevertheless, these economic and political activities by wage-earners for the protection of their living standards and their jobs were bound, as the slaveholders realized, to clarify the workers' comprehension of their problems and tasks and to build the organizations by which they would advance further. The violent reaction of the slaveholders provided an important lesson in this educational process. The working class was ineluctably forced toward opposition to the slavocracy and the whole system of chattel slavery.

John Palfrey wrote in 1846: "So long as the black working man is held in bondage, just so long will and must the white working man be held in miserable darkness and bondage of mind. The momentous issue will soon be seen to be, continued and increased *depression of the non-slaveholding freeman*, or manumission for the Slave."[70] The oppression of the Southern workers and their struggles against it—for the right to work without competition of slave labor, for democratic reforms, for public schools, for equal taxation—gradually led an increasing number of them to a comprehension of the truth of Palfrey' statement. In their education, an important role was played by the Southern abolitionists.

It is significant that, whereas most of the Northern abolitionists ignored the possibility of an alliance with labor, practically all of the Southern members of that fraternity of agitators directed their appeals and their propaganda primarily to the working men and farmers. Although they did not neglect the moral issues they had a much more realistic perception of the economic effect of slavery, and recognized that, apart from the slaves, the workers and farmers were the only force capable of overthrowing the institution. While the Northerners spoke for the rights of the slaves alone, the Southerners preferred to represent the non-slaveholding whites as well. One of these was William S. Bailey, machinist of Newport, Kentucky, "with a large family, and hatred of slavery such as only an experience of its unspeakable oppressions on the white mechanics as well as the negro can engender. . . . "[71] During the last ten years preceding the Civil War, intermittently interrupted by mob attacks on his presses and himself, he edited an anti-slavery newspaper in Kentucky in which he said, "We plead the cause of WHITE MEN and WHITE WOMEN in the South—we ask for their sake, a patient and candid hearing."[72]

Likewise, *The True American*, published in Lexington by Cassius Marcellus Clay, a former slaveowner, was devoted "to

Universal Liberty; Gradual Emancipation . . . the Elevation of Labor Morally and Politically." Deciding to give up his opportunities for a political career, he cut himself off from his own class, emancipated his slaves, and entered his life-long occupation of explaining to the working men that their only path to freedom lay in the overthrow of slavery. Here is a typical example of his vigorous editorial style:

When a journeyman printer *underworks* the usual rates he is considered an enemy to the balance of the fraternity, and is called a *"rat."* Now the slaveholders have RATTED us with the 180,000 slaves till forbearance longer on our part has become criminal. They have *ratted* us till we are unable to support ourselves with the ordinary comfort of a laborer's life. They have *ratted* us out of the social circle. They have *ratted* us out of the means of making our own schools. . . . They have *ratted* us out of the press. They have *ratted* us out of the legislature. . . . What words can we use to arouse you to a sense of our deep and damning degradation! Men, we have one remedy, untried, omnipotent, power of *freemen* left—the ballot box: yes, thank God, we can yet *vote!* Our wives, our sisters, our children, raise their imploring eyes to us; save us from this overwhelming ignominy —this insufferable woe; place us upon that equality for which our fathers bled and died. Come, if we are not worse than brutish beasts, let us but speak the word, and slavery *shall die!*[73]

It is, of course, impossible to measure the effect of this propaganda or the extent of anti-slavery sentiment among Southern workers. It can be said with certainty that the majority of them never attained to such a level of political consciousness, but there can also be no doubt that there was a strong and growing undercurrent of hostility to the system. This is attested to by the observations of a number of American and European travelers, contemporary journalists, and residents of the South,[74] by the hysterical alarm of the slaveholders and their repressive measures, and by occasional public expressions such as the resolution adopted by a mass meeting of the mechanics and working men of Lexington, Kentucky, in 1849. This resolution asserted that

slavery degraded labor, enervated industry, interfered with the
occupations of free laborers, created a gulf between the rich and
the poor, deprived the working classes of education, and tended
to drive them out of the state. While recognizing the right of
property in slaves under existing laws, the statement concluded
that, "as slavery tends to the monopoly as well as the degradation
of labor, public and private right requires its ultimate extinction."[75]

The febrile apprehensions of the ruling class mounted to unprecedented heights in the late 1850's, particularly in connection
with two events. One was the growing restlessness of the slaves
whose real and fancied preparations for revolt produced a panic
in the South in 1856, with the press complaining that the "low
down poor whites" were inciting the slaves to rebellion and joining in their conspiracy to overthrow the government by force and
violence.[76] The other event was the appearance in 1857 of *The
Impending Crisis of the South: How to Meet It,* by Hinton
Rowan Helper, a small farmer of North Carolina. Helper expressed a strong antipathy to the Negroes, a sentiment shared by
many of his class, but he presented a documented damnation of
the depressing consequences of the Institution on the poor white
and a ringing challenge to them to rise up against it.

He warned the farmers, mechanics, and workingmen that the
slaveholders who controlled the government had hoodwinked
them and used them as tools to maintain their power and their
"peculiar institution." By subterfuge and misrepresentation, by
keeping the people in ignorance and inflaming their prejudices,
they taught the people to hate the abolitionists, and thus tempo-
rarily averted the vengeance which was bound to overtake them.
Helper urged the non-slaveholders to join the abolition movement
and rescue the South from "the usurped and desolating control
of these political vampires." He concluded that if the people of
the South allowed the slavocrats to fasten slavery on Kansas, the
entire nation would soon fall prey to their designs; "if you do no

voluntarily oppose the usurpations and outrages of the slavocrats, they will force you into involuntary compliance with their infamous measures."[77] This book struck at a vulnerable point in the armor of slavery, and the heavy artillery of calumny and "refutations" was turned against it and its author.[78]

Two sections of the working class were thoroughly and actively anti-slavery: the free Negro mechanics and the German-American laborers. It required no agitators to convince the former that their salvation depended on the uprooting of slavery, which branded them both as workers and as Negroes. They were correctly regarded by the slave power as a "disturbing element," for they furnished a strong core of participants and leaders in every phase of the anti-slavery movement, and played a prominent part in aiding the slaves to escape, in distributing abolitionist literature in the South, in organizing and leading slave revolts, in the Northern abolition movement, and in assisting the Union armies as servants, scouts, spies and soldiers.[79]

The Germans were recognized as another "danger to the community." The Morehouse, Louisiana, *Advocate* noted that "The great mass of foreigners who come to our shores are laborers, and consequently come in competition with slave labor. It is to their interest to abolish Slavery; and we know full well the disposition of man to promote all things which advance his own interests. These men come from nations where Slavery is not allowed, and they drink in abolition sentiment from their mothers' breasts."[80]

When a group of Turners resolved to secede from the National Association because of its anti-slavery position, they received a spirited reply from the Wheeling society, which said: ". . . it is plain that the Turners must oppose the extension of slavery into the free territories, because they are all free laborers and must seek to preserve the soil for free labor, and because it is only through the emigration of free laborers into the territories that the future great States can be kept free from the institution of slavery, while to make these territories into slave States would be to consign

their soil to the monopoly of a few rich planters and close them
against free laborers." The proposition to form a separate Southern branch of the Turner-Bund was therefore regarded "as a
miserable business, and as a treason to the principles of our
fraternity."[81] The Free Germans of Louisville, led by Karl
Heinzen, adopted a platform in a mass meeting in 1854 calling
for the organization of a reform party embracing all "who want
that liberty now so much endangered." In addition to its demands
for land reform, labor legislation, free schools and free justice, the
platform referred to slavery as a "moral cancer, that will by and
by undermine all republicanism," and demanded the prohibition
of slavery from the territories, repeal of the fugitive slave law,
gradual abolition, and equality of rights for the Negro people.[82]

Even more sweeping in their abolitionism were the German-
American communists, who organized opposition to slavery in
several Southern states. Several anti-slavery papers were published
in Texas by German communist workers, the most significant of
which was the *San Antonio Zeitung,* a weekly abolition paper
published from 1853 to 1856 by Adolph Douai, a leading American socialist.[83] The Social Democratic Society of Working Men
consisting of German-Americans in Richmond and calling itself
"the party of the future," put forward a platform which stated
"Both political parties of our land have proved their incapacity to
develop and build up the true democratic principles of the Constitution. Their fate is inevitable—already the process of dissolution has commenced." The Society's program included universal suffrage, direct election of officials, abolition of the Senate
and Presidency, the recall, a foreign policy in aid of all people
struggling for liberty, complete freedom of religion and separation
of church and state, abolition of land monopoly, tax on property,
public education, an eight-hour law, state ownership of the railroads, and "the supporting of the slave emancipation exertions of
C. M. Clay by congressional laws."[84]

If the Southern working class as a whole was not "abolition-

zed" by the time of the war, it nevertheless had mature spokesmen, and had itself, in the course of many guerilla battles against
the aristocracy, advanced along the path of self-conscious development. This was to prove a matter of considerable significance
during the crisis of 1860-65.[85]

Divide and Rule

The ruling class understood much more clearly than the workers that the interests of the latter were in opposition to slavery and
that, to maintain their subjection (and that of the slaves), it was
necessary to keep them down, keep them ignorant, keep them
weak, and keep them divided from their natural allies. A few
suggested that it might be safer to keep them satisfied, but they
were quickly ruled out of order.

So long as the laboring class was small, scattered and unorganized, there was little possibility of its becoming a serious threat.
But let it grow to a large, concentrated, industrial proletariat, and
it would be time for the slaveowners to book passage for Brazil.
This problem presented the South with one of its great dilemmas.
On the one hand, industrialization seemed to be the only means
of providing decent employment for the poor whites and allaying
discontent. A writer in *De Bow's Review* noted that the poor,
having the vote, might overbalance the rich. They had been content to endure their degraded conditions in plantation labor
because they were satisfied that they were above the slave, socially
if not economically. But the mass of the poor whites were beginning to understand their rights and to learn that there was a world
of industry opening before them by which they could elevate
themselves from wretchedness and ignorance to competence and
intelligence. *"It is this great upbearing of our masses that we are
to fear, so far as our institutions are concerned."*[86]

On the other hand, it was generally accepted that the creation

of a free laboring class was an even greater danger. C. G. Mem‑
minger, a prominent South Carolina statesman, wrote to Gover‑
nor Hammond in connection with this problem, that those wh‑
were "agog about manufactures," like William Gregg, were un‑
wittingly lending aid to the abolitionists. If Negro mechanics an‑
operatives were driven from the cities, he feared, their place‑
would be taken by the "same men who make the cry in th‑
Northern cities against the tyranny of Capital—and there as her‑
would drive before them all who interfere with them—and woul‑
soon raise here the cry against the Negro, and be hot Abolitionist‑
And every one of these men would have a vote."[87] The Richmon‑
Enquirer expressed the same idea somewhat more crudely whe‑
it stated that the South could have industry, but would not hav‑
"your brutal, ignorant and insubordinate factory hands in ou‑
midst, for all the wealth of 'Ormus and of Ind,' " nor exchang‑
its situation "for the countless millions of paupers and criminal‑
who lift up and sustain the cowardly, selfish, sensual, licentiou‑
infidel, agrarian, and revolutionary edifice of free society."[88]

Furthermore, the establishment of manufacturing in the Sout‑
would undoubtedly draw immigrants from Europe and th‑
North, who were considered by the Charleston *Standard* a curs‑
instead of a blessing because they were generally opposed t‑
slavery. Unlike the merchants, who were intelligent and trus‑
worthy and able to discern their true interests, the paper b‑
moaned that the mechanics were *"continually carping about slav‑*
competition . . . most of them are pests to society, dangerous amon‑
the slave population, and ever ready to form combinations again‑
the interests of the slaveholders."[89] Nor was it believed prude‑
by many to employ slaves in manufacturing, for the instructi‑
which they would have to receive, their concentration in larg‑
numbers, and their contact with free labor would "foment di‑
content."

There were many factors which hindered the industrializati‑
of the South, particularly the lack of investment capital, compe‑

on from Northern producers, and the relatively greater returns
om agriculture. But the social consequences of the introduction
f manufacturing was a question that received considerable atten-
on from the leaders of the South. The preponderance of opinion
n the subject was that a slave in industry was already half free,
nd a free laborer already half an abolitionist, and that it would
erefore be better to keep the South agrarian, backward and
slaved than industrialized, prosperous and free.[90]

The guiding principle of the slavocracy was *divide et impera*.
s basic policy followed two lines, the first of which was to con-
nce the white laborers that they had a material interest in the
reservation of the chattel system. They were constantly told that,
consigning the hard, menial and low-paid tasks to slaves, the
hite workers were enabled to constitute a labor aristocracy
hich held the best and most dignified jobs, and that the latter
ere lucrative only because they were supported by the super-
ofits wrung from the unpaid labor of slaves. Unless abolitionism
as "met and repelled as becomes a proud spirited people," the
hites would have to take over the menial jobs and the emanci-
ted slaves would be able to compete with them in every branch
industry.[91] Furthermore, since the South was not blighted by
e curse of industry and urbanization, the workers did not have
compete with the "remorseless and untiring machine" or with
reign pauper labor," they did not suffer unemployment from
riodic business depressions, they did not have to work in
wded cities and in "close and sickly workshops," and, best of
, they were not subject to contact with "all the absurd and de-
ading isms which have sprung up in the rank soil of infidel-
. . . . They are not for breaking down all the forms of society
d of religion and of reconstructing them; but prefer law, order
d existing institutions to the chaos which radicalism involves."[92]
nally, just as Northern workers were taught that they could, by
plication and thrift, become employers themselves, the slogan
s advanced in the South: "Every laborer a slaveholder." It was

argued in the Southern commercial conventions, for example, tha
the slave trade should be revived so that every worker and farm
could own at least one slave, thereby preventing "an antagonis
between slavery and labor, like that between capital and labor i
the North."[93]

No less important as an ideological weapon against lab
militancy was the use of a technique in which the Southern Bou
bon has become a world authority: race prejudice. Every effo
was bent to prove that there was no conflict between rich ar
poor in Southern society, and that, in fact, there were no cla
distinctions at all, the only gradations being those of color. Th
meanest of the "mean whites" was placed, by virtue of his ski
on a "perfect spirit of equality" with the gentlest of the gentlem
planters. Southern society was said by Robert Toombs of Georg
to exemplify the principles of the Declaration of Independenc
for, since that document obviously did not refer to Negroes wh
it said that all men were created equal, "the perfect equality
the superior race, and the legal subordination of the inferior ra
are the foundations on which we have erected our republic.
society."[94] The workers were beguiled by a spurious pride of ca
and social status, and in addition frightened by the specter of ra
war, Negro supremacy and miscegenation. The "purity" of t
races had to be maintained by a strict observance of prescribed re
tions, and any worker who showed signs of treating a Neg
fellow-worker as a human being was likely to be chastised
expulsion or violence.[95] And it was the very degradation to whi
slavery consigned him that made the deluded worker suscepti
to the ideology of race supremacy. Because he was himself reduc
virtually to the status of the slave, he could preserve a modicu
of self-respect only by identifying himself in some way with
master class, with whom he could share the "privilege" of lordi
it over a helpless class of pariahs.[96]

Thus, the workers were blinded in order that their conflict w
the slaveholder might be diverted and directed against the slav

hile at the same time the slaves were used to keep them in
bjugation. (Did not William Gregg assure his fellow slave-
olders and capitalists that there could never be any conflict
tween labor and capital in the South, since ". . . capital will be
le to control labor, even in manufactures with whites, for
acks can always be resorted to in case of need."?)[97] Frederick
ouglass exposed the significance of this racial prejudice:

e slaveholders, with a craftiness peculiar to themselves, by encouraging
e enmity of the poor, laboring white man against the blacks, succeed in
aking the said white man almost as much a slave as the black man him-
f. The difference between the white slave, and the black slave, is this:
e latter belongs to *one* slaveholder, and the former belongs to *all* the
veholders, collectively. The white slave has taken from him, by indirec-
n, what the black slave has taken from him, directly, and without
emony. Both are plundered, and by the same plunderers. The slave is
bed, by his master, of all his earnings, above what is required for his
re physical necessities; and the white man is robbed by the slave system,
the just results of his labor, because he is flung into competition with
class of laborers who work without wages. . . . At present, the slave-
lders blind them to this competition, by keeping alive their prejudices
ainst the slaves, *as men*—not against them *as slaves*. They appeal to their
de, often denounce emancipation, as tending to place the white working
n, on an equality with negroes, and, by this means, they succeed in
awing off the minds of the poor whites from the real fact, that, by the
h slave-master, they are already regarded as but a single remove from
uality with the slave.[98]

a delegation of Negroes explained to President Johnson many
ars later:

e hostility between the whites and blacks of the South is easily explained.
has its root and sap in the relation of slavery, and was incited on both
es by the cunning of the slave masters. Those masters secured their
endancy over both the poor whites and the blacks by putting enmity be-
en them.
They divided both to conquer each. . . .[99]

The Southern obligarchy attempted to smother the develo
ment of the working class and to keep it in blinkers, but it ha
another means of maintaining its power: dictatorship. Every for
of legal and extra-legal repression was employed to prevent t
enlightenment of the people and to crush resistance. Freedom
speech, press and assembly was infringed upon, the mails we
censored, personal liberty was violated, and the entire apparat
of the state, civil and military, was utilized to maintain slavery.
The fact that such methods had to be resorted to more frequen
as the crisis in the South deepened justified the expectations
Douglass that "The crafty appeals to the prejudices of the wh
laborer, against the black laborer, will lose their power to decei
in due time, and that prejudice, so long existing and augmentin
will one day find a new object upon which to discharge its t
rors."[101] This hope was not sufficiently realized by the time of t
war to enable the workers to play a decisive role in the overthro
of slavery, but emancipation created the conditions under whi
both Negro and white workers could more readily learn that l
son which was indispensable for the advancement of both.

CHAPTER III

NORTHERN LABOR CONSIDERS
SLAVERY

Slavery and the Northern Workers, 1830–1845

During the first decade and a half after the inauguration of
the "new" abolition movement in 1830, the attitude of Northern
labor to slavery differed from that of its Southern counterpart
as a result of three circumstances. First, the Northern working
class was much larger, stronger, and more concentrated, and
had developed a higher degree of class-consciousness. Consequently, it was necessarily concerned for the most part with its
own immediate struggles for economic improvement and with
building up and defending its own organizations. Its energies
were engaged in the establishment of a labor movement as such.
Secondly, the workers had little direct contact with slavery and
its consequences, at least until the expansionist program of the
slaveholders became a national problem. The problem of slavery
and the oppressions of the slavocracy did not have for them the
immediacy and urgency that they had for the workers in Dixie,
and their position on the slavery question was determined by
different considerations and took a different course.

Finally, the character of the Northern abolition movement
itself had a considerable effect in defining the role of labor. Because the abolition leadership was predominantly of the middle
class and its attitude to labor generally cool if not hostile, many
workers were repelled from the anti-slavery cause or tended to
take an independent position which would enable them to put

forward their own demands as well. One of the most difficu
problems of the labor movement in the struggle against slaver
like that of the European workers in the democratic revolutio
of the nineteenth century, was to find a way to cooperate wi
the middle class against a common enemy without losing
identity and its independent program.

Although the workers did not satisfactorily solve this proble
in the ante-bellum period, they did contribute greatly to t
movement which finally brought about the destruction of chat
slavery. In fact, the backbone of the abolitionist movement
the 1830's was made up of farmers and artisans in whom t
spirit of liberty was strong, and who, "when the great princip
of freedom are jeoparded can neither be intimidated by Slav
holding bluster, nor bribed by the factorage of Cotton-bales, n
sugarhogsheads however numerous they may be."[1] It was, sa
Thomas Wentworth Higginson, "predominantly a people's mo
ment, . . . and far stronger for a time in the factories and sh
shops than in the pulpits or colleges."[2] It was the support
farmers and artisans that sustained the movement in those d
of mob violence and persecution. But the abolitionists constitu
a small sect, and the majority of the workers, like the rest of t
people, were not deeply influenced by them. Politically immatu
the workers' consideration of slavery was determined largely
its real or supposed effects on their economic conditions, th
things that trade unionists call bread-and-butter issues.

Bread and Butter

When slavery had existed in the North, not long since,
workers had the same problem of competing with slave labor
had the Southern workers, and their opposition to this comp
tion was a factor in the abolition of slavery in the Northern sta
As a result of petitions from mechanics, the legislature of Pe

lvania passed a resolution condemning the hiring out of slaves
y their masters, and later embodied this in law. This was a
ow to the slave system, because it virtually confined the use
' the slaves' labor to the personal needs of their owners and
ade it prohibitively expensive.[3] In Massachusetts, John Adams
serted that the real cause of the abolition of slavery was the
crease of white workers, who would no longer permit the rich
employ slaves because of their injurious rivalry. "If the gentle-
en had been permitted by law to hold slaves," he admitted,
he common white people would have put the negroes to death,
d their masters too, perhaps. . . . The common white people, or
ther the labouring people, were the cause of rendering negroes
profitable servants."[4]

Economic rivalry did not cease when slavery was confined
low Mason's and Dixon's line, for the institution cast its shadow
er the entire nation. As early as 1834 the attention of the
orthern operatives was directed to the appearance in the Phila-
lphia market of cotton yarn manufactured in Virginia by slave
por, and selling at a price which could not be met by Northern
dustry, and they were warned that this was the beginning of
enterprise that would result in reducing the condition of
orkingmen to one "but little better than that of the slave."[5]
the next decade the warning was becoming a reality, and
hen the Southern conventions began to talk of a systematic
velopment of industry, the situation began to cause consider-
le alarm. A political economist pointed out in 1847 that slave
por in Virginia, at a cost of $120 a year, would soon destroy
e Pennsylvania iron industry, which paid $300 for labor.[6]
ring the depression of 1858 it was said that while a thousand
eratives in the factories and rolling mills were unemployed,
ny thousands of dollars worth of the products of Tennessee
n establishments, worked exclusively by slaves, were being
d in the Northern markets.[7]

The anti-slavery papers began to report on the progress of

industrialism in the Southern states, explaining that their produc
would undersell those of Northern factories and either dri
their employees out of work or force them to lower their stan
ards to those of the slaves, and the Philadelphia *Daily Repub*
cautioned the striking workers in that city that if they did n
yield their demands for increased wages and shorter hours t
manufacturers would move to the South and employ slave labo
The Fall River *Mechanic* noted that the demand for a ten-ho
day was being opposed on the ground that competition with sla
labor made it impracticable, and called upon the workers
assemble and express their views on the subject of "white slave
and Negro slavery."[9]

Nor did state boundaries provide protection against the stigr
with which slavery branded labor and laborers. The abolitioni
repeatedly pointed out that "Slavery blights the industry of t
nation by making labor disreputable. It degrades the labori
population assimilating them to slaves. It leads our statesmen
imagine, and sometimes say, that the laboring people are inco
petent to self-government, and thus it emboldens them to tr
them as slaves."[10] Thomas Morris of Ohio charged in the Sena
that the demeaning of labor had gone so far as to inspire attac
on the principle of universal suffrage and warned the work
to take heed of what was happening before it was too late.[11]

Political economists who sympathized with the labor mo
ment likewise noted this phenomenon. Theodore Sedgwick sa
that the taint of slavery was poisoning the blood of the peo
in the free states. "Slavery had given to the common people th
mean names of reproach which have been attached to all w
profess the common man's labours. . . . In our own country,
poorest class in the free states, have been sometimes called 'wh
slaves.'" Thus, he noted, the slavery question was one wh
concerned the white working men of the entire country.[12]

Nor were the workers unaware of the degradation with wh
slavery marked labor. *The Boston Reformer* believed that

sociation of labor with slavery caused labor to be looked down
pon, and that the attitude of the slaveholder was imparted to
e Northerners. "He looks upon the free laborer here very much
  he does on the slave in his own section of the country, and
 e first we know, all those with whom he has intercourse here,
so become unable to distinguish any essential difference between
 e free white, and the enslaved black laborer."[13] A. H. Wood,
 other labor editor, seconded this remark. He added that the
orthern capitalists were inflamed and captivated by the example
  the slaveholding aristocrats who had "no *Saturday nights* in
eir financial calendars, no *Januarries* with the laboring herd.
 o Trade Unions are there, no combinations to raise wages, no
velers are there, but one eternal harvest of productive industry
evails," and that they "have racked their ingenuity to find out
 ays and means to bring the laboring classes of the North, into
e same state of subjugation." The workingmen of the North,
erefore, had a direct interest in the overthrow of slavery.[14]

If this problem seemed somewhat remote both in time and
 ace to many workers, they were faced with another immediate
 d present form of competition that was no less clearly a result
 the continuing existence of slavery in one section of the country,
mely, the competition with the labor of free Negroes. These
ople, branded with the stigma of the auction block and the
ctims of discrimination, persecution and a double measure of
pression, occupied a status only a degree higher than that of
 slaves themselves. The prejudice against them was so intense
 at it became increasingly difficult for them to get employment,
 rticularly after the heavy influx of immigration began in the
 ly 1840's, and a demand arose for new kinds of skills which
 e Negroes did not have and were not permitted to acquire.
 ederick Douglass referred to this situation in his paper in 1853.
 was becoming increasingly evident, he stated, that the free

Negroes must learn trades or perish. The old avocations of t
Negroes were rapidly and unceasingly passing into the hands
whites, whose color and hunger were thought to give them a bett
title to employment. White men were becoming house-servan
cooks, stewards, porters, stevedores, wood-sawyers, hod-carrie
brick-makers, white-washers, and barbers, so that the Negro
could scarcely find the means of subsistence. This would co
tinue, Douglass believed, until slavery and the prejudices nurtur
by slavery were abolished.[15]

This was the case throughout the North. The Negroes we
forced to abandon one trade after another, in one city af
another, were even driven out of the menial offices of whi
they once held a virtual monopoly, and were finally forced
emigrate from the cities in large numbers.[16]

This policy was the result not only of the prejudices of e
ployers but of the workers also, who found themselves pitt
against the Negro workers and taught that their own prosper
depended on the adversity of others. Many workers refused
work with Negroes, and trade unions proscribed the emplo
ment of Negro mechanics and forbade their members to tea
them trades.[17] The Negroes, a disfranchised and unprotec
minority, were the chief sufferers from this suicidal divisi
but the white workers were exploited by it as well, and especia
the Irish laborers who filled the unskilled and low-paid jobs.
failing to unite with the Negroes in a common struggle to i
prove their conditions, they were forced into a mad strife
jobs, and the whites were able to come out on top only at
cost of meeting or underbidding the depressed wages of th
rivals, and even then the losers in the skirmish were held a
club over their heads to keep them in place.[18]

It is not to be wondered that in this brutish contest, the weap
of the brute were employed. In many Northern cities pass
and hunger exploded into fierce riots, most often involv
attacks by Irish against Negroes, as when Negroes were emplo

fill the places of striking stevedores in New York; and some-
mes the warfare spread from the waterfront to the town, and a
lpless population were expelled from their homes.[19] Finally,
mands were heard for the complete exclusion of free Negroes.
practically every Northern legislature laws were introduced
ohibiting their immigration into the state or imposing restric-
ns on them, and some of them were enacted. So the pattern
second-class citizenship spread from the South and engulfed
e nation, and Negro and white workers alike were caught in
e trap.[20]

Few white workers understood that this difficulty was a product
the slave system; instead of seeking a solution in the abolition
slavery, many were frightened by the specter of an emanci-
ted people swelling the ranks of the job-hunters and became
lent opponents of abolition. Some of them even believed that
olitionism was inspired by the capitalists for this purpose, like
e one who wrote in the *Voice of Industry* that the "selfish
pitalists, and those who are disgustingly subservient" to their
stem "seem quite anxious to bring labor of the black slave into
mpetition with that of the whites, by reducing its compensa-
n one quarter. This would be fun to the capitalists, but death
us, who are their slaves."[21] The *Working Man's Advocate*
erted that emancipation would bring the freedmen into direct
mpetition with the white workers, and concluded: "It is not
ficult, therefore, to foresee in whose favor the competition,
tween three millions of blacks and a yet greater number of
ites, would terminate; and who would first suffer from want
employment and the reduction of wages consequent on com-
tition." The editor favored gradual emancipation and coloniza-
n of the ex-slaves in a special state set aside for them in the
est.[22]

Southern politicians and pro-slavery publicists were assiduous
propagating this idea among the workers, and Henry Clay
ote to the Rev. Calvin Colton urging him to write a popular

tract whose purpose should be to arouse the working classes of the North against abolition. He suggested that Colton argue tha the free Negroes would come North, enter into competitio with the free laborer, reduce his wage standards, undermine h social standing and his "racial purity," and reduce him to th "despised and degraded condition of the black man."[23] Th abolitionists worked just as hard to convince the workers th emancipation would not produce these consequences. The pointed out that Negroes only came to the North to escape fro slavery, and that emancipation would remove the motive f their emigration; that the majority of free Negroes stayed the South unless they were driven out; and that their associatio and family ties, their familiarity with conditions and suitabili to the climate, and the high price which their labor would com mand if slavery were abolished, would not only keep the fre slaves in the South but would induce most of those in th North to return, thus redounding to the advantage of the whi laborer.[24]

Special efforts were made to wean the Irish laborers fro their hostility to abolition. Since they had nearly all been peasai in the old world they came to this country with little industr skill and consequently were consigned to the most menial jo They therefore felt the competition of free Negro labor mo acutely than any other group and were more sensitive to t propaganda that emancipation would endanger their standards deluging the North with a flood of low-paid workers. They we even more susceptible to this propaganda because of the sour from which much of it emanated: the Democratic party and t Catholic Church.

The Irish-Americans had always been strongly attached to t Democratic party, whose very name attracted them, while th were repelled by Federalists and Whigs because of the w founded suspicion that those parties represented the mor power and harbored the nativist elements who wanted to esta sh second-class citizenship for the immigrants. The Democrats, pposing nativism and posing as the friends of the workingmen, were able to gather the Irish into their fold. While the Irish workers were less concerned with national than local political ffairs, their loyalty to the party made it possible to keep them a line on all major issues, including the slavery question.[25]

The Catholic Church was officially neutral in the slavery controversy, avoiding any dogmatic position which would result in the kind of schism that had rent several of the Protestant churches. In the South it was unanimously pro-slavery, like every other religion except that practiced by the slaves. In the North the church embraced every gradation of sentiment except outright abolitionism, which was identified with radicalism and strong government—both were feared as encouraging anti-clericalism. Such a large number of the spokesmen for the Church held pro-slavery views that they were generally regarded as reflecting the policy of the Church itself.[26] The Irish Catholic press was, with scarcely an exception, vigorously opposed to abolition, branding it as a British agency whose sole object was to destroy the Union, and even defending mob violence against the abolitionists. These papers also toed the Democratic party line on all issues and supported its candidates in every campaign.[27]

To overcome these handicaps was no small task, but the abolitionists attempted to enlist the Irish love of liberty and deep hatred of oppression in the anti-slavery cause. In this endeavor they had the assistance of Daniel O'Connell, the great leader of the struggle for Catholic emancipation and Irish independence, and many other Irish democrats. In 1841 O'Connell, Father Mathew, the famous temperance reformer, and sixty thousand other Irishmen addressed an appeal to the Irish residents of the United States calling upon them to espouse the anti-slavery cause as part of the fight against oppression everywhere. Mass meetings were held in several cities, at which this address was read and resolutions voted upon. A meeting in Faneuil Hall resolved:

That we rejoice that the voice of O'Connell, which now shakes the thr
kingdoms, has poured across the waters a thunderpeal for the cause
liberty in our own land; and that Father Mathew, having lifted with o
hand five millions of his own countrymen into moral life, has stretch
forth the other—which may Heaven make equally potent—to smite off t
fetters of the American slave.

. . . That we receive with the deepest gratitude the names of the six
thousand Irishmen, who, in the trial-hour of their own struggle f
liberty, have not forgotten the slave on this side of the water; that we acce
with triumphant exultation the address they have forwarded to us, a
pledge ourselves to circulate it through the length and breadth of o
land, till the pulse of every man who claims Irish parentage beats true
the claims of patriotism and humanity.

Wendell Phillips made the keynote speech, which he conclud
by asking, "Will you ever return to his master the slave w
once sets foot on the soil of Massachusetts? [No, no, no!] W
you ever raise to office or power the man who will not pled
his utmost effort against slavery? [No, No, no!]"[28] While ma
Irish-American workers were persuaded by such appeals, t
majority probably retained their hostility to abolition througho
the ante-bellum period.[29]

Our Fair Escutcheon

May the foul stain of slavery be blotted out of our fair
escutcheon; and our fellow men, not only declared to
be free and equal, but actually enjoy that freedom and
equality to which they are entitled by nature.
—"Workingmen's prayer" submitted in 1830 by the trade unions
Massachusetts to the state legislature.[30]

In 1836 the Working Men's Association of England address
an appeal to the American working class, inquiring why "the
and blackest remnant of kingly dominion has not been uproo
from Republican America?"

Why, when she has afforded a home and an asylum for the destitute and oppressed among all nations, should oppression in her own land be legalized, and bondage tolerated? Did nature, when she cast her sunshine over the earth, and adapted her children to its influence, intend that her varied taints of skin should be the criterion of liberty? And shall men whose illustrious ancestors proclaimed mankind to be brothers by nature, make an exception, to degrade to the condition of slaves, human beings a shade darker than themselves?

Surely it cannot be for the interest of the working class that these prejudices should be fostered—this degrading traffic be maintained. No, no; it must be for those who shrink from honest industry, and who would equally sacrifice to their love of gain and mischievous ambition, the happiness of either black or white. We entertain the opinion, friends, that all those who seek to consign you to unremitting toil, to fraudulently monopolize your lands, to cheat you in the legislature, to swell their territory by injustice, and to keep you ignorant and divided, are the same who are the perpetrators and advocates of slavery.[31]

Lewis Gunn, a Philadelphia labor leader, transmitted this address to the workers of America with the admonition that "Our voice should *thunder* from Maine to Georgia, and from the Atlantic to the Mississippi—the voice of a nation of *Republicans and Christians* demanding with all the authority of moral power, *demanding* the immediate liberation of the bondsmen."[32]

The majority of the workers were not yet ready to respond to this appeal, but a growing number began to discern a menace to labor in the oligarchic pretensions of the slaveholders.[33] The labor leader and land reformer, George Henry Evans, was no great admirer of the abolitionists, whom he considered honest but fanatic, but as early as 1831 he had become convinced that the interests of labor demanded that they should exert themselves in the cause of emancipation. Free men could never enjoy equal rights, he maintained, in a nation in which two million human beings were held in bondage. It was therefore the duty of every freeman and every friend of equal rights to save the country from the evils which threatened it by lending their aid in the fight for the total eradication of slavery.[34]

Probably there was no stronger concentration of anti-slavery sentiment anywhere in the United States than among the "factory girls" of New England, whose humanitarianism and devotion to democracy and the rights of labor gave them an ardent hatred of the slavocracy. They were very active in the abolition movement, in spite of intimidation both for their views and for their impudence in transgressing the bounds of female decency by expressing them.[35] The love of freedom and the plebeian virtue of these girls were enshrined by Whittier in one of his more youthful efforts, "The Yankee Girl," written for the *National Enquirer*:

> She sits by her wheel at that low cottage door,
> Which the long evening shadow is stretching before,
> With a music as sweet as the music which seems
> Breathed softly and faint in the ear of her dreams.
>
> . . . .
>
> Who comes in his pride to that low cottage door?
> 'Tis the haughty and proud to the humble and poor,
> 'Tis the great Southern planter, the master who waves
> His whip of dominion o'er hundreds of slaves!
>
> "Nay, Ellen for shame, let those Yankee fools spin,
> Who would pass for our slaves with a change of their skin,
> Let them work as they will at the loom or the wheel,
> Too haughty for shame and too vulgar to feel.
>
> "But thou art too lovely and precious a gem
> To be bound to their burdens or sullied by them.
> For shame Ellen, shame, cast thy bondage aside,
> And away to the South as my blessing and pride.
>
> "Oh come to my home where my servants shall all
> Depart at thy bidding and come at thy call;
> They shall heed thee as mistress with trembling and awe
> And each wish of thy heart be felt as a law."

Oh could you have seen her, that pride of our girls,
Arise and cast back the dark wealth of her curls,
With a scorn in her eye which the gazer could feel,
And a glance like the sunshine that flashes on steel.

"Go back haughty Southron, thy treasures of gold
Are dimmed by the blood of the hearts thou hast sold.
Thy home may be lovely, but round it I hear
The crack of the whip and the footsteps of fear.

. . . .

"Full low at thy bidding thy negroes may kneel,
With the iron of bondage on spirit and heel,
Yet know that the Yankee girl sooner would be
In fetters with them than in freedom with thee."[36]

The anti-slavery press, and particularly the *National Anti-Slavery Standard,* which was first edited by Nathaniel P. Rogers, one of the few abolitionist leaders who actively championed the cause of labor, began to harp on this theme. In his first issue Rogers stated his aim to be to convince the "hard-handed workingmen" that their fate was indissolubly linked to that of the slave and that their progress was dependent on the broadening and deepening of democracy, of which the workers were the greatest beneficiaries and the stoutest defenders. Time after time the abolitionists quoted from the anti-democratic and anti-labor speeches of Harper, Leigh, McDuffie and other Southern spokesmen, and hammered home the precept that slaveholding was the natural enemy of the working class.[37]

That this viewpoint was taking hold in the labor movement was indicated when in 1842 a cargo of slaves revolted on the *Creole,* seized the vessel and took it into a British port where they gained their freedom. The *New York State Mechanic* lauded this blow for liberty and denounced "our Chivalrous southern neighbors—those men who sneeringly call the mechanics and laborers

of the free North *slaves*—these men would rush into war with
England, and then, as they have done before, leave the 'northern
slave' to bear the brunt, and pay the cost with their treasure and
their blood."[38] The workers were not prepared to fight
England in order to maintain the "property" of the slaveholders
nor were they willing to defend the institution against a rising of
the slaves at home. The New England Workingmen's Convention
in 1846 declared that *all* men were entitled to the rights for which
the workers were contending, and that if the "three millions of
our brethren and sisters, groaning in chains on the Southern
plantations," should follow the example of the revolutionists who
resisted British oppression, "we will never take up arms to
sustain the Southern slaveholders in robbing one-fifth of our
countrymen of their liberty."[39]

In 1848 a mass meeting of workers assembled in Faneuil Hall
to hail the revolution in Europe and passed a resolution declaring
"That while we rejoice in the organization of free institutions in
the Old World, we are not indifferent to their support at home,
and that we regard the despotic attitude of the slave power at the
South, and the domineering ascendency of a Monied Oligarchy
in the North, as equally hostile to the interests of Labor, and
incompatible with the preservation of popular rights."[40] The
German communist workers of Cleveland resolved to "use all
means which are adapted to abolishing slavery, an institution
which is so wholly repugnant to the principles of true Democracy."[41]

The attack on the civil liberties of the abolitionists aroused
many more workers to an awareness of the danger from that
quarter. A meeting was called in Lowell in 1835, at which resolutions were presented to muzzle the anti-slavery press, close
all halls and churches to the abolitionists, and to "prevent all
over whom they have any control, from attending meetings or
such discussions." The workers in the hall created such a com-
motion that the speaker was unable to continue and a vote of

he resolutions was impossible. The Southern press was in a
age over this, bitterly lamenting that abolitionism had gained
uch inroads into the working class, and proposing a boycott of
heir manufactures that would cause Lowell to "wither or be
orced to expel the abolitionists."[42]

When the Southern congressmen attempted to put a gag on
he right of petition, the *National Laborer* noted that the petitions
f the abolitionists and those of the trade unions in behalf of
he ten-hour day received the same treatment, and the significance
f their common plight was plain.[43] Especially alarming to labor
vas the mob violence against abolition meetings and newspapers
nd against the Negro people. Even Evans, who did not see
ye to eye with the abolitionists on their program and tactics,
enounced attacks on Negro abolitionists as calculated to create
rejudice between Negroes and whites, "which *might,* in the
nd, produce much bloodshed, and which *must,* at any rate be
ighly injurious to both."[44] The lynching of Lovejoy, the assaults
n anti-slavery meetings, and the destruction of C. M. Clay's
ress likewise drew vigorous protests from the labor press, which
sserted that "when we see the craven tyrants of the South . . .
varring with the freedom of the press and the liberties of the
vhite man, in order to rivet more securely the chains of black
lavery, we will denounce them as the cowardly enemies of all
ational liberty, who dare not tolerate the liberty of the press,
ecause they know that the unrighteousness of their system
vould cause it to be abolished, if exposed to the light of free
iscussion."[45]

Some of the abolitionists tried to show the workers that the
laveholders had designs not only on their civil rights but even
n their personal freedom. Liberally quoting the apologists of
lavery who stated that servitude was the normal condition of the
aboring classes, that the slaves were better off than the Northern
vorkers, and that the free states would have to introduce the
istitution within a few years, the abolitionists proclaimed that

a plot was brewing to actually enslave the entire working class of the United States. They charged that in this enterprise the slaveholders had the willing cooperation of the Northern capitalists, who had a "peculiar affinity" with them and were "in love with the beauties of that system." The struggle was on, they declared, between the antagonistic principles of free and slave labor. The two could not much longer co-exist; one must prevail to the destruction of the other. Either the laborers in the South would be free or the laborers in the North would lose their freedom. "The laboring population of the North have it *now* in their power to turn the scale which way they please. On which side will they place themselves?"[46] The workers would one day take this matter seriously, but at the time most of them were less concerned with the possibility of their future enslavement to the "man-stealers" than with the actuality of what they considered their present slavery to the capitalist class.

"Chattel Slaves and Wage Slaves"

> Remember, too, that wrong is here,
> And give the North one pitying tear;
> Oh! the fruits of love go forth,
> To free the South and bless the North!
> *The Voice of Industry*[47]

The young American labor movement very quickly developed a high degree of class-consciousness. Subjected to a galling yoke of long hours, low wages, and insecurity, the workers naturally compared their conditions with those of the Southern slaves and discovered a startling similarity. Of course, the conditions of the Northern working class as a whole were not as bad as those of the slaves, especially during prosperous business periods, and besides the free workers had the opportunity of advancing or of rising out of the working class which the slaves did not have. Many of the statements were merely fanciful fictions, designed by labor spokesmen to emphasize the deplorable conditions of the workers and by defenders of slavery to apologize for the conditions of the slaves. But the fact that such comparisons could be seriously made indicates what laborers thought about their status, and greatly affected their attitude toward the slavery problem, because it strengthened their tendency to place the abolition of "wage slavery" before that of chattel slavery.

Seth Luther, the outstanding labor leader in New England in the 1830's, doubted if the mill workers were better off than the slaves, and thought that children born in slavery did not work half as long, nor perform one-quarter of the labor that the white children did in the cotton mills, and had many advantages which the latter did not possess.[48] The *Mechanics' Free Press* described the circumstances of the laborer who, working more than the slave, "can not secure to himself and children the necessaries of life; he commences in the morning of his life his daily task, and so long as his breath continues he *may* supply himself and children with food; but when sickness, the oft consequence of over exertion, overtakes him, he is stretched on his bed, his wife can not leave him to obtain work; he has no master interested in prolonging his life, therefore none to send him food or medicine; his children want bread, he has none to give them; and the sons of freedom are oft compelled to go forth and solicit from the cold hand of charity, the crumbs that fall from the rich man's table." The writer concluded that John Adams was right when he considered the difference between the working class and the slaves to be principally a "custom of speech."[49]

Referring to the alarming increase in pauperism the *Voice of Industry* declared that wages were steadily sinking until thousands were reduced to the starvation point, and the workers were subject to "a subtle, indirect slavery rarely acknowledged, but everywhere felt." In this respect, observed the writer, the slaves were better off than the free laborers of the North, for at least their conditions remained pretty much the same from year to year.[50] If the workers were exploited as much as the slaves, they suffered even more in one respect, for they had no means of support during sickness, old age and unemployment other than the meager and uncertain bounties of charity, whereas the slaves were maintained by their masters at all times.[51]

Not only were their conditions as bad or worse than those of the slaves, in the opinion of many laborers, but even the forms of oppression sometimes exhibited a remarkable similarity. The Cabotsville *Chronicle* charged that the mill owners were recruiting labor by "forcing poor girls from their quiet homes, to become their tools, and like the Southern slaves, to give up her life and liberty to the heartless tyrants and taskmasters." They sent a long black wagon, known as a "slaver," cruising about the countryside of Vermont and New Hampshire, with a "commander" who was paid a dollar a head for each operative he brought back, often enticing them under false pretenses.[52] A much more comprehensive analogy between the two forms of slavery was drawn by some. One writer noted that while slave families were sometimes separated by force, the families of working men were likewise often compelled to separate to find employment, and their children were frequently sent into the factories, to the detriment or destruction of their health and morals. The black slave could not choose his own master, but was frequently the same with the white worker, who was indeed thankful to have any master at all. Both the female slaves and the working women were sometimes compelled to submit to the licentious desires of their masters. The slaves could not vote, neither could the white women. Besides, "the black slave is free from the care, responsibility, and perplexity which is the lot of the poor white . . . , nor does he fear that he will be compelled to go to the almshouse for want of employment, or in consequence of old age, sickness, or misfortune."[53]

It seemed to many workers that in the systems of chattel slavery nd "wage slavery" there was a difference without a distinction, or "The poor negro must work or be whipped,—the poor white aborer must work or be starved." While the Southern slave's abor was bought for a certain sum during his life, the Northern lave's labor was bought yearly.[54]

When some labor spokesmen looked beyond the legal sanctions f slavery and defined its essence, they discerned a basic identity etween chattel slavery and the wages system. William Cobbett onstrued a slave as a man who had no property. ". . . any man vho is compelled to give up the fruit of his labor to another, t the arbitrary will of that other, has no property in his labor, nd is, therefore a slave, whether the fruit of his labor be taken rom him directly or indirectly," by force or by fear of starvation. Did this fit the wage-earner?[55] "In what does slavery consist?" sked the *Mechanic's Free Press*. "In being compelled to work or others, so that they may reap the advantage." Did this fit the vage-earner?[56] Mike Walsh summed the matter up in a speech 1 Congress:

he only difference between the negro slave of the South, and the white ages slave of the North, is, that the one has a master without asking for im, and the other has to beg for the privilege of becoming a slave. . . . he one is the slave of an individual; the other is the slave of an inexorable ass. . . . If a dozen of us own a horse in common, we want to ride him as uch as possible, and feed him as little as possible. But if you or I own a orse exclusively, we will take good care to feed him well, and not drive im too much to endanger his health, but just enough to keep him in ood traveling order.[57]

These conclusions, widely held among the working classes, vere drawn primarily from their own experiences and observa- ons rather than from any understanding or investigation of conomic theory. This explains why they almost completely verlooked one of the glaring inconsistencies of the abolition gument. The latter pointed out over and over again that one : the chief advantages of free labor over slavery was that the wage-earner, working under the incentive of reward (that is the necessity of supporting himself and his family) produced twenty-five per cent more than the slave working under the compulsion of the lash. In other words, the slaveholders were virtually told that they could exploit their workers more if they emancipated them and could increase their profits by twenty-five per cent.[58] Some of the political economists who defended the interests of labor made a more searching analysis of the economic basis of the wages system and nearly approached the doctrine of surplus labor as a measure of exploitation, which was later expounded by Marx.

John Francis Bray, in *Labor's Wrong and Labor's Remedy*, stated that labor was the only measure and true title of property and that since wages contained less labor than that incorporated in the product, the surplus went to the owner; whether a capitalist or slaveholder, the process and the result were the same.[59] Stephen Simpson, the author of *The Working Man's Manual,* believed that wages generally amounted to the smallest pittance compatible with the preservation of life. Employers fixed the wages of their workers as absolutely as did the slaveholders those of their chattels, and were no more disposed to dole out more than enough to keep them alive and working. And what was it, he asked, but the principle of slavery that made it a felony for workingmen to ask for just wages, that punished them as conspirators, and that sentenced them to jail as it did the robber?[60]

More important than these works was *The Working Man's Political Economy* by John Pickering, a land reformer.[61] The book opens with the words: "Every where we see toiling millions the slaves of the capitalists; consequently we find unconsumable wealth in the possession of a few, while poverty, discomfort and wretchedness is the lot of the great mass of the people." He found evidence in the entire history of the world for the fact that in civilized countries the rich became richer and the poor became poorer. The greater the wealth of a country, and the greater the riches, power, and splendor of the capitalists, the less was the poor man's share and the harder he had to work for a bare subsistence, until he finally sank into poverty, want, and wretchedness. When the country became completely overstocked with wealth, the workingman could find no work at all. Capitalists would not employ him, being unable to realize a profit from his labor, and he was turned into the street to starve, beg, or steal. But the slaveholder could not do this, said Pickering, for his interest prompted him to keep his slave in a healthy working condition until the surplus wealth was disposed of and he could again be profitably employed.[62] The wages of laborers and slaves were both the same, he argued, namely "such as to enable them to continue the race of journeymen and servants, as the demands of society may happen, from time to time, to require." He cited the authority of Adam Smith for the fact that an employer can realize more profit from the use of free labor than from a chattel slave, and with less risk of capital, and went on to give a detailed analysis of the comparative costs in both cases, the results of which seemed to confirm the theory of Smith.[63] Pickering concluded that the exploitation of slaves and wage-workers was at best identical, and probably greater in the case of the latter. "In neither case would the victims consent to part with the product of their own labor, if they could help it, except for an equivalent; but the masters, having virtually made the laws, have taken good care to protect themselves from violence, while they commit the injustice."[64]

The conditions and status of the workers, and their conception of the nature of that status, were of crucial importance in molding their position on the question of slavery and abolition. An insignificant element in the labor movement came perilously close to defending slavery, like the *American's Own and Fireman's Journal,* which published "A Plea for Slavery" by Las Casas,[65] or the drunken congressman Mike Walsh, whom Frederick Douglass aptly dubbed "that living embodiment of *Subterranean* filth and fury."[66] A much larger number simply paid no attention to the slavery question until about 1845, considering it as a matter of little concern to them, who had their own problems. Their attitude was expressed by a meeting of workers in Massachusetts who said that the slaves were taken care of by their masters—let the workers take care of themselves.[67]

Among those who did take a stand on the slavery question, the great preponderance of opinion was on the side of emancipation, although most labor leaders were not willing to subordinate themselves to the narrow policy of the "pure abolitionists" or subscribe to their philosophy and tactics.[68] The workingmen, believing that their condition was as bad as that of the slaves, were naturally in favor of abolishing "wage slavery" as well as chattel slavery. The most important and the most difficult problem they faced was a matter of strategy: which issue should be given primacy, which was most likely to be accomplished first, and how could they best work for the emancipation of slavery without sacrificing their own cause and retarding its victory? It was a rare labor leader who had the insight to comprehend that the labor movement could not achieve a really independent position until the field had first been cleared by the final overthrow of the slave system and the power of the landed aristocracy—and, as we shall see, the abolitionists hindered their approach to such an understanding. Consequently, the dominant view in the labor movement at this time was that they had to strive for the emancipation of *all* workers, white and Negro, with the immediate and pressing issue being the abolition of wage slavery.

It should be understood that when they spoke of the abolition of wage slavery, most workingmen and their spokesmen did not have in mind the abolition of capitalism. There were some socialists, Utopian and Marxian, in the ante-bellum American labor movement who believed that wage slavery could be ended only by the establishment of a cooperative commonwealth. More commonly, wage slavery was equated not with capitalism but with the worst aspects of it, such as extreme exploitation, narrowing of opportunities for the workers, and disregard for their rights and feelings. To bring these conditions to an end, they proposed such reforms as easy and equal access to the land, public education, a shorter work-day, abolition of monopolies and national banks, and the abolition of slavery. These reforms were intended more to give the workingmen equal opportunity to rise out of the working class than to abolish class society. But in either case the concept of wage slavery was based on a recognition of the existence of classes with different if not opposing interests. This is the essence of class consciousness.

Representative of this viewpoint was the *New England Artisan,* published by the New England Association of Mechanics and Working Men, whose object was to secure the realization of the principles of freedom and equality. The *Artisan* commented on the great exertions made by philanthropists to arouse the sympathy of the white people for the suffering and wretchedness of the slaves. While endorsing these efforts, the paper also called on the philanthropists not to overlook the wrongs inflicted on the white workers every day. The slaves were not the only oppressed and degraded portion of the population, it asserted. "We see oppression all around us; and what is still worse, we see it often inflicted by those very persons who profess to have the most pity for the slaves of the South." The *Artisan* asked the reformers to fight against injustice everywhere and to labor for the destruction of oppression at home as well as for the abolition of slavery in the South.[69] It proposed that slavery, being a "national curse," should be immediately abolished by national means, and suggested that the workingmen petition Congress to accomplish this, possibly by the proceeds from the sale of public land or the surplus revenue of the imposts.[70] A decade later a meeting of 25,000 workers in New York adopted a resolution expressing the same idea: "To slavery in the abstract, slavery in the concrete, to slavery absolute, slavery feudal, and the slavery of wages; to slavery where it is, and where it is not . . . to slavery we are opposed under every phase and modification, and so with firm and solemn purpose will remain until our lives end."[71] The German-American workers generally held the same position, strongly opposing slavery but giving priority to the struggle for the overthrow of wage slavery.[72]

During the 1840's a position of considerable influence in the labor movement was gained by the land reformers, and their attitude toward slavery and abolition strengthened that which was already dominant among the workers. The outstanding leader of the land reformers was George Henry Evans, an English-born associate of Robert Owen, a printer by trade, and a leading figure in the American labor movement from the time of the New York Working Men's Party organized in 1829.[73] During the 1830's he edited *The Man* and the *Working Man's Advocate,* the latter being the foremost labor paper of the decade. In the early 1840's he began to express his views on land reform in *The Radical* and the revived *Advocate,* whose name was later changed to *Young America.* The basis of Evans' program was the belief that labor was enslaved by industrial capitalism and that its only hope of escape lay in breaking the monopoly in land and assuring to every man his share—a quarter-section inalienable homestead. This panacea was to be achieved by political action: "Vote yourself a farm."

Evans had long been an advocate of the abolition of chattel slavery, and he now made this issue a part of his general program for the eradication of all slavery. He believed that it was impractical to attempt to abolish chattel slavery before abolishing "that form of slavery that is nearest home. Having accomplished this, we could with much more effect, it seems to me, turn our attention to that at a distance."[74] Furthermore, he thought it would be foolish to try to "persuade the overworked *white* slaves (supposing they had the power) to vote the *personal* freedom only of the *black,* thereby enabling their former masters, by the lash of want, to get as much labor of two-thirds of them as they formerly got of the whole, throwing the labor of the other third on the already overstocked labor market. Evident, it seems to us, is it the *first* duty of Democracy to decree the freedom of the soil."[75]

Nor would it be of any advantage to the Negroes to substitute wage slavery for chattel slavery, contended Evans. The abolitionists had employed bad arguments, based on false principles, because they failed to recognize man's right to the use of the earth as an essential freedom. They said to the slaveowners, "Free your slaves (retaining your land), and you will compel them to compete with each other for wages, and get more work from them at less cost. . . ."[76] What benefit would be derived, asked another "Agarian," by granting legal freedom to a man who was denied the means by which he must live? "What profiteth the starving operative, who is *free,* indeed, but is only free to starve?"[77]

John Pickering went further than most land reformers in denying that the slavery question was of any practical concern to the workers at all. He believed that the whole slavery controversy was nothing more than "the jealousy and contention of Northern and Southern capitalists—the Northern white slave driver and the Southern black slave driver." The Northern capitalist begrudged the slaveholders the political power they derived from their right to vote in lieu of their slaves; while the slaveholder was similarly aggrieved that the Northern employers were able to cajole or compel their workers to vote as they were directed. The entire question was simply a matter of which was "the best and most certain scheme, by which the wealth producers of all colors, may be plundered of the greatest amount of the product of labor in a given time?"[78]

The Utopian socialists, who also influenced the labor movement in the 1840's, took a similar position on the slavery question, although they had a different panacea for the regeneration of mankind. The most important of these schemes in America was Fourierism, or Association, propagated by Albert Brisbane. Believing that the great evil of modern society was industrialism, which enthralled the workers in disreputable labor to the profit of a handful of capitalists, Fourier proposed that society be reorganized into phalanxes, cooperative agrarian communities which would gradually spread until they encompassed all of society. The text-book of the American Fourierists was Brisbane's *Social Destiny of Man,* published in 1840.[79] In it he attacked slavery as an infringement of both "Divine law which proclaims the equality of human nature before God, and of Human law which declares an equality of political rights." But slavery was only one of the defects of the social mechanism, and was rooted in the same system of industrial servitude which made labor the serf of capital. It was merely a symptom of a vast social malady which must be cured in order to eradicate the numberless evils including slavery, which were the disgrace and scourge of humanity. That malady was "repugnant industry." "If labor be repulsive, degrading and but poorly rewarded," Brisbane asked "how are the mass to be forced to it otherwise than by *Constraint?*" Therefore, concluded Brisbane, chattel slavery should not be attacked first, and above all not separately, but as part of a complete social reformation.[80]

The Fourierist brief against the abolitionists was that the latter attacked slavery violently, endangering both property rights and the Union, and strove for the most meager results— mere dabbling in effects. The Associationists, on the other hand, would proceed gradually and peacefully, with compensation for the slaveholders, and the underlying cause of slavery would be extirpated rather than simply changing one form of servitude for another and more aggravated form.[81] In 1845, Horace Greeley a prominent convert to Fourierism, was invited to attend the anti-slavery convention at Cincinnati. His declination, together with the letter explaining his action, threw the abolitionists into a furious rage.

> I understand by Slavery [wrote Greeley] that condition in which one human being exists mainly as a convenience for other human beings—in which the time, the exertions, the faculties of a part of the Human Family are made to subserve, not their own development physically, intellectually and morally, but the comfort, advantage or caprices of others. In short, wherever service is rendered from one human being to another, on a footing of one-sided and not of mutual obligation—when the relation between the servant and the served is not one of affection and reciprocal good offices, but of authority, social ascendency and power over subsistence on the one hand, and of necessity, servility and degradation on the other—there, in my view, is Slavery.
>
> You will readily understand, therefore, that, if I regard your enterprise with less absolute interest than you do, it is not that I deem Slavery a less but a greater evil. If I am less troubled concerning Slavery in Charleston and New Orleans, it is because I see so much Slavery in New-York, which appears to claim my first effort. . . . In esteeming it my duty to preach Reform first to my own neighbors and kind, I would by no means attempt to censure those whose consciences prescribe a different course. Still less would I undertake to say that the Slavery of the South is not more hideous in kind and degree than that which prevails at the North. The fact that it is more flagrant and palpable renders opposition to it comparatively easy and its speedy downfall certain. But how can I devote myself to a crusade against distant servitude, when I discern its essence pervading my immediate community and neighborhood?[82]

Another group of Utopians and labor reformers, led by Robert Dale Owen and Frances Wright, had a peculiar solution for the problem of slavery, combining communitarianism and colonization. Fanny Wright had early formed the conviction that slavery was a moral sin and a social cancer, but believed that any plan for its removal must take into consideration the pecuniary interests of the slaveholders and the existing laws of the states, and that the slaves must first be prepared for freedom by education, and, when emancipated, colonized in Africa or some unsettled part of this country. In 1825 she became a convert to Robert Dale Owen's socialist theories and immediately conceived of applying them to the slavery question. Her plan was to persuade the slave-holders to turn their bondsmen over to a cooperative community, where they would be employed in common for five years, thus learning independent industry and at the same time earning enough to buy their freedom (with interest!). Then they would be manumitted and colonized, enabling the poor whites to find a place in Southern agriculture and manufacturing. She estab-lished an experimental plantation at Nashoba, near Memphis, but it was a miserable failure, both in the number of slaves involved and in the results achieved. Ten years later, Miss Wright was saying that the problem must be left to time and the growth of public opinion.[83]

Owen also opposed slavery chiefly on moral and philosophical grounds, and supported Wright's emancipation scheme. He believed that the slaveholders could be persuaded to adopt it just as he supposed the capitalists would accept his plan for the reconstruction of society. He constantly attacked prejudice and encouraged the education of the Negroes, but in his own colony at New Harmony Negroes were excluded, except as helpers "if necessary" or "if it be found useful, to prepare and enable them to become associated in Communities in Africa. . . ."[84] He was an anti-slavery advocate all his life, but his views were always tempered by constitutional reservations and his ties with the Democratic party, as a member of which he served two terms in Congress. He remained a gradualist and a colonizationist long after the latter had been exposed as a pro-slavery device. His greatest service to the cause came only during the war, when he helped to push Lincoln along the path to emancipation.[85]

Orestes A. Brownson was another radical labor reformer (in the late 1830's and early 1840's) who insisted that the wage system was a worse form of oppression than chattel slavery; he called it "a cunning device of the devil, for the benefit of tender consciences, who would retain all the advantages of the slave system, without the expense, trouble, and odium of being slave-holders." Therefore it would do no good to emancipate the slave, for he would be "a slave still, although with the title and cares of a freeman." The best way to hasten abolition, he argued, was not by direct efforts in behalf of the slaves, but by the development and realization of democratic freedom in the non-slaveholding states. "Let us correct the evils at our own doors, elevate the free white laborer, and prove by our own practice, and by the state of our own society, that the doctrine of equal rights is not a visionary dream. O we have much to do here at home."[86]

The abolitionists could simply not understand this language. They were a heroic band of martyred men, defying poverty, social ostracism, the venom of the press and the priesthood, and the violence of lynch mobs to do battle for the downtrodden slaves. Some of them believed they should keep their nose to the abolition grindstone, while others eagerly embraced the multitude of reforms that engaged the "frantic 'forties": women's rights, temperance, world peace, spiritualism, vegetarianism, and the cold-water cure. But whether "one idea men" or "universal reformers," they had, almost without exception, a blind spot for the ills that beset the working men, except as the abolition of slavery would benefit them. The abolitionists of course denied resolutely that wage-earners could be compared with the slaves, and devoted much space in their literature to prove it. Scarcely an issue of any of their papers lacked an article or poem demon-strating the nobility of free labor, refuting the arguments of labor leaders and reformers that the wages system was a disguised form of slavery, and presenting evidence of the constant improvement in the condition of the proletariat. Every time they heard some

one say a laborer was a slave they saw red, and occasionally their
indignation stirred them to a literary explosion such as this:

> And is *this* the man, thou vaunting knave!
> Thou hast dared to compare with the weeping slave?
> Away! find *one* slave in the world to cope
> With him, in his heart, his home, his hope!
>
> He is not on thy lands of sin and pain,
> Seared, scarred with the lash—cramped with the chain;
> In thy burning clime where the heart is cold,
> And man, like the beast, is bought and sold!
>
> But O, thou slanderer, false and vile!
> Dare but to harm his garden-stile;
> Dare but to outrage his lowly thatch;
> Dare but to force that poor man's latch;
>
> And thy craven soul shall wildly quake
> At the thunder peal the dead shall wake;
> . . . [87]

Not content with proving the superiority of free labor over
slavery, the abolitionists often went further and denied that there
was any real labor problem at all, at least in this country. Gar
rison received the shock of his life when he visited London for
the World's Anti-Slavery Convention in 1838 and was handed a
leaflet reading: "Have we no white slaves?" and signed by "A
White Slave." Reading this to his audience, he answered em
phatically "No." But he admitted that the British operatives were
"grievously oppressed" and dying of starvation, and when he
asked his listeners if the abolitionists did not show their friend
ship for all humanity by their sympathy with the laborers, he was
nearly knocked off the platform by a resounding "No!" Feebly
recovering his composure, he said he was sorry to hear it, but
assured the audience that "it is not true of the abolitionists in the

United States, for they are sympathetic with the oppressed, as well as the enslaved throughout the world." This incident gave him food for thought on the voyage home, but after an intense soul searching he concluded that his words "throughout the world" were somewhat hasty—he really meant throughout the British Empire. He told his welcoming committee when he disembarked: "In England I have seen dukes, marquises, and earls, and royalty itself, in all the hereditary splendor of an ancient monarchy, surrounded with luxury and pomp, and the people impoverished and oppressed to sustain it all; but here, in New England, one looks for such inequality in vain. . . ."[88]

Garrison had always been hostile toward the labor movement. In the very first issue of the *Liberator* he wrote:

An attempt has been made—it is still making—we regret to say, with considerable success—to inflame the minds of our working classes against the more opulent, and to persuade them that they are contemned and oppressed by a wealthy aristocracy. That public grievances exist, is undoubtedly true; but they are not confined to any one class of society. Every profession is interested in their removal—the rich as well as the poor. It is in the highest degree criminal, therefore, to exasperate our mechanics to deeds of violence, or to array them under a party banner; for it is not true, that, at any time, they have been the objects of reproach. . . . We are the friends of reform; but that is not reform, which, in curing one evil, threatens to inflict a thousand others.[89]

A few weeks later he returned to the subject to deny that wealth and aristocracy were allied and that they were the natural enemies of the "poor and vulgar." There was no evidence, he asserted, that the wealthy were hostile to the interests of the working classes, and those who inculcated that "pernicious doctrine" were the worst enemies of the people. "It is a miserable characteristic of human nature to look with an envious eye upon those who are more fortunate in their pursuits, or more exalted in their station."[90]

Garrison finally had to admit that there was poverty and suffering in the United States, and he brought forward a solution for the difficulties of the poor: "They must be sought out by personal effort, and their want be made known, and then enough ready hands and willing hearts can be found to give relief." Rich women especially should "forsake, awhile, the gaieties and follies of your parties of pleasure, to enjoy the bliss of relieving distress. . . . 'GO ABOUT DOING GOOD.' "[91]

Wendell Phillips, after the war to become an outstanding labor reformer, was embarrassed when mistaken for one in 1847. He was misquoted (and still is) as having said that "the great question of Labor, when it shall fully come up, will be found paramount to all others, and that the rights of the peasant of Ireland, the operative of New England, and the laborer of South America will not be lost sight of in sympathy for the Southern slave." *The Harbinger* hastened to hail him for taking "the high road to the principle of social reform," but Phillips shortly corrected the misapprehension. He had spoken of the workers in *England,* not *New England;* the latter he did not regard as wage slaves. In fact he denied that they were wronged or oppressed, and if they were they could remedy it by voting and by practicing economy, self-denial, temperance, morality and religion, eventually becoming capitalists themselves.[92]

C. M. Clay also had an "impartial word" on the subject of the "elevation of labor." He was quite sure that society would never be organized differently than it was then or ever had been. As for trade unions and strikes, while he would not outlaw them, he was convinced that they rarely, if ever, did the workers any good, and often did "infinite evil." And the practice of strikers hindering other workers from taking their jobs by force he regarded as "the most infamous despotism—another name for lynch or mob law, which is at war with all order and human society. . . ." The solution: "Repeal all laws which obstruct man in the use of all the powers which God has given him; and then render those powers as perfect as possible!"[93] Other abolitionists had occasion o give their views on the labor question from time to time. Ebenezer Hunt, an abolition candidate for office in Lowell, replied to a questionnaire: "I am in favor of limiting Labor to such hours, as are mutually agreed upon by the laborer and his employer.... As a general rule salaries should be low."[94]

When they were face to face with the workers, the abolitionists were willing to hold their tongues on the issue of labor reform and tried instead to persuade them that the abolition of slavery must precede any improvement in the status of labor. In 1847 the Labor Reform League of New England held its convention in Boston, the headquarters of Garrisonianism. Among the resolutions to be voted on was one advocating the abolition of *all* slavery. But the abolitionists packed the meeting, took over the leadership, and introduced a substitute resolution stating "That American Slavery is an evil of such gigantic magnitude, that it must be uprooted and overthrown, before that elevation sought for by the laboring classes, can be effected." There was some discussion, but the resolution never came to a vote—the workingmen had all gone home.[95]

The abolitionists pointed the finger of shame at the workers for their selfishness in striving for their own salvation and failing to join in the crusade for emancipation,[96] and the working men in turn accused them of sheer hypocrisy for ignoring the merits of the labor question. "What say, friend Garrison?" asked the *Voice of Industry*.

re we not more liberal than you had supposed? Affinities find each other, ou say, and we shall understand each other in due time. Till then let us exercise charity for each other, and not claim for ourselves more of the genuine spirit of reform, than we are willing to award others, who are laboring as sincerely as ourselves, if not in the same department, in some other, to bring about the glorious era, when wrong and injustice shall cease, and universal rights shall be recognized from East to West, from North to South.[97]

The Boston *Pilot* attacked the false philosophy of the abolition-ists whose "hearts were as soft as butter towards the oppressed laborers in the South, but as hard as flint towards a large portion of the white laborers,"[98] and many labor papers admonished the abolitionists that "charity begins at home."[99]

Many working men believed that the abolitionists not only overlooked the labor question but that they were the bitterest opponents of labor reform and were themselves exploiters of labor in their kitchens and in their factories. The Fall River *Weekly News,* commenting on the thirteen-hour day at Lowell, said: "The owners of the factories hand round the paper for the girls to sign against black slavery in the South, while at the same time they are over-working the free white laborers, of the North, that they may swell their gains and revel in aristocratic pride."[100] George Henry Evans observed that if the alleviation of human suffering were the real object of the philanthropists, they could find ample room for their work close at home. "When they shall have ceased to oppress and grind in the dust the widows and orphans whom Providence has placed at their mercy—when they convince us that the laborers in their factories are better clothed and fed, and in truth enjoy the boasted rights of freemen in a greater degree than the slaves of the South, we will give them that credit for sincerity, and honesty of purpose which we cannot now award to them."[101]

A poem widely printed in the labor press told of the death of a factory girl from overwork and ended:

> That night a chariot passed her,
> While on the ground she lay;
> The daughters of her master
> An evening visit pay—
> Their tender hearts were sighing
> As negroes' woes were told;
> While the white slave was dying
> Who gained their father's gold.[102]

Suspicion of the abolitionists' sincerity was not alleviated when a group of Negroes applied for employment at their places of business, and were either rejected or given menial jobs.[103] Some workers went so far as to charge that the abolitionists were motivated by a desire to "divert you from the protection of your rights and interests, by occupying your attention upon the condition of the colored men while they are enslaving the whites."[104] Others accused them of wanting to emancipate the slaves in order to reduce the wages of their employees.[105]

In this atmosphere of mutual recrimination, in which exaggeration and needless vituperation were employed on both sides, and in view of the opposing philosophies of the two groups, the possibility of cooperation was remote. The Associationists urged unity among all reformers,[106] and the Lynn *Pioneer* suggested that the Massachusetts Anti-Slavery Society and the New England Workingmen's Association should be composed of the same persons, for until they united to work for their common objectives, neither could expect to accomplish much.[107] Some of the abolitionists likewise urged that they should take up the laboring men's cause and thus enlist them in the anti-slavery movement.[108] But the abolitionists were only willing to unite on the condition that the workers abandon their own struggle, and this they would not do.[109] A rapprochement could not be effected until the workers became convinced that the slavery question was of immediate and vital concern to them and the abolitionists learned that they could not go it alone. Talk was useless—only the events of the next decade could bring this about.

Lords of the Lash and Lords of the Loom

Just as the slaveholders feared the revolutionizing effects of industry in their midst, they also took alarm at the growth of capitalism in the Northern states. The conflicting interests and

needs of the Southern planters and Northern middle class ha
furnished the dominant theme in American history since th
founding of the Republic, and while they had been able to wor
out a *modus vivendi,* however uncomfortable at times for one c
the other, a showdown was clearly approaching in the not tc
distant future. "The truth is," admitted Pickens of South Care
lina, "the moral power of the world is against us. It is idle t
disguise it. We must, sooner or later, meet the great issue that
to be made up on this subject."[110] Both sides began polishin
their weapons, including the ideological weapons aimed at rallyin
the support of the people. One of the sharpest in the armory c
the slaveholders was the propaganda assault against the "failure c
free society."

This campaign had three principal components, the first c
which was an attempt to demonstrate that the conditions of th
slaves were superior to those of the Northern workers. Jam
Hammond exposed the absurdity of the view that slavery w
"unpaid labor," and repelled the accusation that the slaveowne
were robbers because they did not pay wages to their slaves. I
fact, he said, slaves received more in return for their labor tha
did the wage-earners. Men labored only to support themselves ar
their families, he contended, and the reward of manual labor w
seldom sufficient to provide more than a bare subsistence. As ev
dence he pointed to the factory workers of England, most c
whom "drag out a miserable existence, and sink at last under a
solute want." What is the value, he asked, of going through t
form of paying wages when they amounted to only a pittan
which was not enough to feed, clothe, and lodge them in reaso
able comfort? Though the slaves were not paid their wages
money, Hammond insisted that they were actually better i
warded with the necessaries and comforts of life, in sickness ar
in health, than the wage earners.[111] In proof of this the statist
of the Northern states were borrowed liberally and paid back wi
interest.[112] The figures on pauperism and crime were report

avidly, and they exhibited a shocking incidence and an even more alarming tendency to increase rapidly.[113] Wide publicity was given to exposures of starvation wages paid to Northern laborers, the extreme poverty and destitution that were suffered by large numbers of workers in the cities, the breakup of families, the prevalence of prostitution, and the abominable conditions in the factories—". . . overheated rooms, containing a hundred persons each, confined to spaces of five feet square, for thirteen hours a day. . . ."[114] During the hard winter of 1855, the slaveholders of Alabama infuriated the Northern press by raising a subscription among their slaves for the relief of destitute workers in Northern cities.[115]

One of the most telling indictments against Northern society was its complete failure to provide insurance against the vicissitudes of unemployment, sickness and old age, which left the laborer at the mercy of meager and uncertain charity, in contrast to the paternalistic chattel system which allegedly provided the necessities of its wards throughout life. The defenders of slavery claimed this as among the greatest boons it conferred upon the slaves. Chancellor Harper thought that wage-earners would appreciate it if some superior power imposed upon them the necessity to be temperate and to perform regular and healthful labor, in return for which they would be saved from the torturing anxiety of their future support, be amply provided with their natural wants, become parents without fear of being unable to support their children, be relieved in sickness, and in old age wear out the remains of existence among familiar scenes and accustomed associates, without being driven to beg, or to resort to the hard and miserable charity of a work-house. . . ." And this, he boasted, was the actual condition of the Southern slaves![116]

The literary masterpiece of this pro-slavery argument was William J. Grayson's long poem, *The Hireling and the Slave*.[117] The object of the poem he stated in the preface: ". . . I have merely

desired to show that there is a poor and suffering class in all
countries, the richest and most civilized not excepted—laborers
who get their daily bread by daily work, and that the slave is as
well provided for as any other. The poor we shall have with us
always. . . ." The poem begins with an assertion of the divine
injunction on man to earn bread by the sweat of his brow:

> Fallen from primeval innocence and ease,
> When thornless fields employed him but to please,
> The laborer toils; and from his dripping brow
> Moistens the length'ning furrows of the plow;
> In vain he scorns or spurns his altered state,
> Tries each poor shift, and strives to cheat his fate;
> In vain new-shapes his name to shun the ill—
> Slave, hireling, help—the curse pursues him still;
> Changeless the doom remains, the mincing phrase
> May mock high Heaven, but not reverse its ways.
> How small the choice, from cradle to the grave,
> Between the lot of hireling, help, or slave![118]

After describing the poverty and misery of the English laboring
class, Grayson mocks the Pharasaism of the British philanthropist
for their attack against slavery, which is the best agency discovered for "civilizing" the Negroes in accordance with God's command. A diatribe against the abolitionists follows, and then he
gets down to his main object of showing the slave to be better
off than the hireling.

> If bound to daily labor while he lives,
> His is the daily bread that labor gives;
> Guarded from want, from beggary secure,
> He never feels what hireling crowds endure,
> Nor knows, like them, in hopeless want to crave,
> For wife and child, the comforts of the slave,
> Or the sad thought that, when about to die,
> He leaves them to the cold world's charity,
> And sees them slowly seek the poor-house door—
> The last, vile, hated refuge of the poor.[119]

Idle dreamers like Fourier and Owen seek a scheme for elevating the workers, but much more useful would be an angel descending from heaven and offering them the answer to their prayers—

> Food, clothing, free from the wants, the cares
> The pauper hireling ever feels or fears;

which can be provided only by chattel slavery.

> How freely would the hungry list'ners give
> A life-long labor thus secure to live!

The poem ends with a lengthy panegyric on the happy life of the slave, with all his needs provided, working happily in the fields by day, enjoying the warm society of his family in the cabin at night, idling through life in "the summer shade, the winter sun," and without fear of the poor-house at its close. The description grows more rapturous line by line until we finally find the slave "luxuriating" in a "lotus-bearing paradise."[120]

These arguments were misleading because they were based on the conditions of the most exploited workers, often used statistics of conditions during depression years, and frequently employed illustrations of English factory workers but gave the impression that they were typical of all American workers. However, there was just enough truth in them to make a plausible argument that the status of the working class was as bad as that of the slaves.

It was but a short step from this proposition to the next, that the so-called free laborers were actually slaves in all but name, and the socialists (St. Simon and Fourier) were given credit for having discovered the true character of capitalist exploitation. In fact, the slaveholders' argument on that score diverged very little from that of the workingmen, except in the conclusions they drew from it: the former thought it would be just as well to reduce all workers to chattel slavery, while the latter proposed to abolish all forms of slavery. James Hammond said in the Senate that in all social systems there must be a class to perform the mean duties, the drudgery of life. That class required vigor, docility, fidelity, little skill, and a low order of intellect. Its exertions made possible the existence of a leisure class which provided progress, refinement, and civilization. "It constitutes the very *mud-sills* of society and of political government; and you might as well attempt to build a house in the air, as to build either the one or the other, except on the *mud-sills*." Fortunately for the South, he stated, the Negro race had been found at hand, well adapted to fill that role. "We use them for that purpose, and call them slaves. We are old-fashioned at the South yet; it is a word discarded now by ears polite; but I will not characterize that class at the North with that term; but you have it; it is true; it is everywhere; it is eternal." All the powers on earth could not abolish slavery until God repealed the fiat that "the poor ye always have with you." The man who lived by daily labor, and had to sell it in the market for the best price he could get, was truly a slave. The only difference was that the Negro slaves were hired for life and well paid, while the white slaves were hired by the day, not cared for, and scantily compensated.[121]

Calhoun, Edmund Ruffin and Chancellor Harper defined slavery in much the same way, that is, as the latter put it, a system whereby "a man is compelled to labor at the will of another, and to give him much the greater portion of the product of his labor ... and it is immaterial by what sort of compulsion the will or the labor is subdued," whether by force or by starvation. They also agreed that in all cases the laborer received for his labor only enough to maintain existence.[122] All "good and respectable people," said Fitzhugh, "who do not labor, or who are successfully trying to live without labor, on the unrequited labor of other people," are cannibals, and the capitalists were the greatest cannibals of them all, for they did not even allow their slaves to retain enough of the proceeds of their labor to maintain themselves when they could no longer work—the wage-earners were slaves without masters. All were striving to obtain "property in man, he asserted, and why should they not be obliged to take care of men, their property, as they did their horses and their cattle? "Now, under the delusive name of liberty, you work him, 'from morn to dewy eve'—from infancy to old age—then turn him out to starve. You treat your horses and hounds better. Capital is a cruel master. The free slave trade, the commonest, yet the cruellest of trades."[123]

The final argument in the Southern gravamen against capitalism was that it bred an irrepressible conflict of classes that threatened to destroy the property relations of both the capitalist and the slaveholding systems. This was what they really meant when they spoke of the "failure of free society"—its failure to control the "mudsills." And this was what the slaveholders regarded as the real difference between slavery and free labor: while both might be exploited in the same degree, and while both might be virtually slaves, the former had no legal or political rights, but the latter were able to conduct an economic and political struggle for the improvement of their conditions. The propagandists pointed to the working class revolutions in Europe and were "haunted by the specter," for they saw signs of the same development in the United States. They noted the growing concentration of capital in a few hands, the steady deterioration in the conditions of the workers, and the increasing difficulty of their rising from the ranks of the working class. In the rise of the labor movement, the spread of socialist doctrines, the outbreak of strikes, and the growing class- and political-consciousness of the workers they saw visions of an impending social upheaval.[124]

The slaveholders held to the stake-in-society doctrine of the Federalists, that the government must in effect be controlled by one class or group of property interests and that its principal function was to protect those interests against the "jealousy and licentiousness" of the "lower orders." In an agrarian society such as existed at the time of the founding of the Republic, it might be possible to maintain republican forms of government, for the majority of the people were property-holders. But with the development of capitalism and the creation of a large and growing class of propertyless workers a "dangerous element" was introduced into society, a "reckless and unenlightened" population which would use its unbridled liberty and its votes to plunder the rich. There were two possible solutions to this menace of a "rampant and combative spirit of discontent," and in the last analysis they were really the same. One was to abandon the pretense of democracy and establish an undisguised dictatorship of the "rich and the educated," excluding the "poor and the ignorant" from all participation in the management of public affairs, and maintain order by a standing army.[125] The second solution, most effective if applied along with the first, was to abandon the pretense of freedom and establish an undisguised slavery for the laboring classes. The advantages seemed almost too obvious to name: it cured the workers of their habit of contracting "deep and inveterate hatred against society; at least, against the prosperous portion of it . . . ;"[126] it established "order" in society; it restored the "true relations between capital and labor," that is, the capitalist owned the laborers, and "the problem is solved; there is no further contest; all that is conflicting gives way, and there is harmony between them. . . ."[127] As Grayson wrote:

> No mobs of factious workmen gather here,
> No strikes we dread, no lawless riots fear;
> . . . not where slaves their easy labors ply,
> Safe from the snare, beneath a master's eyes;
> In useful tasks engaged, employed their time,
> Untempted by the demagog to crime,
> Secure they toil, uncursed their peaceful life,
> With labor's hungry broils and wasteful strife.
> No want to goad, no faction to deplore,
> The slave escapes the perils of the poor.[128]

The slaveholders did not quite have things in such perfect "order" in their own domain as they pretended, but they enjoyed taunting the capitalists with this picture of an employers' heaven, and gave them something to think about. And the workers also gave it more than passing thought.

This pattern of anti-capitalist propaganda was no mere philosophical excursion or intellectual exercise, although it was no doubt inspired partly by a sensitive compulsion to rationalize an institution against which the moral power of the world was turned. It was a planned campaign designed to assist the slavocrats in their losing battle to maintain political supremacy in the national government.[129] What was their game?

There was some loose talk about an alliance between the Southern planters and the Northern working class directed against the "swindling bankers," the speculators, and the "mushroom aristocracy," and the words of the Sage of Monticello that the Northern democracy was the natural ally of the South were frequently recalled. But few responsible Southern statesmen had really taken this seriously since John Taylor, the die-hard exponent of pure Jeffersonianism. Of course, they had to maintain a base of popular support in the North, and they appealed to it for aid in the fight against the national bank, the sub-treasury, protective tariffs, abolition and slavery restriction, and against centralized government.[130] In this policy they were highly successful, chiefly through the instrumentality of the Northern wing of the Democratic party. The Federalists and their successors, the Whigs, had always been considered the representatives of the commercial and monied interests, while the Democrats, tracing their ancestry from Jefferson and Jackson, had taken the popular side on the great political issues of the early nineteenth century and won a reputation as the friends of the common people, gaining additional support from the immigrant workers by opposing the nativist trends of the other parties. Many workers responded with interest to the Southern attack on wage slavery and considered the Southern wing of the party as a strong bulwark against the aggressive designs of the capitalists.[131] They hoped to turn to account the division in the ruling classes in the same way that the English workers did to win the ten-hour law. And many demagogues and ambitious labor leaders and politicians exploited the possibilities for securing "offices of honor and profit" by turning the anti-capitalist sentiments of the workers to the service of the slave-holders.[132]

Brownson, although disapproving of slavery, believed that the factory operatives had more to fear from their employers than from the planters and considered their greatest menace to be the consolidation of the federal government under the hegemony of the capitalist class. Since he did not have confidence in the ability of the workers to emancipate themselves, he proposed, as a policy of expediency, the formation of a political party which would unite the working people and the South under the banner of constitutionalism and state rights. In return he offered to resist the efforts of the abolitionists; but he warned the slaveholders that if they chose to unite with the capitalists instead, the workers would "go *en masse* against slavery."[133] Ely Moore, the first president of the New York Trades' Union, chairman of the National Trades' Union, and the first representative of labor in the United States Congress, agreed with this point of view. The consolidating tendencies of the Federalist school, he said, were calculated to "impoverish, depreciate, and degrade the Democracy; especially that portion who, in obedience to the command of Heaven, ea their bread in the sweat of their face." Successful resistance to these tendencies depended on the maintenance of state rights and on the thwarting of the abolitionist effort to destroy the federal system by employing the powers of the national government to achieve their ends. He therefore joined with the slaveholders in pushing through the gag on abolition petitions and voted for the resolution declaring that the government had no jurisdiction over slavery.[134] Mike Walsh, a Tammany opportunist representing

he Irish working class wards of New York fifteen years later,
followed in his footsteps by endorsing every policy put forward
by the politicians of Dixie.[135]

But while the slavery party made political capital by taking
advantage of the antagonism between Northern labor and capital,
hey had no idea of forming an alliance with the former in the
sense that they should jointly run the government. John Randolph
had long before revealed the meaning of this strategy: "Northern
gentlemen think to govern us by our *black* slaves; but let me tell
hem we intend to govern them by their *white* slaves."[136] They
had no intention that the "white slaves" should govern, either
alone or jointly, as they made abundantly clear, although they
strove for Northern votes to sustain their own supremacy. When
hey spoke of an alliance with the workers, they were engaging in
a game of semantics. Representative Bayly of Virginia, for example, stated that the interests of the two classes were identical
because "the greater part of the capital of the Southern planter,
as the whole of the capital of the indigent white man, is labor."
Therefore the protection of the rights of labor and of the property
of the slaveholders were one and the same problem![137] Pickens
and Calhoun are sometimes represented as being among the chief
advocates of an alliance with Northern labor. But the former defined the meaning of this "community of interests" in much the
same way as Bayly: "When we contend for the undivided profits
and proceeds of our labor, do you not see that we stand precisely
in the same situation as the laborer of the North?" He went on
to affirm that, while the slave owners were identified with the
laborers, "at the same time, we shall ever form a barrier against
breaking up the laws and foundations of society."[138] Calhoun's
line was the same. There is no conflict between labor and capital
in the South because "Every plantation is a little community,
with the master at its head, who concentrates in himself the
united interests of capital and labor, of which he is the common
representative." In the Union as a whole, the South forms "the

balance of the system; the great conservative power, which prevents other portions, less fortunately constituted, from rushing into conflict. In this tendency to conflict in the North between labor and capital, which is constantly on the increase, the weight of the South is and ever will be on the Conservative side; against the aggression of one or the other side, which ever may tend to disturb the equilibrium of our political system."[139]

Furthermore, cooperation with Northern democracy was not only galling to the planters but recognized as very tenuous and unreliable, as Chancellor Harper said in his oration in support of Van Buren in 1840: "Is there anything in the principles and opinions of the other party, the great *democratic rabble,* as it has been justly called, which should induce *us* to identify ourselves with that? Here you may find every possible grade and hue of opinion which has ever existed in the country. Here you may find loafer, and locofoco, and agrarian, and all the rabble of the city of New-York, the most corrupt and depraved of rabbles. . . ." The essential principles of democracy, he stated, were the natural equality and unalienable right to liberty of every human being and the divine right of majorities. These doctrines were not only false but portentous to the future of the slaveholding system. While the Northern democracy might be willing for the present to modify those doctrines in favor of the planters, the spirit of democracy made no such exceptions, and the alliance with the Northern democracy could not be expected to last longer than the latter found it necessary or expedient.[140]

When Harper wrote these words he very likely had in mind the statement made by the *Loco-Foco* not long before. It had repudiated the "dough-faced democrats" who compromised the principles of universal liberty in order to please their Southern brethren, but had succeeded only in gaining their scorn and contempt. Neither Washington, Jefferson, Madison, Monroe, nor Jackson had dared to sacrifice the interests of one part of the Union to the policy of the other, and no true democrat would de so now. The Loco-Focos pledged themselves to use all legal means to eradicate the curse of slavery from the land. Democracy, they declared, might tolerate slavery in deference to Constitutional rights, but it could not brook a union with slavery.[141]

In the days of Jefferson, when the country was largely agrarian, there had been a basis for an alliance between planters and Northern democracy against the incipient capitalist class. John Taylor had said, "The question is, whether the landed interest . . . had not better unite with the other popular interest, to strangle in its cradle any infant visibly resembling this terrible giant."[142] But by 1840 the infant who resembled the giant had grown to a gangling youth who was the spitting image of the monster, and quite plainly it could not be easily strangled. But it could be cajoled, threatened, bribed and bullied, and this the slaveholders set out to do.

An essential part of the strategy was to convince the capitalists that abolitionism was a menace to their property as well as that of the slaveholders. The slaveholders' indictment of wage slavery had shown how easily the assault against the slave system could be directed against the property interest of the North, and slavery apologists repeatedly emphasized that the attack on slavery was inculcating a disregard for property rights that created fertile ground for socialist doctrines. Indeed, screamed Fitzhugh, the abolitionists were only socialists in disguise, stirring up the muddy waters of reform in order to rouse the "Oi Polloi rats" against the very edifice of society.[143] And if the "kindred spirits" of abolitionism and radicalism should ever unite, as McDuffie predicted they would, "no human institution will be regarded as a guarantee of any human right, and the property holders of the North, so far from being able to do anything to secure our property from these fanatics and plunderers, will tremble for the safety of their own."[144] In 1830 Thomas Cooper had warned that "the wealth of the wealthy is in danger," and a generation later Fitzhugh was sounding the alarm "that the North has as much to apprehend from abolition as the South, and that it is time for conservatives everywhere to unite in efforts to suppress and extinguish it."[145]

This was the proposition of the slaveholders: the "gentlemen of property," North and South, should hold the reins of government as an instrument for maintaining order and stability, against slave revolts and fugitive slaves on the one hand and against abolitionism and radicalism on the other; the "conservatism of slavery" would save Northern capital "from the thousand destructive isms infecting the social organization" of the North[146] and the capitalists would suppress the "fanatics" who wanted to destroy the social organization of the South. But within this alliance the South was to be "first among equals," and to insure its supremacy it had a few aces in the hole. The ace of spades was the threat of secession, which, it was avowed, would ruin the business of the North and leave it helpless before the wrath of the masses.[147] Or either of those results might be brought about even without secession: the first by the cancellation of business with those suspected of "heresy," and the second by stirring up class strife. Pickens warned that he might "preach up insurrection to the laborers of the North" and Hammond repeated the threat twenty years later: "You have been making war upon us to our very hearth-stones. How would you like for us to send lecturers or agitators North . . .?"[148]

The strategy of the slaveholders was eminently successful. The bulk of the Northern capitalist class was, throughout the antebellum years, opposed in principle to slavery, the domination of the slave-power in the federal government, and the policies which it carried out. But it was even more perturbed by the tumult aroused by the slavery controversy, by the disturbing ferment of radical ideas, by the possibility that the Union might be disrupted and the Southern market lost.[149] Under the influence of these fears and ambitions, and under the pressure of Southern promises and threats, the merchants relinquished one position

after another, made concession after concession and compromise
after compromise until, by the 1850's, they had become a reliable
support of the slave-power in its projects of supremacy and
aggrandizement. One of the essential terms of the bargain, it
will be recalled, was that the Northern partners should suppress
abolitionism. This proviso was faithfully carried out. In 1837
a "Committee of Fifty" New York merchants, rebuffed by
Van Buren in their demand for repeal of the Specie Circular,
decided to issue an appeal to "the intelligence and virtue of the
people." They would report that Van Buren had acted on the
principle that the poor naturally hate the rich rather than on the
belief that the possession of property was the proof of merit.
They would also appeal to their "brethren of the South" for
their generous cooperation, promising that the property owners
of the North would be the last to interfere with the rights of
property of any kind, and that they would "discourage every
effort to awaken an excitement, the bare idea of which should
make every husband and father shudder with horror. . . ."[150]

What they meant by "discouraging every effort to awaken an
excitement" was revealed in the wave of violence that swept
through the North during that decade. In the destruction of the
press of *The Philanthropist* at Cincinnati, the lynching of Lovejoy
at Alton, the mob attacks against abolition meetings in Boston,
Philadelphia, Utica, Haverhill and other cities, it was the universal observation that the inspiration, organization and often
the perpetration of the attacks were the work of the "respectable
gentlemen of property and understanding" intent on putting
down disquieting innovations and propitiating the slaveholders.[151]

The consummation of the marriage between the "slave power
of the South and the banking power of the North" was announced by Senator Morris of Ohio in 1839. "The cotton bale
and the bank note have formed an alliance, . . ." he declared.
"These two congenial spirits have at last met and embraced
each other, both looking to the same object—to live upon the

unrequited labor of others—and have now erected for themselves a common platform . . . on which they can meet, and bid defiance, as they hope, to free principles and free labor."[152] Of course, part of the business class did not enter into or approve of this alliance, choosing rather to challenge the slave owners for control of the government, and even those who did put on the harness chafed under the restraints. But it required the events of 1845-1860 to disrupt the coalition and throw the two groups into an unreserved contest for hegemony. The same events forced the working class also to re-evaluate its role in the unfolding conflict and its position on the issue that was swallowing up all others—the issue of slavery in the western territories.

CHAPTER IV

THE SLAVE-POWER AND
THE MUDSILLS

Land of the Free

The economy of the United States was bifurcated: in the North a young, vigorous capitalistic order, and in the South an old, decadent slave system. Both were aggressive and expansive —the one because it was young and vigorous, with a rapidly increasing population, stretching forth to reach new markets, trade routes and raw materials, grasping for land to satisfy the yearning hunger of the multitudes of native and immigrant farmers and would-be farmers and the avid appetites of speculators; the other because it was old and decadent, grasping for new lands to replenish the worn-out soil of the seaboard; both because they had to maintain the imperative balance of sections which would assure parity at least in the Senate. For three centuries the white men had been pressing onward, despoiling the Indians of their inheritance and their lives, with scarcely a voice to recall St. Luke 6:31. The new nation by 1840 passed beyond the Mississippi, its cupidity fed by the vision of endless space and blessed with a new name: Manifest Destiny.

But after 1800 it was not enough to seize more land—the division of the booty had to be arranged in advance. While one covetous eye swept the prospective pickings, the other was fixed on the rest of the pack to see that it didn't swallow a larger bite. New England Federalism saw a vision of its tombstone on the plains of Louisiana and fought the Purchase tooth and nail. The campaigns of 1812 to 1815 were shackled by mutual suspicions, and both North and South were baffled in their hopes for Canada and Florida. In 1820 a line was drawn across the map—the Missouri Compromise; and the two sections settled down to enjoy the peaceful repast of new states—one for you and one for me.

For a generation the fearful issue was forgotten as each section developed in its own way within the new limits. But they did not develop at the same rate; the "balance" was becoming lop sided on the Northern end. As Seward noted, the political equilibrium was being upset by the growing physical disequilib- rium. Over two million immigrants came to the United States in the two decades after 1830, most of them staying in the North and by 1850 the Northern population exceeded that of the South by the order of four to three, with every prospect that the numerator would quickly grow larger. In wealth, industry and railroads the disparity was even greater, and as the Western regions were filled, 36° 30′ came to appear to the South less like a dividing line than a restraining rope. The moral balance was turning against her as well, for all the world regarded the chattel system as an anachronism that could not be long for this world. Most Northerners were willing to let it run its course slowly and peacefully out of regard for constitutional guaranties, compromise and property rights, but only because they were satisfied that it was "in the course of ultimate extinction." The assurance of such an eventuality lay in the confinement of the slave area to its then limits, for, as both North and South understood, the law of slavery was Expand or die. But the slaveholders were no prepared for ultimate, let alone imminent, extinction, and in 1845 they got a new lease on life with the annexation of Texas. The irrepressible conflict was under way.

At once the wonted patterns of American life were transfigured. While the dominant section of the Northern business class ful filled its obligations to the alliance, another business group, repre sented by the Northern Whigs, rose up in wrath as it saw the probability of unlimited postponement of its expectations of "ultimate extinction" for slavery and ultimate ascendancy for itself. The appeasement of the slave-power must give way to a firm stand; the contest for control of the Union must be decided in the territories. And the common people recoiled from the perversion of a traditionally democratic foreign policy to one of aggression in the interest of the planter autocracy. For fifteen years the abolitionists had represented the conscience of an apathetic people, but now the still small voice within swelled to a roaring shout of indignation and alarm, and Hosea Biglow took over the job of William Lloyd Garrison. Political parties began to crumble and re-form, as Conscience Whigs and Barn-burning Democrats stood up against the new dispensation, and anti-slavery men experimented with new parties.

The labor movement was no less deeply stirred by these events. Since the time of the Missouri Compromise the American public had shown little interest in the slavery question, and many working people shared this indifference. One can turn the pages of a large number of the workingmen's newspapers, issue after issue and year after year during the 1830's and early 1840's, and scarcely be aware of the existence of slavery. Besides, since the disappearance of the first labor parties shortly after 1830, the working class passed through a period in which political activity was definitely subordinated to economic struggles. In spite of the victories won by those early organizations, it was the opinion of many that the working class was not yet strong enough to maintain an effective independent party, although political action as such was not eschewed. In most of the trade unions of those days the discussion of political questions was not tolerated, for fear of diverting them from their immediate tasks and introducing divisions that would impede a united effort.[1] But the annexation of Texas and the subsequent unfolding of the expansionist program of the slavocracy roused them to a sense of danger and propelled them into the vortex of the political struggles.

Shortly after the establishment of Texan independence in 1836, the Boston *Weekly Reformer* sounded an alarm, warning that by receiving Texas into the Union, "we recognize deliberately and solemnly the right of conquest," and that this would be the signal for the dissolution of the Union. "Much as we love the Union, we love honor, justice, liberty more, and when we are forced to choose between a dissolution of the Union and slavery and national disgrace, we shall not be long in making up our choice."[2] The Loco-Foco legislature of Massachusetts echoed these sentiments, and stated that annexation "will furnish new calumnies against republican governments, by exposing the gross contradiction of a people professing to be free, and yet seeking to extend and perpetuate the subjection of their slaves."[3] The Manchester *Operative* called annexation a base action, "because it would be giving men that live upon the blood of others, an opportunity of dipping their hands still deeper in the sin of slavery. . . . Have we not enough slaves now?"[4] When the act had been consummated, *The Harbinger* branded it as a conspiracy of the slave-power, but added that the slave-power would never have won the day had not the capitalists of the North been willing. "The commercial, manufacturing, industrial, speculating interest of the North fought faintly, trimmed, compromised, conceded; and the instant they could do so with grace, went over with flags flying to the enemy." Northern and Southern capital linked hands against labor under the common war cry, Money before Men.[5]

It is notable that all these expressions came from groups which had until then been indifferent to the slavery issue or decidedly opposed to giving it a prominent place in the consideration of the workers. But now they had their eyes opened to the fact that slavery, particularly in its aggressive phase, constituted a menace to the democratic institutions and principles necessary for the

rowth of the labor movement. All labor spokesmen, of course,
id not react so soon or so fast to the new state of affairs; Robert
)ale Owen, now a congressman from Indiana, believed that
1e benefits accruing to the Union by admitting Texas out-
veighed the benefits conferred upon slavery,[6] and the land
:formers shrugged it off as only another phase of the "contest
etween rich and avaricious planters, and rich and avaricious
1anufacturers, for exclusive privileges."[7] But the rank and file,
ot being wedded to the utopian philosophies of these reformers,
)uld not view it so lightly, and from 1844-1845 they demonstrated
1 the Northern cities against the absorption of the Lone Star
epublic unless provisions were made for the extinction of
avery in her borders.[8]

When the inevitable invasion of Mexico was launched in the
)llowing year, the protests became more vociferous and more
umerous, as workers throughout the North condemned slavery,
1e war and its perpetrators, and demanded the withdrawal of
.merican troops "to some undisputed land belonging to the
nited States."[9] The New England Workingmen's Association,
1eeting in Boston in 1846, resolved that it deeply deprecated
1e "unhallowed war now being waged with such inhuman re-
1lts" and entered its protest against having any part in the
1atter, "having no lives to lose, or money to squander in such
1 unholy and unprofitable cause, to enhance the price of 'Texas
:ript,' and plunder Mexican soil for the United States officers,
aveholders, and speculators to convert into a mart for traffic
1 human blood and human rights."[10]

At the conclusion of the Mexican War—fought, according to
resident Polk, to protect Texas and "to vindicate with decision
1e honor, the rights, and the interests of our country"—it was
)und necessary, apparently as an object lesson to other would-be
ullies, to despoil the Mexican people of an immense chunk of
1eir nation and bring it safely under the wing of the spread-eagle.
'he Texas question thus became the much broader issue of the

expansion of slavery into the territories of the United States, th
control of those territories and, ultimately, the control of th
federal government. This was the dominant political issue of th
next dozen years. The anti-slavery-extension politicians wer
quick to note and to grasp the significance of labor's changin
orientation on the slavery question which resulted from th
Southern policy of aggrandizement and its implications for th
workers; and in the Congressional debates they sedulously cult
vated this development. For the first time since Jackson's ban
war, a major national issue was fought out largely on the bas
of the rights and interests of the wage-earners and farmers.

When David Wilmot of Pennsylvania launched the campaig
to exclude slavery from the territories by the introduction c
his famous Proviso, he remarked, "I would preserve for fre
white labor a fair country, a rich inheritance, where the sons c
toil, of my own race and color, can live without the disgrace whic
association with negro slavery brings upon free labor." Presto
King later reintroduced the Wilmot Proviso with the observatio
"If slavery is not excluded by law, the presence of the slave wi
exclude the laboring white man."[11]

Apart from the Constitutional debate over the right of Congre
to exclude slavery, much of the discussion followed these line
It was asserted that if slavery were permitted to enter the terr
tories, free labor would be virtually excluded from them, "fc
it is folly to think that our Northern men would emigrate to th
most inviting territory in the world where they know they wi
be compelled to labor side by side with the slave." In proof c
this, speakers cited the degraded condition of the workers in th
South, the "lamentable lack of skill in every department c
industry, in agriculture, and the most common branches c
mechanical pursuits," and the mass exodus of Southern workin
men to the free states and territories; in contrast they pointed t
the honor and respect in which labor was held in the North an
the prosperity of the free laborers. Since the territories must b

either all free or all slave, it was demanded that they be reserved
for the benefit of the Southern workers who required them as a
refuge and for Northern workers who, if confined to the already
free states, would become so populous that their wages would
sink to the starvation level. The North, proclaimed Congressman
Tappan, must unite "to preserve the Territories of the nation, yet
unmoistened by the sweat of the slave, to the *free labor* of the
country, which constitutes the greatest element of its prosperity,
its strength, and its future glory!"[12]

David Wilmot warned that if the free laborer did go into the
territories, along with slaves, the ensuing competition would
soon reduce him to the status of the Southern workers, his dignity destroyed, his wages depressed and his means of employment
snatched from him. In the shadow of the planting aristocracy, the
white worker would be forced into the pattern of a fixed social
stratification of lords and vassals, and "if he can not rise to the
condition of the former, he must sink to a level with the latter."[13]
The contest, then, was but a new form of the old fight of popular
rights against privilege and monopoly, of labor against capital,
but this time not the money-power of the North but the "money-
power in the South, more potent and more dangerous than all
other enemies of labor combined." If freedom was overcome in
this contest, Wilmot predicted, it would be the last struggle ever
made against the advancement of the slave power, which would
then overshadow the country and bear down all opposition to
its will. "Holding in its iron grasp by far the larger and better
portion of the soil of the Republic, the great resource of the
laboring man, it will trample at pleasure upon the rights of the
masses, and in the end deprive them of their just influence and
control in the government."[14]

Few Southerners had the hardihood to meet these arguments
on their own ground. The congressmen from Virginia, rising
to the full height of their chivalrous posture, repudiated with
indignation the argument that free labor could not thrive along

with slave labor as a "vile imposture" and a libel against th "industrious and energetic" laboring people of the South.[15] Bu for the most part the Southerners shunned this phase of th controversy, preferring to stick to Constitutional and legal ques tions and the rights of the Southern states. While they wer expounding their doctrine of slavery as the best condition for th working class they undoubtedly felt that, on the score of labor rights in the territories or elsewhere, the less said the better.

The anti-slavery forces were not yet strong enough to stop th slave-power and its Northern allies, and the Wilmot Proviso wa defeated. By the admission of Texas and the Compromise o 1850 the slave territory was doubled, and one of the most infamou laws ever enacted by the United States Congress was wrappe up in the package. The Fugitive Slave Law dedicated the ful power of the federal government to the noisome task of huntin down men and women seeking freedom and clamping thei shackles tighter than ever—all without trial and without th right of the victim to testify in his defense The slave-powe demonstrated that it had secured a firm grip on the governmen and that it intended to destroy whatever stood in its way, in cluding the democratic traditions and the plain sense of decenc of the American people.

But it reckoned without its host. Every victory had its pric —the increasing alarm, disgust and hostility of the people. Th working people were thoroughly aroused over the bargain o 1850. Even the land reformers, who had only a few years earlie washed their hands of the slavery controversy as of no concer to them, now became among the most vociferous opponents o the slave-power's aggrandizement. They could hardly be other wise, for the policy of handing the territories over to slavery wa certainly the greatest blow that could be delivered to their plar for destroying land monopoly and leading the working class t salvation by dividing among it the treasury of merits store up in the unsettled lands of the West. The National Industria

Congress, meeting in the summer of 1850, condemned slavery as a moral, social and political evil and resolved to oppose the further extension of slavery. It repelled the notion that the slave area must be extended in order to satisfy the South and secure the perpetuation of the Union. "Slavery can never be a bond of union and of freedom," it declared.[16] A land reform journal demanded that the slaves as well as the workers be free and the territories dedicated to their use, "without reference to sex, color, or condition."[17] The Fugitive Slave Law gagged them, as it did every person who was not bound hand and foot to the slave-power. The New York Convention of the Industrial Reformers condemned the law "which converts the citizens of the free states into man-catchers for the slave owners of the South" as "a gross violation of the Constitution, an infamous usurpation, and a despotic enactment, not binding in law or conscience on the people, and ought to be resisted, if necessary, to death, by every friend to our country, to humanity, and to justice."[18] *The Monthly Jubilee* declared that this act did "more to stimulate the Northern mind against slavery than all the abolition speeches and excitement that have been made these last ten years," and that it would "be the cause of the overthrow of the 'peculiar institution.'" Then, "another question, of still more importance, will take the field, namely, the Rights of free Labor."[19] The workers, as a result of stern reality, were arriving at a recognition of the fact that their own elevation could be achieved only after the slavery question had been settled by the abolition of chattel slavery.

The nation swallowed the Compromise of 1850, though it stuck in the throats of many. The Compromise was sold as a measure of finality, putting an end to the vexatious problem and preserving the integrity of the Union. After all, the free states had gained California and Oregon, and the slaveholders would never go into the Southwest anyhow—they had fought only for the principle, but really meant no harm. The two sections could

go their own ways, and no one would be the worse for it, except
the slaves. But what were three and a half million slaves compared
with the maintenance of the Constitution and the Union? The
people dozed, restlessly and fitfully to be sure, under the sedative
of these illusions, until 1854, when finality, banality and tran
quillity alike were blasted by the introduction into Congress of
the Kansas-Nebraska bill. The Compromise had involved terri
tory whose status had not yet been settled, but now territories
that had been reserved for freedom since 1820 were to be fed
into the maw of slavery. Promises, agreements and compromises
were all to be discarded; there was to be no sanctuary for freedom
anywhere; the "ultimate extinction" of slavery was to be made
very ultimate indeed. Was it for this that the North had allowed
gangsters to roam its streets in search of fugitives and supposed
fugitives and suppositious fugitives? Was it for this that the
Southwest was being converted into a slave-pen? Was it for
this that timid souls "bit their lips and kept silent"?

Many workers reacted vigorously against the Nebraska Act
In New York, an overflow mass meeting of four to five thousand
laborers was held to consider this question "of the greatest im
portance to mechanics," and protested "That the repeal of the
Missouri Compromise, in order to introduce Slavery into *our*
free territory of Nebraska and Kansas, would be in every point
a crime, a breach of plighted faith, a violation not only of our
just rights but of the rights of man, in defiance alike of Re
publican principles and Christian duties."[20] Huge meetings of
workers assembled in many other cities in New Hampshire
Pennsylvania, Ohio, Massachusetts, Michigan, Vermont, Con
necticut, Indiana, and Wisconsin, passing resolutions simila
to that adopted at Newark:

Resolved, That we view with jealousy and suspicion the bold attempt
which the Slave Power of the country is now making to degrade the labor
ing and producing classes of the people by establishing its system of chatte

or in the Free territories of the West; and that . . . we would repel and
ent the efforts to introduce the black slaves into our workshops. . . .
Resolved, That the people in this city have abundant reason for sustaining
ee and Independent labor . . . and our influence shall never be given
substitute for it slave labor.[21]

The land reformers, meeting at Trenton for the Ninth National
dustrial Congress, were careful not to identify themselves with
anatic abolitionism," but declared that the grasp of slavery was
ffocating the spirit of freedom and was inimical to the interests
labor. They demanded the repeal of the Nebraska Act and the
igitive Slave Law, the protection of "fugitive freemen by the
ghts of our States, and the strength of our arms," the resigna-
n of the politicians "who sold the priceless principle of freedom
the slave power," and the election of representatives who would
sist its aggressions, and invited "workers and foreign immi-
ants to settle in Nebraska in order to thwart the machinations
the slave power."[22]

The German workers were also roused, and began to modify
eir policy of indifference to political action. The previous year
e Arbeiterbund (Workers' League) had been formed under the
dership of Joseph Weydemeyer, one of the outstanding Marx-
s in America, and he had persuaded it to abandon the opposi-
n to political struggles that dominated the German-American
orkers' organizations. At a mass meeting called by the Bund in
ew York, a resolution introduced by Weydemeyer was adopted,
otesting against the Nebraska bill because it favored the
pitalists and land speculators at the expense of the people, with-
ew vast tracts of territory from the benefits of a future home-
ad law, and furthered the extension of slavery. Denouncing
th black and white slavery, the resolution branded as a traitor
the people every supporter of the bill.[23]

This wave of disaffection in the working class caused con-
rnation in the Democratic party, and the latter assigned to their

old wheel-horse, Mike Walsh, the task of putting his finger in t
dike. This would-be labor representative spoke most fluently
this occasion when he rose to denounce the workers' demonst
tions. He set the halls of Congress rocking with laughter when
reviled the opponents of slavery extension as "a set of pear
agitators and Peter Funk philanthropists" whose object was
revolutionize the country but who "could not revolutionize
barber's shop or an oyster box," and when he made a flippa
apology for slavery.[24] Ten years earlier this was the kind of ta
to win votes, but now the workers could not see the joke. Wa.
had not changed, but the working men had. They were fighti
mad over the arrogance and bullying of the slave-power; and t
talk was that they would be next to have chains hung about th
necks.

The Slave-Power Conspiracy

When the working men insisted on the abolition of *all* forms
slavery rather than exclusive and partial emancipation for
chattel slaves alone, the abolitionists had a stock answer whi
in their minds, put an end to the discussion: Why was the Und
ground Railroad a one-way route? Why, when the slaves we
daily risking their lives to follow the North Star, were no wo
ing men making the trek in the other direction to accept t
wardship of the planters? In asking this question the abolitioni
revealed their inability or unwillingness to comprehend t
ideology of the labor movement. In comparing the two lal
systems, the workers were, of course, speaking of a purely e
nomic relationship and noting the scarcely contestable fact t
the workers, like the slaves, were compelled to place their lal
at the disposal of the employers, and that in return for this lab
they, like the slaves, often received only a subsistence. But th
the analogy ended. The workers, like the slaves, understo

early enough the difference between John Calhoun's "thirty
lashes well laid on" and Francis Lowell's pink slips; between the
overseer and the foreman; between "Yes sir" and "Go to hell."
They knew that, however limited, they possessed means for im-
proving their conditions that the slaves did not have—trade
unions, the right to strike, the ballot, the assembly hall, and the
press. They realized that they had the opportunity to rise out of
their class and become farmers or employers themselves, and
many did. Nor were they unaware of the difference between competing with the low-paid labor of immigrants, Negroes, women
and children, and with the labor of slaves.

In fact, so well did the workers understand these things that
they were made the basis for the most comprehensive and effective of all anti-slavery propaganda appeals. This campaign was
constructed of diverse elements, subtle suggestions and varied
formulations, but in its totality it constituted a logical pattern
which imputed the existence of a far-reaching, well planned and
greatly coordinated slave-power conspiracy whose ultimate object
was to destroy the liberty of the American people in general and
of the workers in particular.

The plot rested on a foundation of the allegedly intrinsic hostility of slavery and the slaveholders to the working class. This
was demonstrated by the conditions of the workers in the Southern states—their low wages, their difficulty in finding employment because of the competition of slave labor, their social and
moral degradation, their mass emigration from the slave states,
their lack of public education and political rights, and the
deprivation of their civil liberties. These conditions, it was asserted, resulted not only from the normal operations of the slave
system, but from the aristocratic pretensions of the slaveholders.
Their contempt for the working class was emphasized by the endless repetition of a dozen phrases that became household words:
"We have got to hating everything with the prefix *free. . . .*";
"free society! we sicken of the name. . . ."; "the very mudsills of

society"; "greasy mechanics"; "filthy operatives"; "the poor a
the ignorant"; "sordid, servile, and laborious beings." Extra str
was placed on those expressions which illustrated the slavocrac
opposition to popular government and democratic institutions: '
laborers ever obtain the political power of a country, it is in fa
in a state of revolution. . . ."; "The most degraded classes . . . a
and must be incapable. . . ."; the capitalists must own the wor
ers, "either collectively through the government, or individually
a state of domestic servitude"; ". . . a dangerous element is intr
duced into the body politic." In newspapers, pamphlets, lectu
halls, and in the Congressional forum, these words were reiterat
time without number to prove the actual status of the laborers
the slave states and to suggest the possible status of all workers
they ever fell under the sway of the Southern oligarchy.

The possibility of such an eventuality first became appare
when, during the 1830's, the slaveholders attempted to restr
abolition propaganda by infringing the civil liberties of the pe
ple. On the theory that the primary responsibility of the gover
ment was the protection of property, they held that it shou
take every measure necessary to prevent "incendiary" attac
against the institution, and if constitutional rights stood in t
way of repression, so much the worse for them. The slaveholde
had their own "higher law"—the sanctity of slave property. C
the demand of the Dixie dictators, Congress pushed through t
gag law prohibiting the reception of abolition petitions, and t
postmaster imposed a censorship of the mails to prevent the circ
lation of abolition literature. Their appetite growing by what
fed on, the slaveholders called upon the Northern legislatures
enact penal laws against the "seditious activities" of the abolitio
ists, and in several states such bills were introduced.

The defense of the abolitionists became an urgent necessity
the rights of the working people were to be preserved. T
Massachusetts Anti-Slavery Society defined the issue with pre
sion in its appeal to the legislature against the proposed su

rsion of the Constitution. It asserted that the abolitionists were
gaged in work that was essential for the preservation of the
erties of mankind in general and of the working class in par-
ular. Abolitionism could not be proscribed without destroying
e first principles of republican freedom, for it would require an
t of legislative usurpation that would be fatal to the liberties
d sovereignty of the people. What encouragement, it asked,
ould be left for any men to vindicate the rights of any people,
hen they found themselves under the rod of lawless and un-
ghteous power? What security would there be for the liberties
 mankind when the principle was established that it was "in-
ndiary" and "treasonable" and contrary to law for men to pro-
aim the precepts of righteousness and to plead the cause of the
pressed? "We ask, especially, what security will remain for the
ooring classes of our free Commonwealth, if *legislative censure
d proscription* are to be awarded to those who protest against
e enforcement of involuntary labor without wages?" The object
 the Southern states, concluded the Society, was "nothing more
r less than *the subjugation of the free laboring population of the
n-slaveholding states* to a despotism no less appalling than that
 which the laboring population of the South are now sub-
cted."[25]

This attempt to suppress abolitionism suffered defeat, but what
uld not be accomplished legally it was proposed to do with
tra-legal vigilante committees. The Northern merchant class
ganized mobs to put down the abolitionists, and again the
mocratic rights of the people depended on resisting the assault.
 writer in *The Philanthropist* pointed out the menace to labor in
proposed anti-abolition meeting called in Philadelphia:

> *Pay to the laborer!* Never no never!
> Stoop to persuade whom we love to command;
> Pay to the *laborer* never no never!
> Till God's vialed vengeance be poured on the land.

> Children of Penn! will ye come for the calling
>> Of those who will spurn ye like dogs when ye've done?
> The pitiful Tyrants whose fortunes are falling,
>> McDuffie, and Pickens, and Wise and Calhoun?
>
> They call us "white slaves," aye slaves *shall they* find us
>> With shoulders so patient and souls so subdued
> As to help forge the fetters with which they will bind us,
>> To kiss the same hand our own blood is imbrued?[26]

But the meeting was held; and when, shortly after, the abo
tionists erected Pennsylvania Hall as a forum for anti-slave
meetings, it was burned to the ground by "an orderly, we
dressed assemblage of men" with the apparent connivance of t
police.[27] The invasion of Constitutional rights became bolder a
more far-reaching as the slave-power strengthened its grip on t
federal government, the most notorious instance being the Fu
tive Slave Act of 1850. William Seward warned that this act w
a legislative usurpation which was being boldly enforced by t
courts. Congress had violated the Constitution by compelling nc
slaveholders in the free states to capture and deliver fugiti
slaves. The ancient writ of *habeas corpus* had been made an i
strument for the capture of slaves, and the process of punishme
for contempt made sufficient cause to imprison a citizen witho
indictment, trial or conviction, without bail and without limit
sentence. "Are not these invasions of state rights," he aske
"fearfully premonitory that slavery is to become a universa
ruling power throughout the republic?"[28]

Many believed that slavery had already become the "universa
ruling power," that it was employing its control of the gover
ment to pursue a policy which was utterly incompatible with t
interests of the working class, and that if it were not overthrov
it would completely submerge "the principles upon which t
organization of free labor society rests."[29] Others considered t
supremacy of the slave power to be a matter not of controlling t
government but of extending the area of slavery, and it was t

ansionist program which began in 1845 that awakened them
the danger of its universal dominion. The conquest of Mexico
made the free and slave regions approximately equal, but
n more direful was the Kansas-Nebraska Act, which repealed
Missouri Compromise and established the possibility that all
territories of the United States could be thrown open to
very, so that there would be no place where laborers and
mers could go without subjecting themselves to the competi-
n and degradation that was the lot of the Southern working
ss. These fears were confirmed when, in 1857, the Supreme
urt passed down its decision on the *Dred Scott* case. Going
ond its judicial prerogative, the Court laid down the theory
dear to the slaveholders, that Congress could pass no laws
ich in any way interfered with its most solemn obligation of
arding and protecting the owner in his rights" of holding
perty in man. Consequently the Missouri Compromise was
alid and slaveholders could go into any of the territories and
guaranteed the protection of the government.

Many perceived in the Nebraska Act and the *Dred Scott* dictum
gical pattern which led inevitably to the introduction of slav-
even into the free states. The Mechanics and Workingmens'
ntral Union of New York condemned the decision and saw
it evidence that the slaveholders had a "settled determination"
make their institution legal in all the states, thus depriving free
or of the ability to protect itself against the competition of
ve labor.[30] The "nationalization of slavery" was seen not only
the logic of events and arguments, but as a conspiracy that was
eady in the making. Charles Sumner said that slaveholders
re now claiming the right to carry slaves into New York and
ınsylvania while in transit to slave territory, and that the
rts of the latter state had sustained them.[31] In 1854, Dumas
n Deren, editor of the *Mattoon* (Illinois) *National Gazette,*
ke of free labor as a "novelty" and a "humbug" and proposed
introduction of slavery into Illinois by amending the state
stitution. He wrote to Southerners, urging them to emigrate

to Illinois in order to carry the plot and win for the Southe
people possession of "the key to the western world." Seve
Southern newspapers endorsed the idea jubilantly, one proclai
ing that "The South should not content herself with maintaini
her ground; she should progress. She should expand her insti
tions wherever soil, climate, and products are adapted to them."
If these schemes were executed, the United States would be co
verted into a slaveholding empire which would "blast, as with
sirocco, those influences which make MAN . . . the first gr
aim of Society and Government;" and the workers would
forced "into Canada, Russian America, Australia, and wherev
else, throughout the whole earth, from which industry can fi
refuge."[33] It was this thought that inspired Seward's famous ref
ence to the "irrepressible conflict between opposing and endura
forces." He foresaw that the United States must become, soon
or later, either entirely a slaveholding nation or entirely a fi
labor nation. "Either the cotton and rice-fields of South Caroli
and the sugar plantations of Louisiana will ultimately be tilled
free labor, and Charleston and New Orleans become marts f
legitimate merchandise alone, or else the rye-fields and whe
fields of Massachusetts and New York must again be surrender
by their farmers to slave culture and to the production of slav
and Boston and New York become once more markets for tra
in the bodies and souls of men."[34]

It was this idea also which inspired a correspondent of t
Anti-Slavery Bugle to write "Men of Labor":

> Men of Labor, ho! the battle
>   Calls to action, calls to arms;
> Shall your toil be free or fetter'd
>   In your workshops, on your farms?
> Plough and loom, and ringing anvil,
>   Trowel, hammer, spade and hod—
> Shall they bear the curse of bondage,
>   Or the Freedom born of God?

Lo! 'tis yours to give the answer,
  Yours to say if Slavery's night
Wider o'er this fair Republic
  Shall extend its awful blight—
Blight to speech, and soil, and labor,
  Blight to all that lifts and saves
Freemen—sovereigns in their freedom—
  From the grade and fate of slaves.

Shall the taskman's human chattel
  Here, or over Kansas plains—
Marching, "like dumb driven cattle,"
  To the music of his chains—
Further curse the land your fathers
  Won for Freedom with their blood?
Further, thrice-accursed Slavery!
  Sweep and whelm you with its flood?

Men of labor, shall your labor
  Be degraded everywhere?
Further shall the taskman's chattel
  Three-fifths of your franchise share?
Further shall this cloud of bondage
  Yonder go, or hither come?
On Free Soil, or in Free Senates,
  Further strike your Free Speech dumb![35]

This much of the "slave-power conspiracy" was constructed
from the observed facts of its operation, implemented only by the
imputation of a premeditated design to proceed step by step to a
fixed end. And the end, the capstone of the plot, was furnished
by the slaveholders themselves, namely, the reduction of the free
laboring class to slavery. While they never actually said that the
workers should be literally enslaved, and probably had enough
sense to realize it could not be done, they had predicted that it
would one day be necessary and had clearly expressed their belief
that the world would be a better and safer place to live in if it
were done. From the slaveholders' indictment of the "failure of
free society" it could be inferred that this was in the back of their

minds; from their panegyrics of the slave system, the corollar
could logically be deduced that they could not but favor such
policy; and from their contemptuous references to free labo
it could be supposed that they would one day attempt it. I
could be, and it was.[36] But the pro-slavery propaganda gav
grounds for more than inference, deduction and supposition, an
this propaganda was captured by anti-slavery men and turne
against the enemy.

Calhoun had been one of the first apologists of slavery to defin
the "positive good" doctrine. In the first generation after th
Revolution, the natural rights theory was yet popular even amon
the Southern aristocracy, and many of them could still utter mil
condemnations of slavery. Most of them defended slavery apolo
getically, as an institution that had been bequeathed to them, o
even forced upon them, by the English, and there was nothin
they could do about it except treat the slaves humanely an
colonize those who were emancipated. They admitted that slaver
was an abomination in the sight of man and God, but if it wer
abolished the South would be ruined, there would be no one
raise the cotton, there would be race war, and besides the Negro
weren't ready for it yet. But Calhoun announced that the "fol
and delusion" that slavery was a moral and political evil wer
gone, and that the South now saw it in its true light, as "the mo
safe and stable basis for free institutions in the world." It was
longer an evil, or a relative evil, or even a relative good, but
positive good, for slave, for master and for society. It was
natural progression from this position to a defense of slaver
as the best condition not only for "inferior races" but for "inferi
classes" as well. And the progression was made. The Richmor
Enquirer put it boldly:

Until recently, the defence of slavery has labored under great difficulti
because its apologists were merely apologists, took half-way ground. Th
confined the defence to *mere negro slavery,* thereby giving up the slave

rinciple, admitting other forms of slavery to be wrong, and yielding up
ιe authority of the Bible, and of the history, practices, and experience of
ιankind.—Human experience, showing the universal success of slave
ιciety, and the universal failure of free society, was unavailing to them,
ecause they were precluded from employing it, by admitting slavery in
ιe abstract to be wrong. The defence of mere negro slavery involved
ιem in still greater difficulty. The laws of all the Southern States justified
ιe holding white men in slavery, provided that through the mother they
ere descended, however remotely, from a negro slave. The bright
ιulattoes, according to their theory, were wrongfully held in slavery.

The line of defence, however, is changed now, and the North is com-
ιetely cornered, and dumb as an oyster. The South now maintains that
ιavery is right, natural, and necessary. It shows that all divine and almost
ι human authority justifies it. The South further charges, that the little
:periment of free society in Western Europe has been, from the beginning,
ι cruel failure, and that symptoms of failure are abundant in our North.
'hile it is far more obvious that negroes be slaves than whites—for they
e only fit to labor, not to direct—yet the principle of slavery is in itself
ght, and does not depend on difference of complection.[37]

his article was reprinted in other Southern papers, and some
: them wrote their own variations on the theme,[38] but it received
idest publicity in the North, where it was broadcast with and
ithout comment as the most damning exposure of the true
ms of the slave-power conspiracy.[39]

Even in the case of this final stage of the "conspiracy," people
ιund evidence of attempts here and there to begin putting it
to execution. For example, numerous instances were reported of
ιaves, particularly fugitives, who had no "visible admixture of
egro blood," which was cited as proof that the color line was no
ιrrier to enslavement; and it was said that the language of the
ιgitive Slave Act made it applicable to white apprentices and
ι other white men who owed service, and that one such case
ιd actually been enforced in the courts.[40] The enslavement of
ee Negroes who failed to depart from certain Southern states
ithin a specified time, and of free Negroes in the North who
ιuld not definitely prove their right to freedom, showed that a

legal status of freedom could not be an assurance against the "man-stealers."[41] Some thought that the scheme was to make a wedge by enslaving immigrants, for it was said that Robert Wickliffe of Kentucky had suggested, in case of a labor shortage, that he was "in favor of making slaves of the damned Irish and Dutch," and that William Gilmore Simms expostulated: "Pity it is that the lousy and languishing lazzaroni of Italy cannot be made to labor in the fields under the whip of a severe task-master!"[42] Others thought the indigent might be the first victim of the plot, as indicated by the report that New Mexico had passed a law decreeing corporal punishment for recalcitrant white apprentices and by the proposal of the *New York Day Book* that indigent laborers and their children be sold to anyone who would agree to take care of them "as long as they live." But however it might be perpetrated, it was a common belief that if the aggressions of the slave power—aggressions against democracy, against the territories and against "free society"—were not halted, the end would be the conversion of the United States into a slave empire. This was the theme of one of the most famous poems of the day, "A Letter from Mr. Ezekiel Biglow," by James Russell Lowell:

> Them thet rule us, them slave-traders,
>   Haint they cut a thunderin' swarth,
> (Helped by Yankee renegaders,)
>   Thru the vartu o' the North!
> We beg to think it's nater
>   To take sarse an' not be riled;—
> Who'd expect to see a tater
>   All on eend at bein' biled?
>
>   . . . .
>
> They may talk o' Freedom's airy
>   Tell they're pupple in the face,—
> It's a grand gret cemetary
>   Fer the barthrights of our race;
> They jest want this Californy
>   So's to lug new slave-states in

To abuse ye, an' to scorn ye,
    An' to plunder ye like sin.

Wy, it's jest ez clear ez figgers,
    Clear ez one an' one make two,
Chaps thet make black slaves o' n—s
    Want to make wite slaves o' you.

Tell ye jest the eend I've come to
    Arter cipherin' plaguy smart,
An' it make a handy sum, tu,
    Any gump could larn by heart;
Laborin' men and laborin' women
    Hev one glory an' one shame,
Ev'y thin' thet's done inhuman
    Injers all on 'em the same.

'Taint by turnin' out to hack folks
    You're agoin' to git your right,
Nor by lookin' down on black folks
    Coz you're put upon by wite;
Slavery aint o' nary color,
    'Taint the hide thet makes it wus,
All it keers fer in a feller
    'S jest to make him fill its pus.

   . . . .

Wal, go 'long to help 'em stealin'
    Bigger pens to cram with slaves,
Help the men that 's ollers dealin'
    Insults on your fathers' graves;
Help the strong to grind the feeble,
    Help the many agin the few,
Help the men thet call your people
    Witewashed slaves an' peddlin' crew![43]

Re-forming the Lines

The aggression of the slave-power, and its impact on American
e and politics, cut the ground from under the position that the

labor movement had maintained until 1845 and created the con
ditions which made possible the fulfillment of McDuffie's drea
prediction that the abolitionists and workers would one da
unite. Most working men had been opposed to slavery, bu
many had refused to join the abolition movement because o
their fear that emancipation would produce a mass exodus o
freedmen to the North to compete with them in the labor marke
A large number of workers never shed this fear, but many mor
came to feel that the imminent danger of slave competition i
the territories and possibly even in the states was of greate
concern than the ultimate danger of competition with fre
Negroes. The threat was both more immediate and, if realized
more momentous. Some of the workers therefore were ready t
support abolitionism, while others retained their hostility to
but at the same time were willing to make a stand against th
slave power and thus glided cautiously into the anti-slaver
camp.

A large section of the labor movement had remained aloof fron
abolitionism because it believed that the labor issue must b
settled first, that it was a problem of greater magnitude, tha
abolitionism was a diverting influence, and that slavery was o
the way out anyhow. But the course of events from Texas i
1845 to *Dred Scott* in 1857 made it increasingly apparent tha
slavery was so far from curling up and dying that, on the con
trary, it emerged as the greatest obstacle to the solution of th
labor question, and the plantation masters as the worst enemie
of the working class. This was the case with the land reformer
also, whose program for the emancipation of labor was blow
sky-high by the slaveholders' attempt to engross the territory o
the nation. To a great extent the issue of labor's emancipatio
became merged with the slavery question as the resolution of th
latter became a condition for the success of the former.

There were other factors also that had deterred labor from pa
ticipating more actively in the anti-slavery movement—labor

distrust of the abolitionists and their motives, the abolitionists' hostility to the labor movement, and labor's adherence to the Democratic party. These too were to a large extent eliminated by the events after 1845, and especially by the realignment of political parties and the metamorphosis of the anti-slavery movement.

The abolitionists were one of the most faction-ridden reform movements in the history of the United States. Aside from colonization, which was a bogus anti-slavery scheme, the cause was rent with internecine quarrels which at times became quite nasty. There were advocates of immediate abolition, of gradual emancipation, and of "immediate gradualism," but the brawling of these groups was largely a tempest in a teacup. A more important cause of friction was the extreme egomania of Garrison, born in the self-righteous certainty that he alone knew the will of God, weaned on the adulation of his followers, and matured by criticism which in his eyes could only be the voice of the devil. His pharisaism became insufferable to all but his most loyal adherents. His self-esteem grew to such proportions that he resented the success of Frederick Douglass and opposed any independent efforts of the Negro people to work for their own emancipation, excusing this injury by the insult that "The anti-slavery cause, both religiously and politically, has transcended the ability of the sufferers from American slavery and prejudice, *as a class,* to keep pace with it, or to perceive what are its demands, or to understand the philosophy of its operations."[44] It was apparent that Garrison was beginning to confuse himself with another hallowed name with the same initial.

The first major split in the abolition movement resulted from the controversy between the one-idea men and the universal reformers. Garrison embraced virtually all the social reforms of the day (except labor reform) and insisted on espousing them in the *Liberator,* whereas many abolitionists either could not accept these reforms or felt that they would divert the efforts of the cause and repel potential converts. The most important issue was

women's rights: Garrison gladly accepted the support and assis
ance of women and insisted on their right to hold office in th
Anti-Slavery Society and to speak from its platforms. Chiefly
a result of hostility to this policy a large section of the membershi
seceded and formed the rival American and Foreign Anti-Slaver
Society, which eventually overshadowed the parent body. A
other source of discord was the insistence of many abolitionis
on the exclusive use of passive resistance and moral suasion, thu
denying effective means of struggle to both Northern abolitionis
and the slaves themselves. Frederick Douglass exposed the hop
lessness of such a philosophy, pointing out the futility of usir
moral considerations or reason with slaveholders. "One might
well hunt bears with ethics and political economy as weapon
as to seek to 'pluck the spoiled out of the hand of the oppresso
by the mere force of moral law." Slavery was a system of bru
force, he stated, and must be met with its own weapons.[45]

The philosophy of passive resistance was related to a mo
deep-rooted disease—an organic disease—that infected a larg
body of abolitionists, and not only the Garrisonians: namel
purist and puerile sectarianism. With the Garrisonian school ab
lition was neither a political, a social nor an economic questio
but a moral and religious one. The bottom line of their philosopl
was, "Slaveholding is a *sin*." This could have been, and for mar
was, the beginning of earnest anti-slavery work. But for Garriso
and his adherents it was the end. They started by trying to co
vert the slaveholders, and when that was revealed as a hopele
endeavor, they turned to converting themselves. Every day
their lives was but another opportunity to make public revelatio
of a religious "experience" and renew their dedication to the fait
They rose up with phylacteries on their arms and lay down than
ing God and praising themselves for having lived another da
without succumbing to the temptations of the unclean spirit
Their mission was not to destroy evil—"God will vindicate tI
oppressed"—but to keep themselves from contamination by ev

heir mission was not to free the slaves but to wash their hands
f responsibility for enslaving them.

This peremptory passion for purity was the basis of the Garri-
onian political philosophy—or anti-political philosophy—which
as summed up in the doctrine "No union with slaveholders."
ince the Constitution of the United States recognized and sanc-
oned and upheld property in man, it was a covenant with death
d a compact with hell, and Garrison exorcised the devil every
ourth of July by publicly burning a copy of the Constitution.
ince the Union was an instrument of the compact for the preser-
ation of slavery, by armed force if necessary, the Union must
e dissolved. Since every office-holder must swear allegiance to
e Constitution, no true believer could share in his guilt by
ecting him to office. Did Garrison think that non-resistance,
issolution of the Union, and non-participation in politics would
elp the slaves? That was not his concern. If one vote of his
ould emancipate every slave in the country, he had said, he
ould not cast that vote. What was his plan for emancipation?
e had none, and boasted of it as a mark of his integrity. The
st he could offer was, ". . . let no cement of the Union bind
e slaves, and he will right himself"—by passive resistance, no
ubt.

The American and Foreign Society shared the prophet's bias
ainst political action, but another and growing group came out
r political abolitionism. They were able to break the tyranny of
arrison's logic by the simple process of denying that the Consti-
tion was a pro-slavery document. Since the Declaration of Inde-
ndence, with its proclamation of freedom and equality, formed
integral part of the Constitution, according to their views, the
tter could not possibly be interpreted to sustain slavery. Slavery
fact was unconstitutional and illegal, and it was the plain duty
freedom-loving people to elect men to office who would use the
wers of the government to destroy the unholy institution. This
as a forward step in the abolition movement of inestimable

importance, for it finally placed a traditional weapon in the hands
of anti-slavery men—political struggle on the basis of the liberat
ing philosophy of the Declaration of Independence. The firs
result of political abolitionism was the formation in 1840 of the
Liberty party, organized mainly by the wealthy Tappan brother
of New York, which entered the election campaign on a straigh
abolition platform.

The Liberty men quickly learned the first lesson of the politica
primer, that a party cannot succeed on the basis of one idea, tha
it must present a program with the widest appeal to the people
Winning voters was different from winning converts. They ap
pealed to the working men of the North and South to cast thei
votes for the overthrow of the aristocracy that degraded them
exploited them and reviled them, for the emancipation of labo
through the emancipation of the slaves;[46] and they broadened
their platform to include the special demands of the working
men. Gerrit Smith, himself a wealthy landowner, was converted
to land reform, mainly by George Evans personally, and at the
1847 convention of the party a program was adopted which in
cluded, besides the abolition of slavery, the repeal of all tariffs
the abolition of the military and naval establishments, the ending
of the war with Mexico and the restoration of her conquered
territory, the abolition of all monopolies, restrictions on land
holding, inalienable free homesteads and temperance. The slave
holders and the Northern commercial and industrial aristocracy
were allied, declared the convention, against moral law and
natural rights, and both must be fought. "Every effective blow
struck at either of them, weakens all the rest. . . ." For the firs
time a serious and practical appeal was made for united politica
action by the workers and the abolitionists.

In asking you to assist us in vindicating the claims of the oppresse
colored man, whose wrongs, being most grievous, demand a commensurat
prominence, we do not ask you to stand neutral or non-committal, in you

political activity, and in your votes, in respect to the wrongs, greater or
smaller, of any other class of men. . . .

As a political party, we will hold no truce with a *Northern* Aristocracy
for the purpose of checkmating the *Southern* one. We will take no shelter
under the wing of a *Southern* aristocracy, from the spreading branches of
a *Northern* one. Whether they choose to measure swords with each other,
as rivals, as they sometimes do—or mutually court and strengthen each
other, as at present inclining to do,—we will wage an uncompromising and
exterminating warfare with each, so long as either of them show their
heads in the field, not forgetting to watch after them, if they retire. . . .
When all the elements of aristocracy on the one hand, and of true democracy
on the other, shall thus find their latent affinities, and marshal their
forces, we shall have "an open field and fair play," and we ask nothing
more. . . .[47]

The program and the appeal for a common struggle were per-
fectly symbolized by the party's candidates for president and
vice-president: Gerrit Smith, abolitionist and land reformer, and
Elihu Burritt, "the learned blacksmith," worker and pacifist. The
party was endorsed by the New England Labor Reform League
and the National Industrial Congress—McDuffie's fearful forecast
was on its way to realization, though not in the manner he had
supposed.[48]

There was yet another problem that the anti-slavery men had
to solve, namely, the relationship between the ultimate goal and
immediate issues. The purists, the "ultra-leftists" in the abolition
movement, had no conception of political strategy. They maintained the naive conviction that if they only kept up their agitation for immediate abolition long enough and loud enough, the
light would one day break through the minds of the benighted
people and slavery would crumble to the ground like the walls of
Jericho before the trumpet-blasts of righteousness. They did not
understand that most people would arrive at a realization of the
need for abolition only as the result of a fight against the slavocracy on issues that touched their immediate interests, and that in
the course of this fight they could become organized and united

for the eventual overthrow of slavery. Although the working class
was opposed to slavery, it was not yet ready to engage in an active
fight for its destruction. But it was ready to fight to confine it to
the states where it existed and to wrest the government from
the hands of the slave-power and the money power. That was not
enough for the purists, even among the political abolitionists; in
fact it was in their eyes nothing less than "union with slaveholders." They would make no compromises, accept no half measures,
never retreat one step in order to advance two. Nor could they
countenance cooperation with men who were not animated by
the same noble and philanthropic motives that drove them to
battle with the legions of darkness. In the 1830's the abolitionists
had performed a service that entitles them to a place beside the
great heroes of mankind's fight for liberty; they raised the banner
of immediate and unconditional freedom for the slaves and kept
it flying in the face of a host of enemies, traducers and faint
hearts. In the 1840's and '50's and the war years they made a
contribution of no less importance: they kept ever before the
people the final goal towards which their efforts must lead. But
they could not lead the people to that goal, for they ran too far
ahead and lost contact with the people.

The Liberty party could not make the transition, and after
garnering a few thousand votes in two Presidential campaigns
sank into oblivion. The new party would have to be one that
could absorb the progressive elements in the old parties and
among the independent voters as well as abolitionists, and must
be based on the issue that could unite them against the slave
power. That issue was the exclusion of slavery from the territories, and the party assumed the appropriate name of Free Soil
which suggested not only its major plank but also its endorsement
of free homesteads for farmers and workers. Some of the Liberty
people came into the new party, forming its abolitionist wing.
Like its predecessor, the Free Soil party represented itself as the
champion of the slaves as well as the farmers and workers—both

ose in the South, "more trampled upon, if possible, than the
ery Africans themselves," and in the North, the "children of
il . . . who would annually seek a new home and a refuge from
ant and oppression in the vacant territories" and whose pro-
ction "in their rights to political and social equality, and in
e secure enjoyment of the fruits of their industry" was the true
bject of government.[49]

The "children of toil" were ready to welcome such an appeal,
or they were becoming increasingly aware of the restraint that
e slave-power was exercising on all their cherished reforms.
The question of slavery is in truth the question of labor," asserted
e *Voice of Industry,* for whenever the rights of labor or any
ther reform was advanced, the influence of the slaveholders was
rown against it. "Do we ask for a Free Soil, a land limitation
w, or any other measure which looks to the protection and eleva-
on of the laboring class, we are told by the McDuffies and the
alhouns that slavery is the natural and necessary condition of
e producing classes. . . ."[50] Another labor paper, viewing the
fluence of slavery in the same light, drew the logical conclusion
which the working men were being propelled. The slavery
uestion could not be downed, it asserted, but was becoming daily
ore vexing, and was now the only issue before the country.
Vhether the question was one of free trade, taxation, internal
nprovements, peace, free soil or anything else, "this enormous
ragon" of slavery had something at stake. It was clear to this
riter that "Either slavery must have full liberty and sweep to
xpand itself in influence or else it must meet in fell encounter
ith death. . . . We go for direct and internecine war with the
onster."[51] Throughout the North workers continued to flow
ito the anti-slavery camp at an accelerating tempo. In Vermont,
e advocates of land limitation condemned both land monopoly
nd slavery and joined the abolitionists to form the state Free
oil organization, and in every other state anti-slavery men and
orkers joined forces on a program of opposition to slavery,

homestead exemption, and the freedom of the public domain; in industrial centers such issues as the ten-hour day were also endorsed by the Free Soilers.[52]

The formation of the Free Soil party was a symptom also of the disintegration and reorganization of the old parties that began in 1845. Both Whigs and Democrats were heterogeneous parties made up of members of all classes in all sections of the country. Neither could withstand the impact of the slavery and territorial issues when they came to overshadow all others. The Northern wing of both parties had to make a decision sooner or later: either capitulate to the planters and accept their ascendancy in the Union, or resist them and establish its own hegemony. The natural inclination was toward the latter policy, and many made the decision by transferring their support to the Free Soil party in 1848 and the Republican party in 1856. This group represented mainly the farmers, the lower middle class, and the small industrialists on the make.

But others could not make the decision—not yet, at least. Bankers, merchants and cotton manufacturers were bound to the slave system by a network of commercial links, and could not take the risk of antagonizing business associates and possibly disrupting the Union—they believed that the South meant business, in both senses of the term. Besides, many of them were convinced that as the South had warned them, abolitionism was a species of radicalism that must not be encouraged; men of property must hang together or they would hang separately. The first and greatest concern of conservatives everywhere and at all times is to "maintain the stability of political institutions against the disorganized excitement which [takes] possession of men's minds the immutability of principles. . . . The stability of the laws, and their uninterrupted action—never their change."[53] How could they go into upstart parties tainted with the dangerous ideas of abolition and agrarianism? These elements, with a few exceptions, stayed in the old parties, possibly hoping to keep control in their hands but willing to temporize, compromise and accommodate themselves to the planters' wishes. The Democrats found this easiest to do, for they had rooted political ties with the South and a traditional policy of state rights, whereas the Northern Whigs had always been a high-tariff, pro-bank and internal improvement, strong government party in the tradition of the Federalists. Furthermore, their opposition to the Mexican War and support of the Wilmot Proviso had been too vociferous, too much tinged with abolitionism. So the Southern planters migrated wholesale into the Democratic party and called it their own. The Whigs floundered in the sea of confusion and indecision, with only one claim on people's loyalty—they had saved the Union by the Compromise of 1850; when that was torpedoed by the Kansas-Nebraska Act, the Whig party was dead.

As the Democratic party made the transition from Jackson to Calhoun, and as the workers became more concerned about the menace of the slave-power, the party found it increasingly difficult to maintain its hold over them, and they began to look for more congenial associates. One symptom of this was the revolt of the Barnburners from the New York organization. This faction of the party was a lineal descendant of the Workingmen's party of 1830 and the Loco-Focos of the Jacksonian days. In 1848 the Barnburners joined the Free Soil movement in protest against the defeat of the Wilmot Proviso, and their leader, former President Martin Van Buren, became its candidate in that year.

Another example of what happened to the Democratic party was revealed in the history of the Fall River *Weekly News,* published by a Mr. Almy and John C. Milne, who was apparently the chief editorial writer. The *News* was a Democratic organ and Milne was decidedly pro-labor. He supported the ten-hour day, wage lien laws and free homesteads, gave full notices of local and New England labor meetings, was sympathetic with Associationism and opposed the anti-union policy of the capitalists—"that miserable race of parvenus, parasites and popinjays"—who "hated everything connected with labor, except its dividends." From the time of the annexation of Texas, the editorial policy of the paper reflected the dilemma of the editor: it tried to maintain "the principles and doctrines of the democracy, as inculcated by Jefferson" and at the same time retain its loyalty to the Democratic party, which was rapidly abandoning those principles as it fell under the domination of the slaveholders. Milne was strongly opposed to slavery and, while he disagreed with Garrison's disunion doctrine, he praised him for his power and ability, and gave lengthy and sympathetic reports of local abolition meetings. However, during the same years he was supporting the annexation of Texas and the Mexican War, as party measures.

Milne was convinced that the workers could achieve their demands only through the Democratic party, and therefore remained loyal to it and supported its national policies, but he did not like the growing symptoms he saw of "fawning sycophancy upon the slaveholders of the South; and this disposition to sacrifice any man at the North who dares to be a thoroughgoing and consistent democrat, in holding the doctrine 'that all men are created equal. . . .'" In 1847, the *News* unequivocally supported the Wilmot Proviso, stating that the territories should be "speedily purified from the presence of the Slave system, a system so opposed, so antagonistic to every interest and principle upon which our Liberty and happiness are founded." If the slave-power was strengthened by gaining control of the territories, "The North will then be a servant of servants—and democracy may exist here, but only in name—equal rights will die here among the democrats, as it has long ago died at the South among those called by this name." Milne demanded that the Democratic party take a stand against slavery extension, and if it failed he would favor the organization of a new party made up of all friends of freedom.

But the next year he was again supporting the Democratic candidate, Lewis Cass, whose policy called for popular sovereignty in the territories. By 1850 he was willing to give up the fight on the Wilmot Proviso and come to a settlement with the South in the interests of peace and the Union. However, this mood soon passed, and the arrogance of the slaveholders and the complete submission of the Democratic party on the Fugitive Slave Act particularly disgusted him. He was giving up his hopes for saving the party. The North had reluctantly had the slavery question forced upon it, and had determined to decide it in favor of freedom. "Let us do everything in our power," he wrote, "to put an end to a system which permits and enjoins such accursed deeds, and first and immediately to blot and erase forever from the statute books of our own nation, the infernal slave act of 1850."[54]

In 1851 Milne supported the election of Sumner to the Senate: " . . . there are some crises when party considerations should be sunk, or kept out of sight, in view of some commanding and all-worthy object." He gave considerable attention to the proceedings of the Free Soilers and finally, in 1852, broke with the Democratic party and dissolved his connection with the *News*. In a farewell statement to his readers he said that he had supported the party while it was the party of progress and liberty; even when the majority had been derelict to the principles of the democratic faith, he remained with it in hopes that it would return. But he had been disappointed in that hope when the party gave its support to the fugitive slave law. "The respective democratic and whig conventions at Baltimore, seemed to vie with each other in humility to the degrading and unconstitutional measure, both declaring it a finality, and each denouncing its repeal. My judgement abhors the measure, and my feelings revolt at the dereliction vinced by those who bow to it and support its atrocious provisions."[55] Milne was typical of many workers and workers' leaders who were driven out of the Democratic party by its subservience to the slaveholders.

The Free Soil party was composed of farmers, workers and the progressive elements among the middle class and the industrial capitalists who were determined to halt the progress of the slave-power; and by the latter term was meant not only the slaveholders but the Northern business classes that were allied with them. As Sumner said at the Massachusetts Free Soil convention in 1849, the efforts to place the national government on the side of freedom had received little sympathy from the wealthy, but had encountered their opposition. It was easy to explain this, he stated, for the instinct of property was stronger than the instinct of freedom. "The money-power has joined hands with the slave-power. Selfish, grasping, subtle, tyrannical, like its ally, it will not brook opposition. It claims the Commonwealth as its own, and too successfully enlists in its support that needy talent and easy virtue which are required to maintain its sway."[56]

The hostility of the early abolition movement to the worker had made it impossible for the latter to join it without sacrificing their own demands. But now it was clear that the greatest enemies of labor were ranged against them on the side of the slave mas-ters; the exploiters of the chattel slaves and the wage slaves, "the lords of the lash and the lords of the loom," had joined hands and the workers and the slaves were fighting each other's battles whether they knew it or not. The fight against the slave-power became "a battle against conservatism, reaction, aristocracy, and the power of capital—in Ohio and Massachusetts as well as in South Carolina."[57] The lines were forming for the Second American Revolution.

Free Soil and Free Labor

With the defeat of the Free Soil party in the election of 1848 many of the Barnburners and Conscience Whigs returned to the haven of party regularity, and the alleged "finality" of the Com-

promise of 1850 caused others to return. The Free Soil party, with
those influences removed, became again mainly a coalition of
anti-slavery men, workers and farmers. But the conditions which
inspired its organization were recreated in 1854 by the Nebraska
Act, this time on a much larger scale. The Nebraska Act not only
destroyed the compromises of 1820 and 1850 but, in the eyes of
most people, precluded the possibility of future compromises.
This time the exodus from the Democratic and Whig parties
was of mass proportions and a new party was required to organize
the dissidents—not a third party but a party to replace the defunct
Whigs and challenge the supremacy of the Democrats. The Free
Soil organization could not fill the requirements, because it had
suffered the loss of prestige that comes with defeat, and was too
"radical" for most of those looking for a new home. Thus the
Republican party was born; spontaneously and simultaneously
through the North organizations were formed, and then coalesced
into a national body.

The Republicans took over their predecessor's slogan: Free soil,
free labor, free men, and (for the campaign of 1856) Fremont.
But it no longer had precisely the same meaning. The term "free
soil" had connoted three different things with the Free Soil party:
its dislike of slavery, its determination to keep the territories free,
and its support of a free homestead law. With the Republican
party, the first and last of these were relegated to a minor position.
The party was not, strictly speaking, an anti-slavery party at all in
the sense that it avowed opposition to the institution itself; in fact
it was specifically pledged not to interfere with slavery in the states
where it was recognized.[58] It was anti-slavery only in the sense
that it challenged the supremacy of the slaveholders in the territories and in the Union and, if successful, must bring about the
downfall of the slave system, willy-nilly; and in its fight against
the slaveholders it could not avoid, if it wanted to, a criticism
of the institution as such. It was precisely this that dismayed the
abolitionists: from Garrison to Smith to Van Buren to Fremont to

Lincoln the anti-slavery creed was steadily diluted and adulterated until it became too distasteful for strong men to swallow. On the other hand, with each dilution the number of men who came to participate was multiplied. From the point of view of some, the process appeared as a steady corruption of the nation's moral character; others could see only the growing strength of the array of hosts come to battle against the slave-power. As for free homesteads, the Republicans scarcely mentioned them in the campaign of 1856. The big issue, almost the only issue, was the exclusion of slavery from the territories, and their preservation for the free laborers of the North and South. As the Cleveland *Leader* stated, the question to be decided at the forthcoming election was whether the unsettled territory would be devoted to the use of free workingmen or whether it would be taken from them and be cursed by the establishment of slavery throughout its entire extent.[59]

The term "free labor" likewise did not have the same significance on the Republicans' banner as it had on the Free Soilers'. The latter party had supported many of the specific demands of the labor movement and was, in truth, a farmer-labor party; the Republicans kept only the homestead plank and consigned it to a dark corner. Farmers and workers made up the bulk of the Republican party, but it was dominated by the middle class leadership and outlook imposed by the Democrats, Whigs and Know-Nothings who swarmed into it. It represented the interests of the working class only in that it was ranged against the money power and the slave-power, the greatest enemies of labor, and in that the slavery question itself was the issue of greatest importance to the labor movement at that time. In fact, the guiding theme of the campaign was the representation of the Republican party as the party of labor. In his letter of acceptance, Fremont wrote that his policy "would leave no aliment to that sectional party which seeks its aggrandizement by appropriating the new Territories to capital in the form of Slavery, but would inevitably result in the triumph of Free Labor—the natural capital which constitutes

he real wealth of this great country, and creates the intelligent
power in the masses alone to be relied on as the bulwark of free
institutions."[60]

From press and platform this idea was harped upon. Seward
asserted that the history of the United States was determined by
the conflict between slaveholders and nonslaveholders. The slaveholders had sought to fortify themselves with a blind disregard of
the rights and interests of non-slaveholders. The latter, increasingly conscious of the danger of slavery, sought to counteract the
policy of the slaveholders by diffusing the spirit of freedom. Only
the Republican party upheld the cause of the nonslaveholders.[61]

The interests of the Southern workers were also said to be
defended by the Republicans. The Cleveland *Leader* congratulated the working men of St. Louis on their turning a Republican
victory, and hoped that their example would be emulated in the
slave states. Asserting that the interests of labor and Republicanism were identical, the paper declared that the Republican party
was the working man's party, its object being to protect free
labor from degrading and unfair competition with involuntary
labor.[62]

While some of the Republicans expressed the hope that the triumph of free labor would also result in striking the shackles
from the slaves, most of them made no pretense of being concerned with the fate of the Negroes, and many went out of
their way to insist that theirs was the party of *white* labor. Although the experiences of the Liberty and Free Soil parties had
indicated that many workers might be brought to strike at the
roots of the slave system in the fight to overthrow the slave-
power, the conservative elements in the Republican party introduced the note of white supremacy, and in doing so hoped to
win the votes of Negrophobes and anti-abolitionists who were
opposed to slavery extension. For example, Senator Trumbull
said, at the party's national convention, "It is not so much in reference to the welfare of the negro that we are here, but it is for

the protection of the rights of the laboring whites, for the protec tion of ourselves and our liberties."[63] The Hartford *Courant* ex pressed the attitude of the more chauvinistic sections of the party The Republican party was the white man's party, it asserted. I did not oppose the progress of slavery from any feeling of sym pathy for the Negroes. On the contrary, it did so because i liked the white men better than the Negroes. "We believe th Caucasian variety of the human species superior to the Negr variety—and we would breed the best stock, and fill this nobl land of ours . . . with the noblest race of human beings possible . . . The Republicans mean to preserve all of this country tha they can from *the pestilential presence of the black man*."[64]

While the Republican party presented itself as the champio of free labor, it portrayed the slave power as labor's mortal fo Its spokesmen carefully spelled out the effect of slavery on th conditions of the Southern workers,[65] and emphasized especiall the "northerly direction to the development of the negro race. the threat of slave competition in the territories, and the harmfu influence that it already exerted on labor in the free states. widely circulated pamphlet was devoted to proving that Souther slavery reduced Northern wages by its employment in industri that competed with Northern products. "The system of reducin the laborer to a bare subsistence, is hostile to the individual an personal well-being of the great mass of the fifteen millions people who wield the political control of the free States; and will be passing strange if they do not so wield it as to prote themselves and their own."[66]

A great deal was said about the Southern aristocracy's contem for labor and laborers, and one of the popular campaign son; went:

> The great "F.F.'s" are nobly born,
> A whip each baby waves;
> Our base mechanics they hold in scorn—

They are but *whiter slaves!*
They raise their cash by chain and lash,
And trade and toil ignore.
Why wasn't I born in old Virginia,
On old Virginia's shore?[67]

Much political capital was made when the Democratic congressman Philip Herbert of California shot and killed Thomas Keating, the Irish head-waiter at Willard's Hotel in Washington, allegedly for refusing to serve his breakfast after hours. Herbert was acquitted by Judge Crawford of the Criminal Court of the District of Columbia, and efforts to expel him from the House and to investigate the affair were defeated. This was bad enough, and some of the Southern newspapers added fuel to the flames by defending Herbert, as the *Alabama Mail* did: "It is getting time that waiters at the North were convinced that they are servants, and not 'gentlemen' in disguise. We hope this Herbert affair will teach them prudence."[68] The New York *Tribune* wrote that the doctrine laid down by Crawford was "slaveholder's doctrine and slave driver's law."

. . is a customary, natural, and perhaps necessary part of the slavedriving system, that the driver should go armed—should carry a pistol or bowie knife in his pocket, to enforce his command, and to punish all audacious resistance, and especially all insolent demeanor. . . . 'tis a part of the law of slavery that the servant thus chastized for his insolence, has no right to make any reply, retort, or resistance . . . [which] may be forthwith punished by the instant shooting or stabbing of the insolent servant, the killing, so far from being murder, or even manslaughter, will be excusable homicide. . . .

Our laboring people at the North may see in these rulings of Judge Crawford, the natural consequence of the ascendancy which slaveholding and slavedriving have already obtained in our policy, and which the party calling itself Democratic is seeking so eagerly to extend and perpetuate. . . . [69]

Buchanan was portrayed in the 1856 campaign not only as the candidate of the labor-hating oligarchy, but as a man who per-

sonally favored the degradation of labor. He was accused of
having advocated a daily wage of ten cents and thereby won the
sobriquet "Ten-Cent Jimmy." Several campaign songs were composed on this theme, like "Buck Shooting":

> Can poor men forget to remember,
> When old Buck was willing to greet
> The day when mechanics should labor
> For ten cents a day and no meat?
> He may take in his horns and forswear it,
> Can he blot out the record? Not he!
> Our platform is *Freedom for Kansas*!
> Our motto, "*Free Homes for the Free*!"
>
> Oh! the Free Working Men of the Union
> Can think! and will act for themselves!
> They'll slaughter Old Buck for his antlers,
> And let him dry up on the shelves.[70]

A major role in Republican campaign tactics was assigned to
the propagation of the "slave-power conspiracy." McDuffie, Calhoun, Pickens, the Richmond *Enquirer, et al.,* were trotted out
and put through their paces again. One of the most widely circulated and copied broadsides of the campaign was one entitled
"White Slavery. The New 'Democratic Doctrine.' Slavery not to
be confined to the Negro Race, but to be made the universal
condition of the Laboring classes of society." Most of it consisted
of the choicest quotations from the Southern press about the
mudsills and greasy mechanics. An editorial in the New York
Tribune was typical of what was written in hundreds of Republican and abolition papers. It asserted that the slavery question was
not a Negro question, a question of the abstract rights of man,
or even a question whether slavery should continue to exist; it
was rather a question whether the mass of Americans would
retain their liberty or whether it would be nullified like that of
the poor whites in the South. "It has come at last to this; that the

free millions of the North insist, before everything else, and at all hazards, Slavery shall not extend another step. 'Why?' Because there is but one step more for it to take, and after that there can be no more free labor at the North."[71]

It is very difficult to judge the effect of the 1856 campaign on the workers. It seems certain that the majority of immigrant laborers, and particularly the Irish, did not vote for Fremont, not only because of their traditional Democratic affiliation, but because of the strong nativist strain in the Republican party. After the Southerners captured the Know-Nothing party, most of its Northern members joined the Republicans and furnished them some of their outstanding leaders. In New York and Massachusetts nativist influence in the party was particularly strong, and immigrants could hardly be expected to give their votes to a party which harbored such elements and did not repudiate their hatred of the foreign born. Furthermore, the appeal of free territories could not have much effect on workers who did not have the means to emigrate to the West even if they wanted to.[72] The Germans, however, deserted the Democratic party in large numbers after the Nebraska Act was passed, and most of them went into the Republican fold. The "Forty-eighters" were aggressively anti-slavery, and the Turnvereine, the socialist Turnerbund and the German labor unions, which were all outspoken in their opposition to slavery, gave their support to the Republican party.[73]

Edward H. Rogers, a worker who was active in the abolition movement, stated that the working class played a crucial part in the anti-slavery movement in the 1850's, attributing this largely to the fact that the ten-hour day was won by many workers during that decade, enabling them to participate more actively than before.[74] 25,000 workingmen of Pittsburgh, including German, Irish and native Americans, addressed the workers of Pennsylvania, calling upon them to protect their rights, which were imperiled by the slaveholding aristocracy. If the latter succeeded in extending slavery over all the territories, warned these workers of Pittsburgh, they would establish their supremacy over the government and extend the sway of slavery over the free work ingmen. The only hope of the workers was in the Republican party, under whose banner would be fought the battle of the rights of man. The working men were urged to lay aside mino differences in the face of the great danger, and to unite for the preservation of the territories against slavery.[75]

If the Republican party had taken a more positive stand on labor issues other than the territorial question, it would have won more support from the workers. But then it wouldn't have been the Republican party.

In many respects the campaign of 1860 was a carbon copy of 1856; but there were important differences, for while the issue were essentially the same, the developing crisis had reached new stage. The attempts of the administration to force slavery on Kansas, the attempt of the Supreme Court to force it on all th territories, the demands for reopening the slave trade, the increa ing talk of secession, the Ostend Manifesto, the filibustering expe ditions—these events convinced the Northerners more than eve that compromise was impossible, that the decision to submit o make a stand could not be avoided much longer. It was becomin clear to those who wanted nothing more than concord and orde that the price demanded by the slaveholders was too high. Man businessmen wanted a high tariff, a Pacific railroad, river an harbor improvements, a national banking system, and control o the national resources and the national market; while the Dem crats were in power they could not get them, but the Republican promised them all. The majority of Northern businessmen, an particularly the merchants, bankers, and cotton manufacturer remained in the Democratic party, and in fact a number of Whi among them moved into the Democratic camp as their only hop for defeating the Republicans. But a significant section of th

apitalist class, especially among the iron masters of Pennsylvania
nd New Jersey and others who had no business connections
vith the South, shifted their support to the Republican party,
letermined to end the domination of the slave power.[76] As the
Republicans gained in strength and bade fair to win the next
lection it became even more important to jump on the band-
vagon and convert the party to their own purposes. The depres-
ion that set in after the panic of 1857 produced a wave of militant
bor struggles; the unions folded up but the unemployed work-
rs demonstrated in the streets for relief and jobs. Their discon-
ent might be siphoned off by directing it against the slave power.
oliticians too, sniffing victory in the air, scampered to join the
inning side. Lincoln put "the man before the dollar," but by
860 the idealism of his party was tempered by the realism of
usinessmen who considered the man a means of making the
ollar, and of politicians who saw him only as a means of making
otes. The platform of 1860, the Republican legislation of the war
ears and the subsequent history of the party bear witness to this
ct.

The rank and file had their own reasons for supporting the
arty: they were "the man" in person, the common people to
hom the Declaration of Independence was more than "glittering
neralities" and "self-evident lies." It was the creed of their life
d the foundation of their liberties; it was given life by the
volution against King George, and it would be preserved by a
cond revolution against King Cotton. They would return Amer-
a to the path of democratic development. Many workers believed
at a democracy instituted and managed by the Republican
rty would be spurious, and refused to give their support to it:
he capitalists have no sympathy for the Negroes or the white
orkers, wrote one worker; their only purpose in joining the
epublican party was "that capital shall obtain political power to
rect the legislation of the Federal Government as it does now
at of New England, and thus enable the few to govern the

many.''[77] But this was the issue of the future; the immediate job was to save the country from the slave power. And since the workers were not strong enough in numbers and organization or mature enough politically to carry on the fight independently they attached themselves to the party of the middle class and accepted its leadership in the fight against the common enemy.

In the struggle against reaction, waged by a coalition of farmers workers, middle class and capitalists, inevitably the ideology of the coalition was expressed in a curious amalgam of conservatism and liberalism, property rights and human rights, the dollar and the man. It represented antagonistic forces, yet they were united in a common fight for progress, each attaching its own meaning to the term. A perfect embodiment of this unity of contradiction was found in the standard-bearer of the party, Abraham Lincoln He was a firm believer in the philosophy of the Declaration of Independence, but maintained that the Negro was inferior to the white man and opposed their right to be citizens, voters, juror or office-holders or to have social equality. He was opposed to slavery on moral grounds, but when he introduced a bill in Congress proposing gradual emancipation in the District of Columbia he added a strong fugitive-slave clause for the restoration of slave escaping into the District; later he said, "I confess I hate to see the poor creatures hunted down . . . but I bite my lips and keep quiet." He had a profound faith in democracy and the common man, but during most of his political career he was a Whig regular. His views and his actions were at all times governed by caution, moderation and expediency, but he always tempered them with Christian morality, justice and humanity.[78]

Lincoln's deep fellow-feeling for the workingmen was merged with the ideology of the middle class. His sympathy for labor and his understanding of the labor movement were greatly exaggerated in his own time and have been ever since. One of Lincoln widely quoted expressions was that "To secure to each laborer the whole product of his labor, or as nearly as possible, is a worthy

bject of any good government."[79] This sentiment was written
during his Whig days in the course of an argument for a protec-
ive tariff, and if it were translated into modern terminology, it
would be more accurately rendered as "To secure to each manu-
acturer the whole profit of his production . . . is a worthy object
of any good government." In Lincoln's view, a manufacturer
was a laborer, and the product of his employees' labor was the
roduct of his own labor.

The most radical-sounding of all his pronouncements on labor
was contained in an address to the Wisconsin State Agricultural
ociety in 1859, in which he said, " . . . labor is prior to, and inde-
endent of, capital; . . . in fact, capital is the fruit of labor, and
ould never have existed if labor had not first existed; . . . labor
an exist without capital, but . . . capital could never have existed
ithout labor. Hence . . . labor is the superior—greatly the su-
erior—of capital."[80] What was the context of this remark?
incoln was refuting two other labor theories, both of which were
ased on the assumption that "labor is available only in connec-
on with capital—that nobody labors, unless somebody else own-
g capital, somehow, by the use of it, induces him to do it." If
e single word "else" were deleted from this passage, its assump-
on would have been more correct, but Lincoln was talking about
borers (not wage-earners) who owned their own "capital,"
ther in the form of tools or, especially, in the form of land—that
, the farmers whom he was addressing, who did not labor for
pitalists but did their own work on their own land. Those
ho held this assumption, Lincoln continued, were divided into
o groups: those who thought it best "that capital shall hire
borers, and thus induce them to work by their own consent,"
d those who preferred to "buy them, and drive them to it,
ithout their consent." The latter system, chattel slavery, of course
disapproved. The wages system he found quite unobjection-
le, providing it was not based on the premise that "whoever is
ce a hired laborer, is fatally fixed in that condition for life."

As long as class stratifications were fluid, a laborer could save hi
money and become a capitalist himself, thus proving that labo
was "independent of capital" and "superior to capital." This wa
really but another way of saying that there was no contradictio
or conflict between capital and labor.

This was the sum of Lincoln's labor philosophy, and he ac
verted to it many times. The mudsill theory was false, he asserted
because "There is no permanent class of hired laborers among u
Twenty-five years ago I was a hired laborer. The hired labore
of yesterday labors on his own account today, and will hire othe
to labor for him tomorrow. . . . "[81]

He did not realize that he was admitting one of the basi
contentions of the mudsill theory when he went on to say: "Th
power of hope upon human exertion and happiness is wonderfu
. . . The slave whom you cannot drive with the lash to brea
seventy-five pounds of hemp in a day, if you will task him t
break a hundred, and promise him pay for all he does over, h
will break you a hundred and fifty." In short, Lincoln wante
workers to become capitalists, and he wanted slaveholders t
become capitalists—the world would be a bourgeois heaven fo
every one except those who were working twice as hard as th
slaves under the compulsion of "the power of hope" that they to
would one day join the charmed circle.

In 1860 Lincoln made a speaking tour of New England, whe
he found a shoemakers' strike in progress. In Hartford, he tol
his audience, "Thank God that we have a system of labor whe
there can be a strike."[82] This was hardly in the category of bo
assertions, particularly for a Presidential aspirant in an electio
year. The next day he repeated this remark to the New Have
strikers and explained it more fully:

. . . I am glad to see that a system of labor prevails in New England und
which laborers can strike when they want to, where they are not oblig
to work under all circumstances, and are not tied down and obliged

bor whether you pay them or not! I like the system which lets a man quit
hen he wants to, and wish it might prevail everywhere. One of the rea-
ns why I am opposed to slavery is just here. . . . I want every man to
ave the chance—and I believe a black man is entitled to it—in which he
an better his condition—when he may look forward and hope to be a
red laborer this year and the next, work for himself afterward, and
nally to hire men to work for him. . . . I desire that if you get too
ick here, and find it hard to better your condition on this soil, you may
ave a chance to strike and go somewhere else, where you may not be
graded, nor have your family corrupted by forced rivalry with negro
aves. I want you to have a clean bed and no snakes in it![83]

Thus, Lincoln conceived of labor's advancement in terms of
dividual betterment rather than through group action. Even his
onception of a strike was very narrow: it meant to him merely
e right to quit and "go somewhere else," presumably to the
rritories where one could get a homestead and become "inde-
ndent of capital." He held to the Calvinist doctrine that pros-
rity was a sign that one was a chosen vessel of God, and that
ilure was a mark of disfavor and a result of indolence, prodi-
lity and careless work habits.[84] His outlook was that of the
urgeois who believes that every man holds in his two hands
e means of salvation (that is, prosperity) through hard work,
rift and ambition—in short, it was the philosophy of rugged
dividualism. It was not the men of toil that Lincoln extolled,
t "those who toil up from poverty"[85]—a distinction that was full
meaning.

Lincoln's philosophy of labor was not essentially different from
at of many abolitionists, but he differed from them in one
portant respect: whereas they had counterposed the labor ques-
n and the slavery issue and made the abandonment of one the
ndition for accepting the other, Lincoln merged them into a
gle problem and made the resolution of the latter a condition
r the solution of the former. Lincoln's position was much more
actical from the viewpoint of both capitalists and Republican
liticians, and more realistic from the viewpoint of labor's inter-

ests. His ideology was a reflection of the alliance between labor and capital in the fight against the slave power. It is noteworthy that every expression of his labor philosophy was coupled with a refutation of the mudsill theory, and often with the issue of keeping the territories free of slavery.

Lincoln was quite concerned with the Southern attack on "the failure of free society." He clipped the worst anti-labor articles from the Southern press and pasted them in his scrapbook, and when he read Fitzhugh's *Sociology for the South* he "revolted in anger and disgust." This was unquestionably a sincere reaction, but Lincoln also perceived the propaganda value of such arguments, especially if some of the Northern papers would endorse them. In 1856 he arranged, through his partner Herndon, to have the *Conservative* reprint the famous article from the Richmond *Enquirer* which defended the principle of slavery for all laborers regardless of race. In the same issue of the paper, however, appeared an editorial denouncing the doctrine that slavery was the best condition for all laborers. Lincoln used the article throughout the campaign to show the danger of the slave-power conspiracy but never mentioned the editorial.[86] He was reported to have drawn the ultimate conclusion from the slave-power conspiracy in his speech to the Illinois state convention of the Republican party in 1856:

. . . if the safeguards to liberty are broken down, as is now attempted, when they have made *things* of all the free negroes, how long, think you, before they will begin to make *things* of poor white men? Be not deceived. Revolutions do not go backward. The founder of the Democratic party declared that *all* men were created equal. His successor in the leadership has written the word "white" before men, making it read "all *white* men are created equal." Pray, will or may not the Know-nothings, if they should get in power, add the word "protestant," making it read "all *protestant white men*"? . . .

But we cannot be free men if this is, by our national choice, to be a land of slavery. Those who deny freedom to others, deserve it not for themselves; and, under the rule of a just God, cannot long retain it.[87]

In the debates with Douglas, however, and in his own campaign
f 1860, he only hinted at the possible enslavement of all workers,
hoosing rather to emphasize the probability of the institution's
ecoming nationalized. This was most clearly expressed in his
amous House-Divided Speech:

'e are now far into the first year since a policy was initiated with the
owed object and confident promise of putting an end to slavery agitation
The Nebraska Act]. Under the operation of that policy, that agitation has
t only not ceased, but has constantly augmented. In my opinion, it will
t cease until a crisis shall have been reached and passed. "A house
vided against itself cannot stand." I believe this government cannot en-
ire permanently half slave and half free. I do not expect the Union to
dissolved—I do not expect the house to fall—but I do expect it will
ase to be divided. It will become all one thing, or all the other. Either
e opponents of slavery will arrest the further spread of it, and place it
here the public mind shall rest in the belief that it is in the course of
timate extinction; or its advocates will push it forward till it shall become
ke lawful in all the States, old as well as new, North as well as South.
Have we no tendency to the latter condition?[88]

has been said that Lincoln tried to "forget" this speech as being
o radical for a Presidential candidate, but he repeated its es-
nce several times in 1860,[89] and his party rode it hard and fast
roughout the campaign.

On the basis of Lincoln's remarks concerning labor, he was
ilt up by the party as a great champion of the working class.
it even more, his own origins and his homely demeanor were
ploited to picture him, in Ben Wade's words, as "the very
carnation of American labor."[90] He was already known among
e Swedes as "the son of a working man," and the campaign
anagers made a brilliant effort to impress this image on all the
orkers. The Chicago *Press and Tribune,* for example, proclaimed
at Lincoln was a man of the people, that he had been a laborer
ring all of his early life, and that he consequently had sympa-
with the men who toiled. "Himself an outgrowth of free insti-

tutions, he would die in the effort to preserve to others, unim
paired, the inestimable blessings by which he has been made
man."[91] The omnipresent symbols of the campaign were the ra
and the ax, and every one in the world knew, as little Tad sai
that Abe was a rail-splitter. Banners were carried in parade
reading: "SMALL-FISTED FARMERS, MUDSILLS OF SOCIETY, GREAS
MECHANICS, FOR A. LINCOLN."[92]

As in 1856, the Republican party was presented as the par
of free labor ranged against its only enemy, the slaveholders. '
say to you, men of Massachusetts, slavery is the one enemy of t
free laboring men of America, of the North and of the South
declared Henry Wilson; its mouthpiece, the Democratic part
has ceased to talk of the rights of man "and speaks now solely
the rights of property in man." The contest is "between the i
terests and claims of the few, who eat their bread—not in t
sweat of their brow, but by the forced and unrequited toil
bondsmen—and the enduring interests and indefeasible rights
millions of toiling men who eat their bread in the sweat of th
faces."[93] Seward was more explicit. He stated that slavery w
objectionable not only on account of the slaves; on the contra
the Negro was only an incident to it, a subject of disputes b
not one of the litigants—like a horse in a justice's court when t
neighbors were litigating about its ownership. The controver
was not with the Negroes, but with two classes of white m
those who had a monopoly of the slaves, and the others who h
none. The pith of the conflict was that the former wanted
extend themselves over the new territories in order to retain th
power, while the latter intended to resist that extension. "It is
eternal question between classes—between the few privileg
and the many underprivileged—the eternal question betwe
aristocracy and democracy."[94]

The Democrats were assailed as "the same men, who born w
a silver spoon in their mouths, and entertaining a supreme c
tempt for all who are not rich, think to beat the honest masses

he voters by specious appeals to their prejudices;" and Herschel
ohnson, Douglas' running mate, was accused of having declared
hat "capital should own labor."[95] The central issues, of course,
vere the exclusion of slavery from the territories, the complete
ncompatibility of the interests of the slaveholders and those of
he workers, and the halting of the slave-power conspiracy.[96] In
ddition, the Republicans made an appeal to the workers on three
ther issues.

First, a concerted effort was made to prove that the party had
een purified of all traces of Know-Nothingism—an effort made
specially difficult by the Massachusetts law passed in 1859 by a
.epublican-Know-Nothing coalition, which required a two-year
vaiting period before immigrants could vote, and by the circula-
on as a campaign document of Helper's *The Impending Crisis,*
vhich contained a scurrilous attack on the Irish Catholics. But the
amage was counteracted by the repudiation of the Massachusetts
w by Republican state conventions, by the assurances of party
:aders, including Lincoln, by the numbers of German leaders
vho held fast to party loyalty, and by the special "Dutch plank"
f the party platform, written by Carl Schurz: "The Republican
arty is opposed to any change by which the rights of citizenship
eretofore accorded to immigrants from foreign lands shall be
oridged or impaired, and in favor of giving a full and sufficient
rotection to all classes of citizens, whether native or naturalized,
oth at home and abroad."[97]

A second important issue was the homestead bill, which the
epublicans not only endorsed but actively campaigned for. The
outh was opposed to such a law, primarily because it would pro-
10te the occupation of the territories by native and immigrant
vorkers and farmers; this would assure the freedom of the terri-
ories more certainly than any act of Congress, thereby annihilat-
1g any hope of new slave states and upsetting the political bal-
1ce. Twice in the 1850's the homestead bill was defeated, once
v Southern votes in Congress, once by the Democratic President

Buchanan. The Republicans interpreted this as a clear demonstration of the slaveholders' hostility to free labor. Representative Windom declared that it was a struggle between the Republican party, as the friend of the toiling millions, and the Democratic party, as the champion of the aristocratic few who regarded the laboring men as slaves. And this was merely a new version of the age-old, irrepressible conflict between the workers, struggling for food, raiment and a humble home for their families, and "grasping, insatiate capital, seeking to erect for itself luxurious palaces upon the bones and muscles and heart's blood of those whom it is pleased to call the 'mud-sills' of society."[98] The Republicans would make the laborers independent freeholders, while the Democrats would enslave them![99]

Finally, the tariff was presented as a labor plank on the ground that its primary purpose was to protect American workers against the competition of cheap foreign labor, and that it would relieve the distress resulting from the depression. The Hartford *Evening Press* turned this issue, like all others, into a conflict between slavery and free labor. Since the slave states could not engage extensively in manufactures, it asserted, the slave-power had always opposed such tariffs as free labor desired. But since free labor had an immense preponderance of numbers and wealth, why should it not have such legislation as it wanted? This was the position of the Republican party, stated the writer.[100] This type of appeal was so effective that the Democrats in Pennsylvania actually promised a tariff in order to steal the thunder of their opponents.[101]

The Democrats tried to counteract the tremendous appeal that the Republicans made to the laboring men by playing on their prejudices and especially by raising the old bugaboo of emancipated Negroes flooding the North to compete with them. They also emphasized that if Lincoln were elected the South would withdraw its trade, and probably secede from the Union, throwing Northern industry into paralysis and bringing unemployment and ruin to the workers.[102] By the latter threat they attempted also to scare the capitalists into swinging the election for them. An Indiana Douglas journal warned that following a Republican victory, "soon the cry of the strong man for *bread* will be heard in accents of woe and dread, in every part of the land. A people who have never heard *that cry,* have but a poor conception of the gloom and terror it will carry to every heart. And what shall follow it? Can we hope that such a day of tribulation would pass, without bringing with it fire and blood—the torch of the incendiary, the blow of the assassin, the war of the poor for food, the struggle of men for life?"[103]

As the election approached and a Republican victory appeared probable, the New York *Herald* urged manufacturers to use "pressure" to secure the votes of workingmen against Lincoln. The employers who manufactured for the Southern market did not require much coaxing to carry out this assignment. In every Eastern state they poured out lavish expenditures to turn the tide, attempted to bully and intimidate their employees by threatening their dismissal in case of Lincoln's election, told applicants for jobs that no hiring would be done until after the election and then only if the anti-Republican ticket carried. A circular sent to every workman in the clothing houses of New York a few days before the election, printed in German for the numerous German-American employees in the trade, urged the workers to vote the Union ticket in the coming election, and to persuade their friends to do likewise. By doing so, they were assured, they would get plenty of work at good wages. But if the Republican candidate were elected, they were warned, the South would withdraw its patronage and unemployment and low wages would follow. On election day, practically every store and shop in the city was closed, and many had signs posted: "Closed—gone to vote and work for the Union."—that is, against the Republicans.[104]

These efforts unquestionably had their effect, but it seems clear, nevertheless, that the majority of Northern workers, with the

exception of the Irish, voted the Republican ticket. Although
there were many demonstrations of Irish workers in support of
Lincoln, they voted by an overwhelming majority for Douglas
but their vote was not for slavery, but rather against the party
which they were convinced was the party of nativism, capitalism
temperance and disunion.[105] The German working men, on the
other hand, were a strongly anti-slavery and pro-Republican
group, the principal exceptions being the Catholics among them

During the 1850's the German-American workers were influenced by men of varied and conflicting views, and there was considerable confusion among them on the slavery question. Kar
Heinzen, a leader among the Free Germans, was a radical abolitionist and made his paper a crusader for Negro freedom;[106] bu
Hermann Kriege violently opposed abolition as a measure, supported by "sentimental philistines" and "liberty-intoxicated ladies
which would not improve the lot of the Negroes by converting
them into wage slaves but would depress labor "to the last extrem-
ity."[107] Wilhelm Weitling, a utopian communist, strongly condemned slavery and the theories of racial supremacy, but alway
retained the position that was so popular in the 1840's, that abolition agitation could only divert the workers from their struggle
against the wage system, and consequently he gave little attention
to the issue.[108] This confusion was reflected in the shifting position of the Arbeiterbund. That organization had been led on to
the path of political action and opposition to slavery by Weydemeyer, but in 1857 it was reorganized and fell under new leadership which was not interested in the slavery question, believing
the institution to be firmly intrenched, and it warned against
overlooking "the other burning issues of the day." A splinter
group headed by W. Banque became a virtual advocate of slave
imperialism. However, after his influence was cast off, the Bund
began to take a stronger position, pledging itself to combat slavery
"in whatever form it may appear . . . with all the means at ou

disposal." In the last months before the war it came to be a vigorous champion of abolition.[109]

A more consistent anti-slavery element in the German-American labor movement were the socialists. Most of the German-
American unions in the East, as well as the Sociale Turn-Vereine,
were under their leadership and they were all uncompromising
opponents of slavery and the slave power; and the German Communist Club was active in spreading abolition propaganda.[110]
Joseph Weydemeyer, the leading Marxist in America, believed
that the free labor movement could not develop as long as slavery
existed and hampered the growth of industrial capitalism. He
wanted labor to play an active and independent part in the anti-
slavery political movement, especially in the Republican party, so
that the workers, while hastening the downfall of slavery, would
also strengthen their organization for the subsequent fight against
capital. Through his positions in the German labor organizations,
his articles in the Illinois *Staats-Zeitung,* and his lectures, his
arguments gained widespread recognition among the German-
American workers.[111]

By 1860 the great majority of the German-American laborers
had become committed to a radical anti-slavery position and to
support of the Republican party. In fact, they played a crucial
role in paving the way for the nomination of Lincoln. There was
a strong tendency in the party to nominate a conservative ticket,
and German workers feared that in such an event the party's position on slavery extension and a homestead bill would be compromised and that nativist elements would strengthen their
influence in the party. Consequently the German-American
workers of New York called a special meeting in which they
announced that they could support the party only if it nominated
candidates on the basis of those principles, and they called for a
national conference to prevent the ascendancy of conservatism.[112]
Such a conference was held in the Deutsches Haus in Chicago two
days before the opening of the Republican convention. It included

representatives of the German workers, particularly Weydemeyer
speaking for the Chicago Workers' Society, and Adolph Douai
shortly arrived from Texas with a pro-slavery mob on his heels
The conference insisted on a firm anti-slavery stand, opposition
to the Massachusetts amendment, support of a homestead act
the admission of Kansas as a free state, and the nomination of
candidates who would defend these planks. The importance of
the German-American voters was universally recognized, and
their influence was reflected in the party platform and in the
defeat of such men as Judge Bates who were being groomed by
the conservative forces in the party for the Presidential nomination.[113]

The German workers were not intimidated by the employers'
bullying. In October, the manufacturing establishments of New
York began to curtail production, fire workers and restrict
supplies to the tailors, who were nearly all German-Americans
on the pretext that the South was not placing orders for fear of
Lincoln's election. They were told that if he were elected, operations would cease entirely. The employers called a meeting of the
tailors for October 30, but several days before, the tailors' union
issued a leaflet condemning this "stupid trick" of the "lackeys of
the slave power" and called on the workers to "stand by Lincoln
and freedom and do not be intimidated into voting for the
Fusion ticket." When the employers arrived at the scheduled
meeting, they found that it had already been organized by the
Turners, and they were unable to make their speeches because
the audience interrupted them. Some of the tailors had prepared
a circular warning their fellow workingmen of the plot to make
them vote against their interests. "Do not let slide the banner of
free labor, of free homesteads, and the protective tariff—to go in
hand with dealers in human flesh." The tailors' union took over
the meeting and turned it into a demonstration for Lincoln
Weydemeyer making the main speech. Many other German
American unions also held Lincoln-for-President meetings.[114]

In all the Northern cities labor leaders organized Republican workingmen's clubs, conducted mass meetings in support of Lincoln, and worked actively to bring out the labor vote. Their efforts were highly successful, for the Republicans carried the day or at least increased their vote in practically every city. The workingmen received praise for their activities from party spokesmen, and one leader declared at a victory celebration that "We owe a debt of gratitude to the laboring class who gave us this victory, not to the mass of the merchants who were frightened by the cry of wolf."[115]

CHAPTER V

"THE UPRISING OF A
GREAT PEOPLE"[1]

The Secession Crisis

The slaveholders had been preparing a long time for the contingency that faced them at the end of 1860, and now they stepped up their efforts to nullify the will of the people: The Republicans must be forced to submit to their demands or they would destroy the new administration by unleashing civil war. To accomplish the former objective, they hoped to take advantage of the economic distress that was spreading through the Northeast. This was a result partly of the continuing effects of the depression that had been hanging over the country since 1857 and partly of the uncertainty and hesitation that accompanied the political crisis; but the immediate aggravation of the decline was due at least in part to the deliberate policy of the planters and their Northern business associates, first to prevent Lincoln's election and then to undo it.

Again the slaveholders employed the dual tactic of intimidating the workers and frightening the capitalists. At the time of the crisis in 1850, the South had attempted to force the workers to accept slaveholder domination of the territories by threatening secession. The fall of wages would be heavy and instantaneous were the union dissolved, wrote a Southern pamphleteer, for the North would have to assume the $20 million of taxes that the South was paying, and $140 million of Southern capital which was giving employment to Northern laborers would be withdrawn. The workers were warned that they would have to bear the entire burden of this loss of business. For the capitalists would send their capital to the South, where profits were higher, until the wages of Northern workers had been reduced to the point which would again permit the profitable investment of capital. The employers would thus escape the burden of new taxes and throw it upon labor.[2]

In 1860, *Anticipations for the Future and Lessons for the Present* was written by Edmund Ruffin, who fired the first shot on Fort Sumter. In this "prediction" of future events, Ruffin foresaw horrible calamity for Northern workers as a result of the cessation of purchase of Northern goods and the employment of Northern ships, the diminished supply of cotton and the sequestration of debts. In spite of unprecedented relief efforts, he envisioned huge demonstrations, succeeded by plundering mobs and riots in every city, ending in complete anarchy. The troops sent to suppress the revolts would be paralyzed by mutiny and desertion; Boston, New York, Philadelphia and Lowell would be the scenes of hitherto unknown bloodshed and carnage, and at last would lie in ruins, burned to the ground, and every man of property butchered. Finally, after the defeat of the North, on "April 7, 1869," it would be reported that "many politicians, and others, and some newspapers, openly maintain the Southern doctrine of the benefits of the institution of negro slavery, not only for the South, but also for their Northern region, (for domestic and menial services,) and argue in favor of slavery being permitted and protected in their states."[3]

Perhaps this was not in the realm of purely fanciful speculation. In December, 1859, a circular was sent in the mails to many Irish-Americans in New York, presumably by Southerners. It stated:

The South looks to its Irish friends in the large free cities to effect a diversion in its favor; and for this purpose the Union Constitutional Irish Association has been formed, of which some of you are (and doubtless

all will be) members. In the great cities prominent free soilers and abolitionists own large factories, stores and granaries, in which vast sums (made
out of the South) are invested. This fact furnishes a means of checking
their aggressions in the South, and the Irish friends of the South are
relied on to make the check effective.—Property is proverbially timid.
Whenever a hay stack or cotton gin is burned at the South by free soil
emissaries, let a large factory, or a plethoric store, or an immense granary
be given to the flames. . . .

Let us urge you to disseminate among your fellow-laborers the idea that
you have not wages proportionate to the present high scale of prices.
When once the mass of our countrymen are filled with the notion that the
free soil capitalists are withholding the price of Irish labor, while trying
to incite the negro of the South to rebellion, it will be easy enough to
gather large mobs of your brethren, . . . [4]

Was this the beginning of the long-threatened invasion of the
North by agitators to "preach up insurrection to the laborers"?

Many Northern business men shared, or pretended to share,
these apprehensions. The Detroit *Free Press* prophesied that the
approaching conflict "will not be with the South, but with tens of
thousands of people in the North. When Civil War shall come it
will be here in Michigan, and here in Detroit, and in every
northern state."[5] Another Democratic paper thought that, in case
of war, the slaves would be found true to their masters, but not
the laboring classes of the North. With the removal of the restraints of law, which presumably would follow in the wake of
war, mobs of starving and desperate men would strike out to
redress their grievances. "So these Republican agitators who have
been sowing seeds of disunion by appealing to the hearts of the
people instead of their heads; playing upon their passions, arous-
ing their sympathies, all to get their votes for places of pelf and
preferment, had better look to their own homes and hearthstones
when the evil days which they have brought about shall come."[6]

The Democrats accused the Republican party of playing with
the prosperity and the very lives of the working class in order
to enrich the capitalists and of proposing "to overthrow this white

Republic in a vain search after 'negro freedom.' "[7] They tried to inflame the workers against their employers and the Republicans, and the New York *Herald* urged the workingmen to express their sentiments in mass meetings "in such a way that the South will see that the rabid republicans, who, with their mad cry of elevation of the negro, would destroy the prosperity of the nation, cannot rely upon them to back them up in this wild crusade, that will land us—Heaven only knows where."[8] The workers did hold mass meetings, but they did not read the lines that the Democrats had written in the script.

The majority of the workers were intensely loyal to the Union, and placed its preservation above all other considerations. But they fervently desired its maintenance by peaceful means if possible, and were willing, in order to avoid war, to make concessions consistent with the sovereignty of the federal government. They knew, of course, that they would have to bear the brunt of the sacrifices demanded by war, they did not believe that the conflict could be solved only by a resort to force, and they were reluctant to take up arms against their fellow workers on the opposite side of Mason's and Dixon's line. It had been only a few months since a revival of unionism had begun, and a number of unions embraced both Northern and Southern mechanics; war would disrupt the bonds of fraternity and seriously set back the progress of the labor movement. The resolution of the Painters' Society of Brooklyn represented the sentiments of the workers: they saw "with regret the crisis brought on . . . by extremists of the North and South," but reluctantly declared their willingness "to fight if need be, for the maintenance of the flag of our country."[9]

The Irish-American, which was not a workingmen's paper but reflected the attitudes of the Irish working men in a distorted way, called upon its readers to stand by the Union. It was steadfastly opposed to secession and poured its contempt upon

Buchanan for his vacillating and submissive policy toward traitors, demanding that the government take a firm stand against the disunionists.[10] The German-American workers likewise stood firm in their loyalty to the Union and the President-elect. When Lincoln passed throught Cincinnati on his birthday in 1861, he was serenaded by the band of the German Workingmen's Society, whose leader, Frederick Oberkleine, read an address. On behalf of the German free workingmen of Cincinnati, he assured the President-elect of their sincere regard. They had voted for him as the champion of free labor and free homesteads, and firmly adhered to the principles of liberty without compromise. They assured Lincoln that if he needed men to maintain those principles, they and other workers "will rise as one man at your call, ready to risk their lives in the effort to maintain the victory already won by freedom over slavery." Lincoln made a rather noncommittal reply, agreeing that workingmen were the basis of all government, because they were the most numerous class, and giving his assurance that he favored a homestead law, free immigration and "those means which will give the greatest good to the greatest number."[11]

The workingmen in the slave states were among the staunchest opponents of disunion. As early as 1849, when there was talk of secession, a leading Georgia Democrat wrote confidentially: "It is impossible to rally the working people of the country to dissolve the Union for the protection of the slaveholders against a measure which three-fourths of the slaveholders will be sustaining and justifying"; another complained that the non-slaveholders could not be excited about the protection of slavery.[12] When the crisis actually came in 1860-61, Southern politicians were again bemoaning the fact that the workers had no interest in defending the human property of the rich and could not be depended on for supporting the plot to subvert the Union.[13] This helps explain the refusal of the secessionists to submit their actions to popular ratification.

It was in the border slave state of Kentucky that the workers initiated their broadest independent political campaign up to that time. On December 27, 1860, workers in all branches of industry assembled in the largest hall in Louisville, on the initiative of the Iron Molders' Union. The guiding thought of the workers was the preservation of the Union "as it is," for on it depended "our hope of happiness and future security." Disclaiming any interest in the "mere abstract questions which have been used . . . to distract and divide the honest masses," they could recognize no just cause or pretext for questioning the election of Lincoln or for abandoning "the gallant old ship of Union—freighted as she is, with the liberty, happiness and prosperity of more than twenty-five millions of human beings—so long as one timber remains above the surging sea, or one shred of the glorious emblem of our national unity is to be seen at her masthead." The meeting viewed "with scorn and deep indignation the course being pursued by the disorganizing traitors who are now at the Federal Capital plotting treason against the greatest and best government instituted by man," and hoped that the public sentiment of an "outraged and indignant people, may reach and overwhelm them." Since the workers had no hope that the politicians would solve the problem, they called upon their brothers throughout the nation to abandon party affiliations and to take united action to prevent the "ultra or sectional men" who were imperiling the safety of the nation. A committee was appointed to prepare an address to the working men of the United States, to urge the calling of meetings in every congressional district and to hold a national labor convention at Philadelphia in February.[14]

The response to this appeal was immediate and widespread, possibly encouraged by the opinion of the Cincinnati *Commercial* that it was "the heaviest blow which the secessionists of Louisville have received from the workingmen of that city." Meetings were held in many cities in the slave states, such as Kentucky, Tennessee, Virginia and Maryland. They all endorsed the resolutions of the Louisville workers, emphasizing their loyalty to the Constitution and the Union, denouncing secession as treason, which was being engineered "by designing and mad politicians, calculated to deluge the Valley of the Mississippi with the blood of freemen," and warning that the federal government and the working people were strong enough "to punish transgressions of every kind." Most of these meetings elected delegates to the coming national labor convention in Philadelphia, and the workers of Baltimore selected James Touchstone, well known for his strong anti-slavery views.[15]

In many cities throughout the North, the workers held similar meetings during January and February, expressing their confidence that "The remedy of all grievances can be had under the constitution and the only way to safety is by the maintenance of it." In many places, the workers went farther, as at Pittsburgh, where they deplored party spirit and recommended the acceptance of any mutually satisfactory agreement, but resolved that it was the President's duty to take prompt and energetic measures to quell treason and rebellion; in Cincinnati one worker was applauded for saying that every rebel should be hanged and that he was ready to put down rebellion by force of arms.[16] A meeting of working men in New York resolved that "the Union must and shall be preserved," by all lawful and constitutional means, and the government sustained and protected. The resolution favored any conciliatory settlement which would be just to all sections and would secure peace and union, *after a fair and candid discussion before the people.* It further proposed that the slavery question be removed from the realm of partisan politics, leaving it to the settlement of each state. The resolution also reiterated the workers' demand for a homestead act.[17]

On the other hand, some of the meetings were dominated by Democrats, and while they too expressed their earnest support of the Union and the Constitution, they often blamed the crisis impartially on the politicians of both parties and sections. Most

of them favored concessions to the South, usually by endorsing
the Crittenden plan to divide the territories into free and slave
areas along the line of 36°30′.[18]

Such was the case in Boston, where a mass meeting was held in
Faneuil Hall on February 20. Of the thirty-five sponsors of the
meeting, only twenty were laborers, the remainder being lawyers
and businessmen; Jonathan Preston, who presided, was the head
of an architectural firm. The first and only worker who addressed
the meeting was Daniel Kelly, a shipwright, and he was indiscreet
enough to deride the Republican leaders because none of them
"ever did any work or ever taught any of his sons to labor, or
ever allowed his daughter to marry a mechanic or a laborer." He
went on to blame the abolitionists for unemployment among the
Boston workers, and to praise the living standards of the Southern slaves, who "know nothing of the cares and responsibilities
that torment their white brethren, and so live a happy, peaceful
life." The main speech furnished the substance of the "Address
of the Workingmen of Massachusetts to their brethren throughout the United States." It blamed the threatening disruption of
the Union on the politicians who betrayed the people of both
North and South by fomenting sectional hatred, and singled out
the abolitionists for special vilification. If the Southern states
chose to return to the Union, they were assured that the workingmen would give them a hearty welcome and endeavor to protect them in their rights. If they preferred to remain out of the
Union, the workers would bid them go in peace. "We wish no
Union but a Union of friendship, not of force. . . ." The resolution
concluded by endorsing the Crittenden compromise.[19]

In Philadelphia, workers held meetings in their shops and then
paraded to Independence Square, carrying banners which read:
"The Union is the keystone of the country." "The Union and the
Crittenden resolutions." "We want Working Men not talking
men in Congress." 5,000 workers stood in the snow for four hours
listening to speeches by labor leaders and employers. The meeting

was conducted in a very arbitrary manner, and because of this some of the delegates, including Jonathan Fincher, the outstanding leader of the Machinists' and Blacksmiths' Union, disavowed their connections with it. There was considerable disagreement over the endorsement of the Crittenden compromise, but none on that part of the resolution which stated "That, if after all fair and honorable means have been exhausted without effecting the desired object so earnestly cherished by all Union-loving citizens we as workingmen, will sustain the Federal Government in all just and legal measures to enforce the laws of our land and nation." Machinery was set up to prepare for the national convention to meet there the following month.[20]

William Sylvis, president of the Iron Molders' Union which had initiated the Louisville meeting, wrote about the national convention in the *Mechanics' Own* ten days before its opening "Under the leadership of political demagogues and traitors scattered all over the land, North and South, East and West, the country is going to the devil as fast as it can. And unless the masses rise up in their might, and teach their representatives what to do the good old ship will go to pieces." He urged workers in every state to send delegates to Philadelphia, where they would "make one more strong pull for the Union."[21] Workers from a large number of cities in eight states—four free and four border slave states —responded, and on the morning of Washington's birthday a huge parade marched to the old State House. Ten divisions were formed by mechanics representing some two score of trades; floats symbolizing the Union were carried, and banners reading "Concessions not secession." At Independence Square a mass meeting was held, in which pleas were made to sacrifice political partisanship for the sake of the Union, and the Crittenden compromise was approved.[22]

The convention sessions were held the following day, when James B. Nicholson welcomed the delegates in behalf of the Philadelphia workingmen. He urged the setting aside of partisan ship in favor of a conciliatory attitude in order to preserve the Union and "transmit to our children the inheritance bequeathed to us by our patriotic sires." He believed the Crittenden plan could be honorably accepted as a basis of settlement. One of the Virginia delegates, who had voted for Douglas in 1860, said he would support any party capable of saving the Union; he opposed secession and proudly labeled himself a "submissionist." Several speakers urged the immediate organization of a farmer-labor party and the election of workers to office as the only way to save the Union, but this question was not permitted to come to a vote. Finally, an eight-point resolution was presented and adopted: (1) the Crittenden compromise was endorsed as a Constitutional settlement of the territorial issue; (2) devotion to the Union and defiance to traitors were reaffirmed; (3) disunion was denounced as repugnant to the people; (4) the politicians of both North and South were anathematized and it was determined to replace them with men who would truly represent the people; (5) the right of secession was denied, but the preservation of the Union by coercion was deprecated; (6) the workers pledged to vote against any candidate who opposed compromise; (7) the repeal of personal liberty laws was urged as a conciliatory measure; (8) a committee was chosen to organize the nation's workers for political action.[23]

As the convention prepared to adjourn, James Touchstone of Maryland rose and delivered a stinging broadside against the Southern aristocracy who were organizing treason for the purpose of "placing their feet on the necks of the mechanics," overturning Constitutional liberty and rearing a despotism on its ruins. He thought the workers' convention should say so, instead of deceiving the people by "a contemptible subterfuge." He therefore submitted resolutions for upholding the Constitution and the laws by all measures, and expressing the sympathy of the convention with their brother workingmen of the seceded states and . . . pledge to them their effort to regain their constitutional rights,

which have been wrested from them by violence." These resolu
tions were greeted by loud applause, but when it was pointed ou
that their passage would wreck the compromise platform already
adopted, Touchstone withdrew them. It is evident that politica
forces on the resolutions committee had distorted the real feeling
of the workers by softening the opposition to the slave-power an
the determination to defend the Union and over-emphasizing th
desire for conciliation.[24] Considering all the manifestations o
labor's attitude from the election to the inauguration of Lincoln
the conclusion is inescapable that, while the depression, the desir
to prevent war and the activities of the Democratic party had re
sulted in some defection from the Republican ranks, the nev
administration could take a firm stand against the slave-powe
with the assurance that the working class in the North woul
rally to the support and defense of the Union, and that the South
ern workers, particularly in the border states, would constitute
potent deterrent to the schemes of the disunionists. The working
men were not committed to any political party, but they wer
committed to the defense of their country and their liberties.

Labor, Emancipation and the Civil War

When the war began with the attack on Fort Sumter, th
workers rose to the defense of their country. Many military unit
of native-, German- and Irish-American workers had alread
offered themselves to the President and they now rushed to th
colors, as did a Polish-American and an Italian-American work
ingmen's guard. Trade unions organized fighting companies an
enlisted as a body, posting notices on their union halls: "Close
for the duration." Behind the lines the workers labored lon;
hours under difficult conditions to turn out the materials of wa
for their brothers at the front. As William Sylvis said at the clos
of the war, "I presume it is hardly necessary for me to enter int

ny arguments to prove that the workingmen, the great body of
he people, the bone and muscle of the nation, the very pillars of
ur temple of liberty are loyal; that, I take it, would be sheer
mockery, would be adding insult to injury; for the evidence of our
loyalty one need only point to the history of the war; to the fact
that while armed treason and rebellion threatened our institutions
with destruction, while the proud and opulent of the land were
plotting the downfall of our government, the toiling millions
stood like a wall of adamant between the country and all its
foes."[26]

The Negro workers also made an outstanding contribution to
the victory of the Union. From the very beginning of the war they
offered their services to the government, and as soon as they were
allowed, joined the army, recruiting their own men, and sometimes refusing pay, as did the 54th Massachusetts regiment which
served for an entire year. In spite of their receiving half the regular pay, in spite of being consigned frequently to menial services
in the army camps, and in spite of unfriendly commanders in
many cases, they did whatever they could—and in a manner
which evoked the highest praise. General Rufus Saxton, for example, reported: "It is admitted upon all hands that the Negroes
fight with a coolness and bravery that would have done credit to
veteran soldiers. There was no excitement, no flinching, no attempt at cruelty when successful. They seemed like men who
were fighting to vindicate their manhood and they did it well."[27]
Some 80,000 Northern Negroes served in the Union armies,
and they were joined by 125,000 slaves who escaped to the Union
lines and joined the army as soldiers, workers, and scouts. In the
latter capacity they performed an indispensable job that could
have been done by no one else. That the Negro people played a
decisive role in the struggle for their emancipation was attested
to by many authorities, and by none less than President Lincoln,
who said in 1864: ". . . the experience of the present war proves
their [the South's] success is inevitable if you fling the compulsory

labor of millions of black men into their side of the scale. . . .
Abandon all the posts now garrisoned by black men, take 150,000
men from our side and put them in the battle-field or corn-field
against us, and we would be compelled to abandon the war in
three weeks."[28]

The workers, of course, were fighting for the purpose, as the
Troy Iron Molders put it, of "maintaining the supremacy of Law
and Order and defending the Constitution so wisely drafted by
the Sons of '76 and also the Federal Capital and last but not least
to protect that good old flag, the Stars and Stripes. . . ."[29] But
they were motivated by more than patriotism alone. By their
political struggles for over a decade they had shown that they
understood the character of their enemy and the fact that they
were defending the democratic tradition of their country, although
some of them did not yet realize that the fulfillment of that
tradition was dependent on the overthrow of chattel slavery.
They identified the fight against the slave-power with the defense
of the labor movement—the word "Union" had a double meaning for them. When the delegates to the National Typographical
Union convention held their annual dinner in Cleveland in 1862
they drank a toast to "Our brethren in the field—True to their
love of 'Union,' they fearlessly stand face to face with its
enemies."[30] The New York local of the same union defined
the issue similarly if not so concisely: if the workingman would
be free "and enjoy the blessings of liberty for himself and his
children—if he would be true to himself and the workingmen
of the South—if he would be true to the interests of labor
throughout the world he must work and vote to overthrow
rebellion and treason and maintain the government at every
cost."[31]

It was only their patriotism and understanding of the issues
of the war that enabled the workers to make the contribution
they did in the face of provocations and injustices from their
employers and from the government. During the elections the

Republicans had worked hard to convince the workers that labor had only *one* enemy, the slave-power; but by their conduct during the war they seemed to be trying to reverse this attitude—everything they did lent credence to the opinion that it was "a rich man's war and a poor man's fight." While working class families were suffering from the absence and death of their breadwinners, the masters of industry were making fortunes from war contracts and increasing their profits by the manufacture of shoddy uniforms and shoes that disintegrated in the rain and rifles that blew off the hands of the soldiers. While living standards deteriorated under the impact of runaway inflation, the rich were getting richer by profiteering and speculation. While workers were promised the benefits of the Homestead Act, the railroad manipulators and stock-jobbers were grabbing millions of acres of the best land and being paid to build the roads. While soldiers and workers received depreciated greenbacks for pay, government bondholders were guaranteed payment in hundred-cent dollars. When workers were forced to strike for a living wage, their strikes were broken, sometimes by foreign laborers imported under the terms of the new Contract Labor Law, sometimes by hastily enacted state legislation which virtually outlawed the right to strike, as in Minnesota and Illinois, sometimes by Federal troops, as in the strike at the Parrott Gun Works in Cold Springs, New York, the walk-outs of machinists and tailors in St. Louis, the engineers on the Reading Railroad, the miners of Tioga County, Pennsylvania, and two hundred mechanics in Tennessee.[32] And while the workingmen were fighting their country's battles, the government and the army brass were honeycombed with Copperheads and pussyfooters who vacillated, temporized, hampered the prosecution of the war and sowed confusion and defeatism.

This state of affairs provided grist for the mill of the Copperheads, who sought to turn labor's discontent with the manner in which the war was conducted into opposition to the war itself.

For example, when two hundred workers in Louisville refused to work at the wages which were offered to them, the New York *Daily News* reported that General Thomas, commanding the region, had arrested them. He is "employed in freeing the Negro," said this Democratic organ, "even at the expense of transferring the chains to the limbs of free laboring men," and the punishment of the workers would last "as long as the Abolitionists can keep up the war spirit, and run riot on the money they fleece from the government." During the election campaign of 1864, when the Copperheads were attempting to save the slaveholders by a negotiated peace, they directed their propaganda to the workers who were suffering as a result of the "aimless strife." They pointed out that while the war was enriching the "shoddy contractors, shoulder-strap politicians and bounty jumpers," it was starving the workingmen and tearing them from their families to bleed and die in an unnatural and patricidal strife. Only peace would put an end to the slaughter, the demoralization of industry, and the starvation wages of labor.[33]

This quisling campaign had little effect on the organized workers of the country, who understood that, even though the rich were using the war to get richer, it was still a war for the liberties of America and the working people. But the propaganda of the Copperheads undoubtedly did influence many of the unskilled and unorganized workers, whose economic conditions were the worst, who did not have the guidance of the most advanced working class leaders and the labor press, and who were still attached in large numbers to the Democratic party. It was to this group especially that the Copperheads, Peace Democrats and Negrophobes directed their propaganda, and they used with greatest force the old tactic of frightening the worker with exaggerated predictions of the free Negroes flooding the Northern labor market. An editorial in the Columbus (Ohio) *Crisis* in 1861 was typical. It reported that a large-scale imm-

gration of free Negroes had already begun and claimed that
the Republicans desired to emancipate all the slaves. This would
send an influx of a million Negroes into Ohio, predicted the
writer, "to mix with the white population, and compete with the
white laborers for a living, or steal from those who have got
property. . . ." He protested against such an interference with
the prosperity and manhood of the farmers and laborers and
expressed the desire that the Negroes be kept in slavery.[34]

During the election of 1862 this was a major theme in the
Democratic campaign. The state organizations of the party
adopted resolutions which designated the Republican party as
"the party of fanaticism or crime, whichever it may be called,
that seeks to turn the slaves of the Southern States loose to over-
run the North and enter into competition with the white laboring
masses, thus degrading and insulting their manhood by placing
them on an equality with negroes in their occupations. . . ."[35]
The Democratic press reported instances, often false, to show
that this was already happening. It was alleged that some hotel
keepers had discharged white employees to make jobs for
Negroes who had escaped into the Northern lines, and that the
abolitionists were working to secure positions for all of them,
each of whom would replace a white worker. The Philadelphia
Public Ledger warned laborers to "beware of the contractors,
jobbers and jobbers who were fattening upon the spoils of their
hard earned labor" and who wanted the war continued in order
to introduce cheap labor into the North. Another Pennsylvania
paper reported that the Cambria Iron Works in Johnston had
employed several "contrabands" at twenty-five cents a day, thus
provoking a strike by the white employees. "The Government
was made for the benefit of white men," decreed the editor, "and
the white men will not submit to be crowded out by the worthless
runaway negroes of the South. Our friends can see in this the
beautiful workings of the Emancipation policy of President
Lincoln." This story was refuted by the employees of the company

themselves, but it was nevertheless reprinted in almost every Democratic paper in the state.[36] The Democrats in many Northern states conducted a campaign to prohibit the immigration of free Negroes or to retain such exclusions where they already existed, as in Illinois, Indiana and Ohio.[37]

The Republicans and abolitionists denied that free Negroes would come North once slavery was abolished, and asserted that those who came during the war were needed to fill the labor shortage, and that they were being employed at standard wages. General D. H. Hunter, who as commander of the Department of the South declared all the slaves in South Carolina, Georgia and Florida free,[38] issued a specific denial of the Democrats' charges, stating that he had given passes north to all Negroes asking for them, but not more than a dozen had applied for them. "My experience leads me to believe that the exact reverse of the received opinion on this subject would form the rule, and that nearly if not quite all the negroes of the North would migrate South whenever they shall be at liberty to do so without fear of the auction block."[39] Lincoln made a special point of this in his annual message to Congress in 1862, pointing out that whether free or slave, there would still be the same number of Negroes doing the same amount of work. Besides, he asked why should emancipation send the free people North? "People of any color seldom run unless there be something to run from . . ." As evidence of the truth of this statement, he pointed to the abolition of slavery in the District of Columbia, which had not produced any influx of Negroes to the North.[40] The Republicans would perhaps not have been in such an embarrassing position if they had not, for eight years past, made their contribution to anti-Negro prejudice by insisting that theirs was a white man's party, that their object was to preserve the territories for white men, and that the Negroes were "no party" to the controversy at all.

Although the Democrats magnified and embroidered the probem, a problem did exist—not in emancipation, but in the anti-labor and anti-Negro policies of employers who could be counted on to create divisions and to employ Negroes in order to depress the wage standards of both white and Negro workers, as they had done in the past both North and South, and as they were doing with immigrant contract labor, with women and children, and with convict labor.

Fincher's Trades' Review, the outstanding labor paper edited by Jonathan Fincher, placed the blame for the problem on "the cupidity of the more avaricious" who would seek to employ the Negroes to "gratify their notions of economy." Fincher did not allow his apprehensions to blind him to the fact that the rebellion was an "attempt . . . to establish a government on the destruction of the rights of labor," and that the workers had to make every necessary sacrifice to win the war, and he did not question the propriety of emancipating the slaves. But, he said, "we will not conceal our fears of the injury likely to be visited upon the innocent, in the attempt to punish the guilty. It will be but a poor return, indeed, to the mechanics and workingmen of the North, who are now fighting the battles of the Union, to find on their return, every source of employment choked up by the freed negroes of the South." He proposed that the government "repay the patriotic thousands who have responded to their country's call by placing proper restrictions upon the ingress of emancipated slaves into the Northern states. . . . We demand that protection from the Government, which we have won by our sacrifice of life, blood and treasure, and which we will continue to give in her defense."[41]

Misgivings were naturally strongest among the unskilled and unorganized workers who would feel any competition the worst, who had the least means of protection, and many of whom were already experiencing such competition. Having learned from hard experience that they could rely on no one to defend them, having no trade unions to help preserve their wage standards, and

being subjected to the anti-Negro propaganda of the Democratic
press, they sometimes turned their resentment against their
rivals, using whatever weapons came to hand. Thus in Cincinnati
in the summer of 1862, Negroes were hired on the river boats
for $30 a month when the current rate was $40 to $75. The Cin
cinnati *Enquirer* reprinted an article from a Philadelphia paper
which reported that Negro labor there was causing a decline in
wages and alleged that Negro workers pouring in from the
South were willing to work for ten cents a day. "Like causes will
produce like results here," wrote the *Enquirer*. "How do our
white laborers relish the prospect that the emancipation of the
blacks spreads before them?" A few days later, the white boat
men, mostly Irish, attacked the Negroes and rioting raged over
the waterfront for five days. The Cincinnati *Gazette* denounced
both the assaults and the agitation that incited them, saying that
"the very men who today are endeavoring to incense the honest
white laboring men in Cincinnati against black competition, are
the supporters of Slavery, and would tomorrow initiate slave
labor into every workshop in your city, if it were possible." Such
agitators who "wilfully excite the worst passions of the
white workers," recommended the Cleveland *Leader*, "deserve
halter."[42]

Similar occurrences took place in many Northern cities, often
as a result of the introduction of Negroes as strike-breakers. In
Chicago the workers in the slaughtering and packing industry
met to protest "the intention of one or more of the leading
packers of this town to bring negro labor into competition with
that of the white men for the purpose of reducing the wages of
the latter to the lowest possible standard." They pledged not to
work for any employers who hired Negroes and voted to expel
from the union any members who violated the pledge.[43] When
the commanding general in Illinois tried to find employment for
"confiscated" Negroes sent north by the Union armies, there
was considerable protest. Workers in Quincy held a mass meet

ag and announced that "we hereby give notice to those engaged
a this business of attempting to ride down and crush out the
ee white workingmen of Illinois, by thus seeking to bring free
egro labor into competition with white labor, that we cannot
nd will not tolerate it; that we will seek our remedy, first,
nder the law; second, at the polls; and third, if both these fail,
e will redress our wrongs in such a manner as shall seem to
s most expedient and most practicable."[44] Many other instances
f this kind could be cited.[45] In the spring and early summer
f 1863 there was a wave of riots between Negro and Irish
ngshoremen in Chicago, Detroit, Cleveland, Buffalo, Albany,
ew York, Boston and other places, almost invariably produced
y the employment of Negroes to break strikes. In June 3,000
ck workers in New York struck for higher wages to meet
e increased cost of living, and their jobs were filled by Negroes
ought in under police protection.[46]

These conditions were aggravated to the bursting point by the
ssage of the first conscription act in March 1863, for it virtually
tablished by law that this was to be a "poor man's fight." In
oviding that any person subject to the draft might be exempted
furnishing a substitute or paying a $300 commutation fee,
permitted men of means to avoid service and saddle their
are on the backs of those who could not pay. The labor move-
ent was not opposed to conscription, but it was vehemently
posed to this discriminatory feature of the act; and while de-
anding the democratization of the law, it urged complete
edience to its provisions. William Sylvis thought Congress had
perfect right to compel the workers to serve in the army if
cessary.[47] Jonathan Fincher agreed that the government had a
ght to appropriate the lives of its citizens and that the people
ved it to their government to give their lives in its defense and
yield obedience to ALL laws enacted by the proper powers,
en if the most objectionable. . . ." But in this case, he pointed
t, the government

has committed the unpardonable crime of dividing the people into classe
of the worst distinction—rich and poor . . . We cannot silently see the poo
conscript torn from family and friends, and forced to the ranks, while th
worthless drone upon society, a rich man's son, can, by paying the cost o
a week's debauchery, be relieved from the hardships and dangers of
soldier's life. . . . For the sake of the country let the conscription come
But let it come alike upon the rich as well as the poor. No exemptions
No, not one—either for worth or worthlessness, distinction or obscurity
wealth or poverty.[48]

Again the Copperheads swung into action, striving to tur
dissatisfaction with the draft law into opposition to the war an
the government. The most unconcealed incitement to riot wa
preached, as in an article in the New York *Daily News* o
July 13:

Only a few among the workingmen of this city who may be conscripte
into the ranks of the abolition army, will march to the field with th
proud conscience that they are the soldiers of a Republic about to d
battle for Republican institutions. The very fact that a power exists tha
can *drive them from their homes to the slaughter pen will teach the*
that they are no longer free agents. . . .

If the workingmen of this city are disinclined to be forced into a fig
for emancipation, let them clamor so loud for peace that their voices sha
be potential with our rulers. It is a strange perversion of the laws of sel
preservation which would compel the white laborer to leave his famil
destitute and unprotected, while he goes forth to free the negro, wh
being free, will compete with him in labor. Let the laboring populatio
assemble peaceably in mass meeting, and express their views upon th
subject. Let it be no political gathering . . . but a spontaneous congregatio
of the working class to give vent, within legal bounds, but firmly, to th
sentiments of their fraternity with regard to this odious war. . . .[49]

On the same day that this article appeared, a mob gathere
at the main recruiting office, disrupted the proceedings an
wrecked the building. The mob quickly gained momentum an
soon had the upper hand throughout the city. The rioters attacke
the *Tribune* offices; assaulted factories and foundries whe
Negroes were employed and tried to close them down or dri

out the Negroes; overran the docks and piers, where their strike had recently been broken by the employment of Negro longshoremen, and attacked every Negro in sight. Blind fury took possession of the mob, which was joined by the riff-raff of the city and pro-slavery sympathizers; they roamed the streets looking for victims, attacked Negroes and Republican leaders, destroyed property, and climaxed their frenzy by burning down a Negro orphan asylum. It was not until three days had passed that the rioting was brought under control by Federal troops rushed into the city. Similar occurrences took place in several other cities, but on a much smaller scale.[50]

It is not difficult to fix the responsibility for this eruption in view of all that had gone before. Opposition to the discriminatory features of the draft was only one element in the "draft riots." The outbreaks were a blind revolt against class legislation, against strike-breaking, against intolerable economic conditions, against the orgy of profiteering and speculation at the expense of the workers and soldiers; they were nourished on the white supremacy propaganda of politicians, both Republican and Democratic, and the divisive policies of employers, both Republican and Democratic; and they were stimulated by treasonous agents of the slave-power. Fincher observed that the working men were loyal and patriotic, and their opposition to the draft was not the result of their being puppets of the Democratic party. The mobs in New York, he said, were composed of men who had families to look after and lacked the $300 to purchase their exemption. This is the whole matter in a nutshell. It is an outbreak of the poor against the rich. It is the poor conscript against the rich exempt." The rioting was wrong, he concluded, but the wrong did not begin with the mob. It began with the law, which was "so flaring an outrage" as to invite what happened. If men with families were exempted and the $300 clause repealed, the laborers would give a "hearty acquiescence" to their duty.[51]

These provocations could only have inflamed many people beyond the limits of human endurance. The remarkable fact is

that such a small number succumbed to them. Before, during
and after these outbreaks, the overwhelming majority of the
workers demonstrated their loyalty to the government and their
determination to carry the war to a successful conclusion. That
the majority of workers was not responsible for the riots was
proved, Fincher pointed out, by the fact that thousands of workingmen were driven from their shops by the rioters, and many
others continued at their work at the risk of their lives. Hundreds
of others cooperated with the authorities to restore order. And the
riots were suppressed by the army and militia, 90 per cent of
whom were workingmen, who were always to be found on the
side of law and order. "They suppressed the riots, as they are
suppressing the rebellion—perhaps to be rewarded in the one
case, as they have been in the other, with the ingratitude of
political demagogues."[52]

Working men printed and distributed posters admonishing
their fellow laborers not to fall into the trap of Southern traitors:

Workingmen! when any man asks you to break the law, and tries to
stir up your passions, while he skulks out of sight, you may set him down
as your worst enemy. Spurn him as you would a viper. The patriotic
workingmen of the North can not afford to spend time in killing each
other.[53]

Another leaflet said, in part:

Do not listen to bad men who are only leading you to your ruin. . . . Stand
up as Democratic Workingmen should stand up before the world, and
show the traitors of the South, and the friends of tyranny all over the
world, that *the Workingmen of New York are able to govern themselves.*
Stand by the Union, the Constitution, and the Laws! Then peace, freedom
and prosperity will be secured to you and to your children after you
KEEP HONESTLY AT YOUR WORK! GIVE NO HEED TO BAD ADVICE![54]

After the riots, there were numerous mass meetings of workers
in New York which protested against the demonstrations and

rongly condemned and disclaimed the disloyal sentiments which
were uttered during their progress.[55] Subsequent calls for volun-
teers were responded to enthusiastically by the workers, and
later drafts were welcomed by the labor press and carried out
without incident.[56]

While the Northern workers remained loyal throughout the
war, the laborers in the South were permeated by a profound
and widespread resentment against the slaveholders who had
forced them into a conflict in which they had no interest. The
Confederacy was also racked by profiteering, speculation and
inflation, and had its own brand of discriminatory conscription
which exempted overseers and owners of twenty or more
slaves. But these conditions produced much more opposition than
in the North, because the workers did not have the motivation
to fight that inspired the Northern laborers; they had nothing
to gain and everything to lose by a strengthening of the slave-
power. Senator James Phelan told Jefferson Davis that no law
had ever met "with more universal odium than the exemption
of slave-owners. . . . Its influence upon the poor is most
calamitous, and has awakened a spirit and elicited a discussion of
which we may safely predict the most unfortunate results."[57]
The workers employed every possible means of evading service:
they entered into the exempted jobs and professions in large
numbers, managed to get affidavits of physical incapacity, went
into hiding in caves and swamps, organized shotgun squads to
receive conscription officers, and deserted from the army in
fantastic numbers. In many cases resistance to the draft was so
widespread that the officials were openly defied, and in some
places anti-conscription and pro-Union organizations were formed.
The unwillingness of the Southern workingmen to fight the
battles of the slaveholders was a significant factor in the defeat
of the South.[58] To the activities of the free workers must be added
the struggles of the bondsmen against their enslavers. By strikes,
sabotage and insurrection, by guerilla warfare conducted by out-

law communities of runaways, by supplying Union armies wit
important military information, by serving as scouts for th
Union forces, and by escaping to the Union lines where about on
third of them enlisted in the armies of liberation, the slave
immeasurably hastened the downfall of their oppressors and thu
earned their emancipation by their own efforts.[59]

The events of the war helped to clarify labor's understandin
of the need to destroy the chattel system. Many workingme
earlier had feared that abolition agitation would divert them fror
their struggles for the emancipation of labor, but now it wa
obvious that the aggression of the slave-power and not th
struggle against it was what stood in the way of the labo
movement. Many had believed that the emancipation of labo
must precede the abolition of slavery, and now it was equal
plain that the workers would not be able to advance their cau
until the great issue of the day was settled by the comple
uprooting of the system that had produced it. William Sylvis ha
voted for Stephen Douglas in 1860 and strove to prevent war, b
once it came he knew that it must terminate in emancipatio
"Whatever our opinions may have been as to the cause of th
war," he said in 1868, "we can all agree that human slave
(property in man) was the first great cause; and from the da
the first gun was fired, it was my earnest hope that the w
might not end until slavery ended with it."[60]

As the war progressed it became clear that it not only shou
but must end in freedom for the slaves, and in fact that it cou
not end in victory *unless* the slaves were liberated. Any oth
conclusion to hostilities would have been, by its very nature,
negotiated peace, for the economic basis of the slave-power wou
be left unimpaired (unless the Southern whites and the slav
themselves put an end to it). The North was fighting with o
arm tied behind its back as long as it did not enlist the slav

the struggle by emancipating them and welcoming their support. The logic of war was forcing the adoption of emancipation, if not as a policy of principle, then as a military necessity. Many people who had taken a very conservative position on the slavery question before the war underwent a complete change within a short time. For example, the attitude of John B. Purcell, archbishop of Cincinnati, was typical of the pre-war Catholic view, but he became a staunch Unionist and supported emancipation. His brother, Father Edward Purcell, editor of the *Catholic Telegraph,* shared his views, and added that it was in the interest of the white laboring men of both the North and South to save the Negro workers from slavery. Many Catholics agreed with his stand.[61] The personal experience of the workers was also an important part of their political education. Greeley stated that "The soldiers who, though generally enlisted with strong anti-Negro prejudices, quite commonly experienced a gradual change under the discipline of service at the front, where they found every black their ready, active, zealous friend, and nearly every slave-holder or overseer their quiet but deadly, implacable foe."[62]

Of considerable importance in helping the workers to understand the issues of the war was the action of the European working class. The common people of Europe were lukewarm towards the American conflict as long as the North was professedly fighting only for "the Union as it was and the Constitution as is." Carl Schurz, from his ambassadorial post in Europe, warned Lincoln that the aristocracy of Europe contemplated intervention in behalf of the slavocracy, and that it would be prevented by the people if they knew that the war was being conducted for the emancipation of the slaves.[63] In no place was this more true than in England, for that country could determine the role of the Continent in the war. The aristocracy and the cotton manufacturers were solidly on the side of the Confederacy and were more than once on the verge of throwing their weight into the scale. That they did not do so was due to a large extent to

the unmistakable warnings of the workers that they would not
tolerate a crusade for the perpetuation of slavery and against
their fellow workingmen on the other side of the ocean. The
workers took this stand in spite of the fact that they were suffering the most cruel privation as a result of the Confederacy's
inability to ship cotton to the industrial centers, a situation which
could have been relieved by the British navy.

At the end of 1861 English reaction seized upon the Mason
and Slidell affair as a pretext for war against the United States
but mass meetings in the working class districts of London
warned that "no intervention on the part of the English government will be permitted," and that they would "raise their
voices and, in case of need, their hands for the prevention of
so great a crime." Mason and Slidell were denounced as "slave
holders as well as confessed agents of the tyrannical faction that
is at once in rebellion against the American republic and the
sworn enemy of the social and political rights of the working
class in all countries."[64] When the Emancipation Proclamation
was announced in September 1862, it was greeted with enthusiasm by the English workers. On December 31 a mass meeting
of London workers adopted an address to President Lincoln, in
which they expressed their admiration for the strugggle to
deliver the country from the curse and shame of slavery.

We regarded with abhorrence the conspiracy and rebellion by which
was sought at once to overthrow the supremacy of a government based
upon the most popular suffrage in the world, and to perpetuate the hate-
ful inequalities of race. . . . We have watched with the warmest interest
the steady advance of your policy along the path of emancipation; and on
this eve of the day on which your proclamation of freedom takes effect
we pray God to strengthen your hands, to confirm your noble purpose,
and to hasten the restoration of that lawful authority which engages . . .
to realize the glorious principle on which your Constitution is founded—
the brotherhood, freedom and equality of all men.[65]

On the same day the workmen of Manchester congratulate
Lincoln on his action:

nce we have discerned that the victory of the free North, in the war
hich has so sorely distressed us as well as afflicted you, will strike off the
tters of the slave, you have attracted our warm and earnest sympathy.
'e joyfully honor you as the President, and the Congress with you, for
any decisive steps toward practically exemplifying your belief in the
ords of your great founders, "All men are created free and equal." . . .
eartily do we congratulate you and your country on this humane and
ghteous course. We assume that you cannot now stop short of a com-
ete uprooting of slavery. . . . While your enthusiasm is aflame, and the
de of events runs high, let the work be finished effectively. . . .[66]

a long editorial, the London *Daily News* applauded the
orking class for "maintaining the honor and character of the
ritish nation in the eyes of the world" when others had de-
ulted.[67] Both the address and the editorial were widely re-
inted in the American press, and as broadsides they were
stributed among the workers. So was Lincoln's reply, in which
told the workers that their "decisive utterances" in the face
the severe trials to which they were subjected was "an instance
sublime Christian heroism which has not been surpassed in
y age or in any country. It is indeed an energetic and reinspir-
g assurance of the inherent power of truth, and of the ultimate
d universal triumph of justice, humanity, and freedom."[68]
Also widely publicized in American newspapers and pamphlets
ere the speech of John Bright at a Trades Union meeting in
ondon on March 26 in which he characterized the slaveholders
the foes of labor and democracy throughout the world,[69] and
e remarks of a Trade Union deputation to the American am-
ssador, Charles Francis Adams. They expressed their "abhor-
nce of the American institution of slavery, their disapprobation
the rebellion of the Southern States of that country, their sym-
thy with the North in its efforts to put down that rebellion, and
eir admiration of the general policy—more particularly that
lating to slavery—pursued by President Lincoln." Adams ten-
red his thanks to the workers and observed that it was natural
r a body of workingmen to look with disfavor upon any

party which infringed on the rights of labor. "You perceiv
that in the struggle now going on in America an attempt
being made to establish a government on the destruction of th
rights of labor—a government of physical power to take awa
the rights of labor. . . ."[70]

In January 1865, the International Workingmen's Associatio
congratulated Lincoln on his re-election in a letter writte
by Karl Marx:

If resistance to the Slave Power was the reserved watchword of your fir
election, the triumphant war cry of your re-election is Death to Slavery.

From the commencement of the titanic American strife the workingme
of Europe felt instinctively that the Star-spangled banner carried th
destiny of their class. The contest of the territories which opened the di
epopee, was it not to decide whether the virgin soil of immense trac
should be wedded to the labor of the emigrant or prostituted by the tran
of the slave driver?

When an oligarchy of 300,000 slaveholders dared to inscribe for th
first time in the annals of the world "slavery" on the banner of arme
revolt . . . then the working classes of Europe understood at once . .
they were unable to attain the true freedom of labor, or to support the
European brethren in their struggle for emancipation; but this barrier
progress has been swept off by the red sea of civil war.

The workingmen of Europe feel sure that, as the American War
Independence initiated a new era of ascendancy for the middle class,
the American anti-slavery war will do for the working classes. The
consider it an earnest of the epoch to come that it fell to the lot
Abraham Lincoln, the singleminded son of the working class, to lea
the country through the matchless struggle for the rescue of an enchaine
race and the reconstruction of a social order.[71]

Adams replied in behalf of Lincoln that the American peop
"derive new encouragement to persevere from the testimor
of the workingmen of Europe that the national attitude
favored with their enlightened approval and earnest sympathies

Labor's support of emancipation was greatly stimulated al
by a thorough and well organized publishing program. Th

epublicans and abolitionists made a systematic effort to discuss
avery in terms of its effect on the working class, both in their
gular press and by the publication of numerous pamphlets and
aflets written especially for workers.[72] Prominent in the coordi-
ation and distribution of such literature were the New England
oyal Publication Society, organized in Boston in 1862, and the
oyal Publication Society of New York. These societies gathered
iti-slavery material from a wide variety of sources and sent
 to newspapers throughout the North for reprinting. By the
id of 1863 nearly a thousand papers were using the services fully
id gratefully, expressing praise for the merit and value of the
aterial they received. Many of the clippings and other docu-
ents were printed as broadsides and sent to some five hundred
dividuals and organizations for mass distribution, particularly
nong the workers.[73] A large number of these leaflets were
voted to exposing the conditions of workers in the slave states,
e anti-labor policy of the slavocracy and its intention of establish-
g a universal slave empire. Many of them gave special attention
 the nativist policy of the Confederate leaders, their contempt
r the foreign born, and their aim of disfranchising immigrant
orkers and restricting their rights of citizenship as a prelude to
islaving them.[74]

The pre-war depression and the war dealt a crippling blow
 the labor movement and its press, but at least one important
bor paper managed to survive and in the last two years of
e war there was a revival. These journals, many of them of
very high standard, were able to play an important part in
arifying the issues of the rebellion to the workers. *The Iron
atform,* published by the New York Typographical Union,
nstantly explained to its readers the necessity of overthrowing
eason in order to insure the protection of labor's rights in
merica and throughout the world, and that this could be
hieved only by freeing the slaves. "There is one truth," it said,
vhich should be clearly understood by every workingman in the

Union. *The slavery of the black man leads to the slavery of the white man. . . .* If the doctrine of treason is true, that Capital should own labor, then their logical conclusion is correct, and all laborers, white or black, are and ought to be slaves."[75] *Fincher's Trades' Review,* published in Philadelphia from the middle of 1863, took a similar position on the issues of the war, calling on the workers to make every sacrifice necessary to crush the rebellion which was attempting "to establish a government on the destruction of the rights of labor."

In addition to the labor newspapers, workingmen published many leaflets and pamphlets to mobilize support for the war and emancipation. These were particularly important in 1863 and 1864 when the Copperheads were agitating for a negotiated peace which would save the slaveowners and their property. One series of broadsides published by "A Democratic Workingman" in New York brought to the workers' attention the ambition of the Confederate leaders "to destroy their republican institutions and build up an aristocracy or a monarchy upon the ruins," to disfranchise foreign born workers, to "check the spread over our territory of that spawn of ignorance and crime, which flows in endless issue from the prisons and dens of corruption in the marts of Europe," and to "reduce free white workingmen to the same political, social, and moral condition as their slaves." It admonished the workingmen not to interfere with the vigorous prosecution of the war and thus help the sworn enemies of labor. It urged them to stand by their government until the enemies of the Union and of democracy were overthrown, and peace and prosperity were restored by the victory of the Union." Another leaflet, addressed to the Irish laborers, quoted Daniel O'Connell's remark that "The spirit of democratic liberty is defiled by the continuation of Negro slavery in the United States." It explained the Southern doctrine that "Capital shall own Labor," and asserted that slavery was anti-democratic because it was a war on the interests and rights of workingmen

"We call upon you, in the sacred name of humanity, never again to volunteer on behalf of the oppressor, nor even for any self-interest to vindicate the hideous crime of slavery. . . . Give your votes in behalf of Freedom and not in behalf of slavery!"[77] The last broadside in the series printed the Southern peace terms —complete submission, recognition of the Confederacy, giving up all the territories west of the Confederate states, and reimbursement of the slave states for the costs and losses of the war— and added: "Comrades! Vote for the party that stands by the government, and vote for the man who stands by us, and by your brave brothers in the field, and let the ballot box tell the story of your patriotism and your resolve not to be the 'white slaves' of traitors or their friends."[78]

One other pamphlet may be cited as representing a somewhat different approach to the workers. In a series of questions and answers it explained the means by which the slaveholders controlled and oppressed the white workingmen as well as the slaves, and concluded with this exchange:

Q. 9. Shall we suffer these 350,000 men, who have committed all these enormities, and who are now drenching this nation with blood, to continue to hold their unjust, ruinous power?

A. No! never! They have forfeited their lives and property. Let us free their slaves. . . . Nothing short of this can ever make this nation a Union. Let this be done, and the down-trodden white people of the South will soon feel deliverance and shout for joy. The welfare of the whole nation demands the entire abolition of the slaveholding power. . . . I call upon my fellow working men, and all who desire the welfare of this nation, and entreat them . . . to unite in demanding of the Government the abolition of the slaveholding power.[79]

The publications of the workingmen helped considerably to defeat the plans of the defeatists and Copperheads, to maintain the fighting spirit of the people, to insure the election of the Union ticket in 1864, to bring the war to a successful conclusion and to secure the complete abolition of slavery.

CHAPTER VI

FRATERNITY IN FREEDOM

———————

The United States, and the working class with it, was transformed by the events of the Second American Revolution, by the overthrow of the slave power and by the struggle for freedom by the workers themselves. To spell out the details of this transformation would require another study as long as the present one, but some of the more immediate effects may be traced. The organized labor movement disintegrated under the blows of economic depression and war, as union members lost their jobs or joined the army, labor newspapers were unable to keep their heads above water, and the few national organizations were split by the impossibility of maintaining connections between Northern and Southern locals. But a revival of the labor movement began with the recovery of business produced by the war economy. The real wages of the laboring men and women deteriorated disastrously as prices soared, and they were compelled to organize to protect their living standards. From 1862 to 1865 most of the old unions were reconstituted or reinvigorated and many new ones were established, and steps were taken to restore the Southern unions and secure their renewed affiliation with the national bodies.

But the post-war labor movement did not merely take up where it had left off before the war. It operated under different conditions and was strongly influenced by the experiences gained in economic and political struggle during the conflict. The process of industrialization and consolidation that had been going on for two generations received a tremendous stimulus from the war, and the capitalist class was in firm control of the national economy by 1865. A "shoddy aristocracy," rich and blustering, had grown up from war contracts, fraudulent dealings with the Union and the rebels, sharp speculation in government bonds, cheap labor and industrial expansion. Iron manufacturing, the production of sewing machines, lumbering, textiles and other industries received a momentous fillip from army contracts and vast new capital resources, and other fortunes were made by railroad construction. Tendencies toward consolidation and monopoly were accelerated, and employers in many industries organized associations for lobbying, price agreements and union-smashing. The rapid growth of population in the Middle West increased the home market, and the sale of farm machinery tripled. Furthermore, the new "captains of industry" had also become, through their influence in the dominant Republican party, the captains of the state as well.

The post-war labor movement, developing under these conditions, was pervaded by a higher degree of militancy and class-consciousness than it had previously known. This may be seen, for example, in the case of two of the largest national unions. Both the Iron Molders' Union and the Machinists' and Blacksmiths' Union, and their leaders, Sylvis and Fincher, held to the doctrine of harmony of interests between employers and employees before the war. But in 1865 Sylvis said that society was divided into two great classes, separated by an impassable gulf—"the rich and the poor, the producers and the non-producers; the busy bees in the industrial hive, and the idle drones who fatten upon what they steal."[1] Fincher opposed political activity by labor on the ground that it would blur the antagonism between the two classes and restrain the workers from asserting and maintaining their rights.[2]

For a decade the Republicans had been telling the "hard-handed sons of toil" that their only enemy was the slavocracy, while the Democrats said that it was the capitalists. The workers themselves for the most part agreed that both classes were hostile to their interests. But during the war their primary aim was to defeat the slave-power, and while they did not forget their own immediate economic problems, they subordinated them for the sake of victory. When strikes were broken by the army during the war, Sylvis declared, only labor's loyalty to the Union had prevented "scenes that would appall the stoutest heart." These outrages on the rights of the workers created a profound sensation, he stated, and although "the muttering thunders of the confined volcano were scarcely audible above the surface . . . they were none the less deep because in secret." He warned that the point might be reached where forbearance would cease to be a virtue.[3]

With the defeat of the slave-power, the emancipation of the slaves and the unbridled reign of capital, this question which had agitated the labor movement for a generation was settled once and for all: the field was clear, and capital and labor stood face to face. The continuity of the struggle for the emancipation of the slaves and that for the advancement of labor was symbolized by Wendell Phillips, who devoted his genius and energies to the cause of the slaves and, when that was won, took up the cause of the working class. In 1865 he addressed a mass meeting of workers in Faneuil Hall and recalled the first time he had stood on that platform twenty-nine years earlier at an abolition meeting. He had felt then that he was speaking in the cause of the laboring men, for he was contending not only in behalf of a race that was bought and sold, but against the contention of Harper, Calhoun and Pickens that the laborer must necessarily be owned by capitalists. "That struggle for the ownership of labor is now somewhat near its end; and we fitly commence a struggle to define and to arrange the true relations of capital and labor."[4] When Phillips had concluded his speech, Ira Steward of the Machinists' Union, and leader of the eight-hour movement, proposed the following resolution, which was adopted by the acclamation of the assembled workers:

... we rejoice that the rebel aristocracy of the South has been crushed, that ... beneath the glorious shadow of our victorious flag men of every clime, lineage and color are recognized as free. But while we will bear with patient endurance the burden of the public debt, we yet want it to be known that the workingmen of America will demand in future a more equal share in the wealth their industry creates ... and a more equal participation in the privileges and blessings of those free institutions, defended by their manhood on many a bloody field of battle.[5]

The *Daily Evening Voice,* published by the Workingmen's Assembly of Boston and vicinity, also recognized that the struggle to place labor "beyond the reach of misused power" was but a new phase of the contest between liberty and aristocracy. While the capitalists "whine at the degradation of labor at the South," it declared, they are "at this very time forging a golden chain ... to bind the Free Laborer of the North."

An oligarchy at the South, holding in its grasp the destinies of millions of the human race, and made mad by their lust for additional power, and, from the very nature of things, antagonistic to free labor, has struck a blow at the National life, and men stand appalled at the magnitude of the struggle. And here at the North, where every village, town and hamlet gives evidence of the industry of the people; where we have, through our institutions, instilled into our minds and fixed in our hearts a sacred love of liberty, an oligarchy, comparatively small, strikes a blow at the independence, nay, the very manhood of the industrial classes, when it denies their right to combine for mutual protection and advancement.[6]

William Sylvis forcefully expressed the new tasks of labor in a circular issued by the National Labor Union:

The working-people of our nation, white and black, male and female, are sinking to a condition of serfdom. Even now a slavery exists in our land worse than ever existed under the old slave system. The centre of the slave-power no longer exists south of Mason's and Dixon's line. It has been transferred to Wall Street; its vitality is to be found in our huge national bank swindle, and a false monetary system. The war abolished the right of property in man, but it did not abolish slavery. This movement we are now engaged in is the great anti-slavery movement, and we must push on the work of emancipation until slavery is abolished in every corner of our country. . . . Then will come such a social revolution as the world has never witnessed; honest industry in every department will receive its just reward, and public thieves will be compelled to make an honest living or starve. LET US ALL GO TO WORK.[7]

Even more for the Negro workers, in the North and the South, emancipation inaugurated a new stage in their fight for freedom. They were the most exploited of laborers, and in the South their oppression was trebled by cheating them of their earnings and by the desire of employers to "keep them in their place." Pressed by unbearable economic conditions, and stimulated by the resurgent labor movement and the electrifying effects of the anti-slavery struggle, Negro workers began to organize trade unions and to strike for higher wages. In 1867 a wave of strikes, particularly among Negro longshoremen, swept over the South. Most of these were for higher wages, and one in Savannah, Georgia, succeeded in securing the repeal of a ten dollar poll tax on all dock workers.[8]

By 1869 the growth of Negro labor organizations had been so rapid that they began to consolidate into state-wide bodies which would coordinate the work of the locals, further the organization of the laborers and press for protective legislation. In the four years after the War, conventions of Negro workers were held in Indiana, Pennsylvania, New York, Kentucky, Maryland, and the District of Columbia, and the roster of delegates represented virtually every trade in which Negroes were employed in those places. In December 1869, two hundred and three delegates from every section of the country met at Washington to "consolidate the colored workingmen of the several states to act in cooperation with our fellow workingmen in every state and territory in the union, who are opposed to distinctions in the apprenticeship laws on account of color, and to so act cooperatively until the necessity for separate organization shall be deemed unnecessary." The convention organized the National Colored Labor Union, whose principal activities for the next three years centered around the demands for higher wages, equal employment opportunities, educational facilities, cooperatives, homesteads and equality before the law.[9]

The agrarian laborers of the South, the bulk of the freedmen, also began to organize to achieve those measures which would secure the fruits of emancipation. Realizing that the formal proclamation of freedom would be hollow without the means of acquiring economic independence and securing their political rights, the Negroes demanded that the land of the traitorous slaveholders be confiscated and divided among the landless farmers, and that they be granted the civil and political rights which alone would guarantee the maintenance of their newly won status: the protection of life and property by law, freedom to sell their labor without intimidation, public education, freedom of speech, press and religion, equal suffrage and equality before the law. In order to secure these essential requirements of free people, the Negroes, with many white people as well, organized Union Leagues and militia units, joined the Republican party and assisted in the writing of democratic constitutions and in organizing state governments. These reconstruction governments have been contemptuously designated as "carpet-bag" governments and "Black Parliaments," but never before or since did the South know such a period of progress and democratic attainment: the civil rights of the Negroes were secured, public school systems established, state and county governments were reorganized on a more democratic basis, the tax systems were revised on a uniform basis applied to all property at its full value, fair labor relations were assured, the landless were given

assistance in purchasing homesteads, and aid was granted for
the building of railroads and much-needed public improvements.
The Negro people and their white allies had placed the South
on the high road to democratic progress—until they were betrayed by the Republican party.

Another marked result of labor's struggles in the Civil War era
was the revival of independent political activity. This was an
inevitable result of the exodus from the Democratic party which
began in the early 1850's, for many workingmen, while supporting the Republican party as the party of resistance to the slave-
power, could not identify themselves with it as the party of
capital. This was evident in the anti-war and pro-Union campaign
during the secession crisis. The workers who participated in that
movement had little confidence in either party to solve the problems of the country in the interest of labor and viewed independent political organization as the only solution. The campaign
itself was an example of such action, and from it emerged a
definite movement towards a labor party. Within a few weeks
after the mass meeting in Cincinnati in January 1861, there was a
local labor party ready to participate in the city elections. After
the national convention in Philadelphia, the delegates from Kentucky and Ohio returned home with definite political aspirations
in mind, and the only others from whom anything further was
heard—the Philadelphia workers—held meetings which demanded the establishment of a political body in opposition to both
the Republican and Democratic parties.[10] Sylvis was the corresponding secretary of the committee chosen to implement the
decisions of the convention and to arrange its next meeting, and
on March 23 he wrote: "The business of this committee is to perfect and perpetuate an organization among the industrial classes
of the city and State, for the purpose of placing in positions of
public trust men of known honesty and ability; men who know

the real wants of the people, and who will represent us according to our wishes; men who have not made politics a trade; men who, for a consideration, will not become the mere tools of rotten corporations and aristocratic monopolies; men who will devote their time and energies to the making of good laws, and direct their administration in such a way as will best subserve the interests of the whole people."[11]

Plans for the formation of a separate party were disrupted by the outbreak of the war, but the idea was kept alive. Most laborers wanted to support the war and the government without committing themselves to any party, and as early as 1862 the *Iron Platform* urged the formation of a Democratic-Republican party in New York to unite the Union supporters of both parties, but the Democrats refused to cooperate. In 1864 groups of trade unionists in several cities formed Workingmen's Democratic-Republican Associations with the aim of uniting the workers in support of Union candidates, educating them on the issues involved in the war, and mobilizing support for the administration.[12] The New York Association addressed a letter to both candidates, expressing its belief that the war was a defense not only of the Union but of the principles of democracy and the rights of labor and that it should be fought to a victorious conclusion without compromise.[13] When it became clear that the Democratic party would not prosecute such a war, the Association threw its support to Lincoln and worked energetically to secure labor's vote for Lincoln on the Union ticket.[14] At the same time it attempted to secure support for an eight-hour law, but was ignored by the Democratic party and brushed off by the Republicans with polite phrases about the antagonism between the slave-power and labor and the "hope that the great struggle . . . shall end in the interest of justice and free labor."[15] The campaigns in New York and Massachusetts against the proposed anti-strike bills gave a strong impetus to independent political activity by labor.

As the belief grew that the Republican party was not "the

party of free labor" but the party of big business, demands for a
genuine labor party were heard more insistently. Through 1864
Fincher repeated time and again that the old parties could not be
trusted to meet the new issues that would arise after the war, and
asserted that the workers must form their own organizations
and become a power that could command recognition.[16] Andrew
C. Cameron of the Chicago *Workingman's Advocate* stated that
labor could not win its struggle against capital except by taking
the law-making power out of the hands of the latter and shaping
the law in the interests of labor. "The relation that labor bears
to the state . . . is the great issue. . . . The eight hours movement
is the indispensable inaugural of the new era. But it cannot be
carried, unless the thorough political organization of workmen
and laborers all over the country is perfected."[17]

Many state and municipal trade union bodies organized independent political parties to campaign for the legal recognition of
unions, eight-hour laws, the discontinuation of the importation
of foreign contract labor, and equal pay for women employed at
public expense. In 1866 the National Labor Union was formed,
with Sylvis as its president, and the first convention adopted a
resolution asserting that history had proved that the working
class could not place its confidence in the existing political parties,
and that they must cut themselves loose from party ties and
predilections and organize themselves into a labor party for the
purpose of securing eight-hour legislation. This eventually led to
the organization of the National Labor Party, though not until
1872, and then it was dominated by currency reformers who made
the greenback program the major demand of the party. The
party also called for the eight-hour day, the granting of public
lands to settlers only, an end to the emigration of forced Chinese
labor, and tariff reduction.[18]

The ties of friendship between American labor and the European working class that had been established during the war were

greatly strengthened in the post-bellum years. Several labor papers fully reported the decisions of the International Workingmen's Association (First International) and the activities of its American section, and many leaders of the trade unions and the National Labor Union understood the value of international labor unity, particularly for the purpose of preventing the importation of strike-breakers and checking the immigration of workers when there was no demand for their labor, but also because it was recognized that "the interests of labor are identical throughout the world . . . a victory to them will be a victory to us."[19] Several unions took independent action leading toward cooperation and possible affiliation with the workers in the corresponding British trades, and from its inception the National Labor Union showed interest in furthering international labor solidarity. Its first convention failed to send a delegate to the International only because there was not sufficient time left, but wished them "Godspeed in their glorious work." In 1867 a delegate was chosen to attend the congress of the International, and the National Labor Union promised cooperation to the workingmen of Europe. This delegate did not attend because he could not collect the necessary funds, but in 1869 Andrew C. Cameron was sent to the Basle conference of the International. Proposals for cooperation between the two bodies were accepted, and a resolution was adopted asserting that the National Labor Union adhered to the principles of the International and expected to join it in a short time. But because of Sylvis' death and Cameron's belief that the methods of struggle advocated by the International were not applicable to American conditions, this expectation was never realized.[20]

A month before Sylvis' death in 1869, he received a letter from the General Council of the International, written by Marx, which appealed for labor unity to prevent war between England and the United States over the *Alabama* claims arising from the Civil War. "Another war which did not have for its objective the cause of the working people would prevent the development of an independent labor movement," Marx observed, and he concluded:

"Yours then is the glorious task of seeing to it that at last the working class shall enter upon the scene of history, no longer as a servile following but as an independent power . . . capable of commanding peace where their would-be masters cry war." Sylvis responded promptly in the spirit of international friendship, asserting that the cause of workingmen on both sides of the ocean was a common one: "It is war between poverty and wealth; labor occupies the same low condition and capital is the same tyrant in all parts of the world." On behalf of the American workers, he extended the right hand of fellowship to "all down-trodden and oppressed sons and daughters of toiling Europe" and wished them success in the good work they had undertaken.[21]

The course of events leading to the Civil War had taught labor that its own strivings could not advance materially until the slaves were emancipated, that "The slavery of the black man leads to the slavery of the white man," as the *Iron Platform* said. Would the workers learn now that their interests and those of the Negro laborers were still bound inexorably together? The competition of Negro and white working men before and during the war had wrought serious injury to both, and as Negroes began to enter into industry in larger numbers and to form their own labor organizations, it became urgent that the labor movement give careful consideration to this question. Already in 1864 the Boston *Daily Evening Voice* had declared that it would advocate and sustain "the rights of Labor—without distinction of sex complection or birthplace. . . ."[22] Sylvis also was aware of the common interests of Negro and white workers; in a speech in 1868 he declared that he had rejoiced at the downfall of Negro slavery. "But when the shackles fell from the limbs of those four millions of blacks," he stated, "it did not make them *free* men; it simply transferred them from one condition of slavery to another it placed them upon the platform of the white workingmen, and

ade all slaves together. . . . We are now all one family of slaves
gether, and the labor reform movement is a second emancipa-
n proclamation."[23]

In its first address to the workers of the United States, written
Cameron, the National Labor Union dealt with this matter
rthrightly. The address stated that the Negro people, almost
tirely workingmen and women, must become an element of
ength or of weakness in the labor movement, depending on the
cision of the white workingmen. Would the whites reject the
egroes' offer of cooperation?

committing such an act of folly we would inflict greater injury upon
: cause of labor reform than the combined efforts of capital could
omplish. . . . So capitalists North and South would foment discord
ween the whites and blacks and hurl one against the other . . . to
intain their ascendancy and continue the reign of oppression . . . What
vanted is for every union to help inculcate the grand ennobling idea that
interests of labor are one; that there should be no distinction of race
nationality; no classification of Jew or Gentile, Christian or infidel; that
re is one dividing line, that which separates mankind into two great
ses, the class that labors and the class that lives by others' labor.[24]

This resolution, however, represented the views only of some
the more farsighted men of the labor movement, and even
y for the most part looked upon the Negroes not as brothers
a common struggle but as competitors who must be organized
only for the protection of white labor. The majority of the
rkers, on the other hand, still believed that the menace of
npetition could be met only by the exclusion of Negroes from
labor unions. At the second annual convention of the National
bor Union in 1867, President J. C. Whaley recommended that,
order to deal with the competition of Negro laborers, they
uld be organized into unions and brought into harmony with
interests of the labor movement. A committee appointed to
pare a resolution on the subject brought in a report stating
t there was such divergence of opinion and the matter was so

full of complexity and "mystery" that it was inexpedient to ta
action. The debate revealed that there was truly a wide varie
of opinion on the subject, including advocates of unity betwe
Negro and white labor, of exclusion of the Negroes, and of e
operation between separately organized labor movements. Acti
was avoided, however, by the assertion that the constitution
the National Labor Union invited all laborers to join and the
fore there was no necessity for any special notice of a particu
class. At the session of the following year, no mention of Neg
labor seems to have been made other than a statement in the pl
form: "Resolved, That inasmuch as both the present politi
parties are dominated by the non-producing classes, who . . . ha
no sympathy with the working millions beyond the use they c
make of them for their own political and pecuniary aggrandi
ment; therefore, the highest interests of our colored fellow-citize
is with the workingmen, who, like themselves, are slaves of capi
and politicians, and strike for liberty."[25]

One of the obstacles to unity centered around differences
opinion concerning political action. While the labor movem
as a whole was moving in the direction of independent organi
tion and concentrating on issues like the eight-hour day a
monetary reform, the Negro workers were firmly attached to
Republican party as the bulwark of their hopes for political a
civil equality, and they were more concerned with the proble
of reconstruction. The failure of the National Labor Union
consider the special political demands of the Negroes crea
serious difficulties.

But the principal issue was the admission of Negro work
into the existing trade unions, and at the 1869 convention of
National Labor Union a more positive stand was taken. This
partly because of the constant insistence of such leaders as Sy
Richard Trevellick of the Ship Carpenters' Union and succe
to Sylvis as President of the National Labor Union, and mos
the labor press, and partly because of the widespread organiza

l successful struggles of the Negro unions—the presence of
e delegates from the Negro labor movement demonstrated
impossibility of further ignoring Negro labor. This conven-
n was the first national labor assembly in the United States in
ich Negro delegates participated. The resolution adopted by
congress declared that "The National Labor Union knows
North, no South, no East, no West, neither color nor sex on
question of the rights of labor, and urges our colored fellow
mbers to form organizations in all legitimate ways, and send
ir delegates from every state in the Union to the next con-
ss." A special committee was appointed to organize the Negro
kers into unions to be affiliated with the National Labor
ion.[26]

his action was greeted by the Negro delegates at the con-
tion. Isaac Myers, of the Colored Caulkers Trade Union So-
y of Baltimore, congratulated the delegates on this important
in advancing the unity of Negro and white workers. "Silent,
powerful and farreaching is the revolution inaugurated by
r action in taking the colored laborer by the hand and telling
that his interest is common with yours." The Negro workers,
said, desired the opportunity to labor at wages which would
re a comfortable living and security. They were eager for co-
ration, although it had not always been possible because the
kshops and the unions had been closed to them, and they had
ell their labor for whatever it could bring. "We mean in all
erity a hearty cooperation. . . . Where we have had the chance,
have always demonstrated it. We carry no prejudice. We are
ing to let the dead past bury its dead. . . . Mr. President,
erican citizenship for the black man is a complete failure if he
oscribed from the workshops of the country."[27]

many respects the action of the National Labor Union
esented a forward step, for it recognized the importance of the
ro workers and the community of interests between Negro
white labor and envisioned their cooperation in the future.

But it also reflected the persistence of prejudice against Negroes, the desire to protect white labor against their comp[e]tion, and the refusal to accept them as equals in the labor m[ove]ment. As the *Workingman's Advocate* said on December 1869, "It will take time to eradicate the prejudices of the past overcome the feelings which, it may be, the teachings of a [long] time have inculcated." The Negro workers were forced to org[an]ize their own unions, while at the same time they strove [for] acceptance by white labor. The *American Workingman* of Bos[ton] expressed its sorrow at the necessity for the organization of [the] National Colored Labor Union, and added: "But we are [con]vinced that for the present at least, they could not do better. [It is] useless to attempt to cover up the fact that there is still a w[ide] gulf between the races in this country, and for a time at least [they] must each in their own way work out a solution of this l[arge] problem. At no very distant day they will become united, [and] work in harmony together. . . ."[28]

REFERENCES

Chapter I: THE LABOR AND ABOLITION MOVEMENTS

. Of 5,500,000 immigrants from 1820 to 1860, 1,100,000 (20%) were mechanics and artisans and 2,000,000 (37%) were unskilled laborers. If all were still living and still in the same occupations in 1860 (neither of which was true), they would account for two-thirds of the mechanics and all the laborers in the country, or all of both categories in the free states, where practically all of them settled.

.. The ensuing data are derived from: *Sixth Census of the United States* (U.S. State Dept., 1841), *Compendium of the Sixth Census* (U.S. State Dept., 1841), *Statistical View of the United States . . . Seventh Census* (U.S. Census Office, 1854), *Population of the United States in 1860* (U.S. Census Office, 1864), *Statistics of the United States in 1860* (U.S. Census Office, 1866), *Manufactures of the United States in 1860* (U.S. Census Office, 1865), *The Statistics of the Population . . . 1870* (U.S. Census Office, 1872), *and The Statistics of Wealth and Industry . . . 1870* (U.S. Census Office, 1872). See also Victor S. Clark, *History of Manufactures in the United States* (New York, 1929; 2 vols.).

. This number seems excessively small when compared with the number of persons employed in various industries and with such facts as that there were an estimated 100,000 cotton-mill operatives as early as 1815. See John R. Commons, *History of Labour in the United States* (New York, 1918), I, 105. The discrepancy is undoubtedly due to the fact that there was no definition of a "factory" or clear distinction between factories, mills, and workshops by which census enumerators could follow a common or consistent practice. The manufacturing statistics given below probably give a better picture of the character of the industrial population.

. Counting half of the mechanics, artisans, and skilled laborers as wage earners.

. The extent to which manufacturing had passed out of the home, even in the South, is indicated by the fact that in 1850, less than 10% of all manufactures were produced in families, all others being produced in manufacturing establishments of some sort. In North Carolina the figure was 10%; in Ohio 3%; in New York and Massachusetts 1%.

. See Clark, *op. cit.*, I, 441-445.

. Edward C. Kirkland, *A History of American Economic Life* (New York, 1951; 3rd ed.), 326-327.

8. Commons, *op. cit.*, I, 104-105.

9. Seth Luther, "An Address to the Working Men of New England . .
   (Philadelphia, 1836; 3rd ed.).

10. The following breakdown was given: New York and Brookly
    11,500 members; Philadelphia, 6,000; Boston, 4,000; Baltimore, 3,5(
    Washington, 500; Newark, 750. Commons, *op. cit.*, I, 424; Fra
    Tracy Carlton, *Organized Labor in American History* (New Yo
    1920), 21.

11. Commons, *op. cit.*, I, 424.

12. Philip S. Foner, *History of the Labor Movement in the United Sta*
    (New York, 1947), 222.

13. The following is based on John Hope Franklin, *From Slavery*
    Freedom (New York, 1947), 204 ff., and J. Saunders Redding, *Th*
    Came in Chains (Philadelphia, 1950), 85 ff.

14. *De Bow's Review,* January, 1850, 25-26.

15. *The Voice of Industry,* February 19, 1847, in John R. Commons' Lab
    Collection of Newspaper Extracts in the Wisconsin Historical Soci
    Library.

Chapter II: IN THE LION'S DEN

1. Daniel Raymond, *Thoughts on Political Economy* (Baltimore, 182
   440-441.

2. Cassius Marcellus Clay, *Writings* (New York, 1848), 346-347 and 2
   see also Henry Ruffner, *Address to the People of West Virgi*
   (Louisville, 1847), 19-20.

3. M. Tarver, "Domestic Manufacturers in the South and West," *DeBo*
   Review, March, 1847, 188.

4. Chauncey S. Boucher, *The Ante-Bellum Attitude of South Carol*
   towards Manufacturing and Agriculture, Vol. III of *Washing*
   University Studies (St. Louis, n.d.), 249, 260-261; *DeBow's Revi*
   Jan., 1850, 12.

5. Thomas Marshall, *Speech in the House of Delegates of Virginia*
   the Abolition of Slavery (Richmond, 1832), 6.

6. Frederick Law Olmsted, *A Journey in the Back Country* (Lond
   1860), 17.

7. *The Injurious Effects of Slave Labour* (Philadelphia, 1824), 17.

8. *Niles' Register,* June 15, 1833; Asa Earl Martin, "The Anti-Slav
   Movement in Kentucky Prior to 1850" (unpublished dissertati

Cornell University, 1918), 66-67; Judge Harper's "Memoir on Slavery," cited in *The Philanthropist,* December 11, 1838.

). *Niles' Register,* December 31, 1831; *Congressional Globe,* 24C. 1S., 1835, Appendix, 86.

). Cited in Russel B. Nye, *Fettered Freedom* (East Lansing, 1949), 30.

. Rosser Howard Taylor, *Slaveholding in North Carolina,* Vol. XVIII, *The James Sprunt Historical Publications* (Chapel Hill, 1926), 80; Frederick Law Olmsted, *A Journey in the Seaboard Slave States* (New York, 1856), 564; according to Hinton Rowan Helper, *The Impending Crisis of the South* (New York, 1857), 380-381, and *The Free South* (Newport, Ky.), Sept. 3, 1858, slave labor was paid better than free labor, but this was probably exceptional.

. Clay, *op. cit.,* 234-235.

. "Address to the Non-Slaveholders of Kentucky," in the Louisville *Examiner,* cited in the *Anti-Slavery Bugle* (Salem, Ohio), May 4, 1849.

. Cited by Charles Nordhoff, *America for Free Working Men* (New York, 1865), 10.

. E. S. Abdy, *Journal of a Residence and Tour in the United States . . .* (London, 1835), II, 219.

. Nordhoff, *op. cit.,* 6-7.

. Roger W. Shugg, *Origins of Class Struggle in Louisiana* (Baton Rouge, 1939), 88-89.

. Cited in Charles H. Wesley, *Negro Labor in the United States* (New York, 1927), 19.

. Ernest M. Lander, Jr., "Manufacturing in South Carolina, 1815-60," *The Business History Review,* XXVIII (Mar., 1954), 62.

. Nordhoff, *op. cit.,* 10-11.

. N. A. Ware, *Notes on Political Economy . . .* (New York, 1844), 201-202; also, see Edward Ingle, *Southern Sidelights* (New York, 1896), 77-78.

. Shugg, *op. cit.,* 91.

Seaboard Slave States, op. cit., 84, 349-350, 373; see also Olmsted, *The Cotton Kingdom* (New York, 1861), 113.

Ibid., 112; *The Free South,* Sept. 3, 1858.

Charles Lyell, *A Second Visit to the United States . . .* (New York, 1849), II, 36; Nordhoff, *op. cit.,* 13; Camden (South Carolina) *Journal,* cited in French Ensor Chadwick, *Causes of the Civil War* (New York, 1906), 34.

Olmsted, *The Cotton Kingdom, op. cit.,* 89, 276. The contraction in the spelling of the epithet is mine, as it is whenever quoted in study.

27. *The National Era,* Jan. 11, 1849; New York *Evening Post,* cited *Publications of the New England Loyal Publication Society* (Bos 1862-68), III, 278.

28. Cited in the *Anti-Slavery Bugle,* Dec. 15, 1855.

29. John Hope Franklin, "James Boon, Free Negro Artisan," *Journal of Negro History,* April, 1945, 160-161.

30. Wesley, *op. cit.,* 71; Shugg, *op. cit.,* 117-119.

31. Wesley, *op. cit.,* 32-33, 80-81; Guion Griffis Johnson, *Ante-Bell North Carolina* (Chapel Hill, 1937), 71-72; John R. Commons, *A Documentary History of American Industrial Society* (Clevela 1910), II, 108.

32. Anonymous, *A Summary View of America* (London, 1824), 252-2 see also excerpt from John Finch, *Notes of Travel in the United St* in Commons, *Documentary History, op. cit.,* VII, 63.

33. Quoted in Lorenzo Dow Turner, "Anti-Slavery Sentiment in Amer Literature," *The Journal of Negro History,* October, 1929, 386.

34. See "Letter from a Kentuckyan," in *The True American,* Feb. 11, 1

35. *The Impending Crisis, op. cit.,* 40-41.

36. Olmsted, *Seaboard Slave States, op. cit.,* 543.

37. Shugg, *op. cit.,* 116-117.

38. The Muscogee (Ga.) *Herald,* quoted in the *Anti-Slavery Bu* October 18, 1856.

39. The Richmond *Examiner,* Dec. 28, 1855, quoted in *The Republi Scrap Book* (Boston, 1856), 54.

40. The Charleston *Standard,* quoted in *ibid.,* 53.

41. *DeBow's Review,* XXX, 306.

42. *Republican Scrap Book,* 51.

43. *Congressional Globe,* 24C. 1S., 1836, App., 289-290. See also Ge McDuffie, "Message to the Legislature of South Carolina," (18 J. H. Hammond, "Slavery in the Light of Political Science," in E Elliott, ed., *Cotton is King* (Augusta, 1860), 638-639; *DeB Review,* Oct. 1849, 295-296; *Anti-Slavery Bugle,* Sept. 20, 1856.

44. *Correspondence of Calhoun,* in Fourth *Annual Report* of the Amer Historical Association (1899), II, 399-400.

45. Edmund Ruffin, *Anticipations of the Future* . . . (Richmond, 18 306-307; my emphasis—B.M.

46. See especially Fletcher M. Green, *Constitutional Development in South Atlantic States* (Chapel Hill, 1930); Clement Eaton, *Free*

of Thought in the Old South (Durham, 1940); Henrietta Buckmaster, *Let My People Go* (New York, 1941).

Quoted in Shugg, *op. cit.,* 127.

Harper, "Memoir on Slavery," *DeBow's Review,* December, 1850, 614-616.

December 28, 1855, cited in *Republican Scrap Book,* 52.

See the Address of Robert Wickliffe, in the *Philanthropist* (Cincinnati), October 6, 1837.

Quoted in Clarence C. Norton, *The Democratic Party in Ante-Bellum North Carolina* (Chapel Hill, 1930), 200 ff.

Quoted in *ibid.,* 200 ff. See also William K. Boyd, "North Carolina on the Eve of Secession," *Annual Report* of the American Historical Association for 1910 (Washington, 1912); Henry M. Wystaff, *State Rights and Political Parties in North Carolina*—1776-1861, Ser. XXIV, nos. 7-8, *Johns Hopkins University Studies in History and Political Science* (Baltimore, 1906), 109-111.

The *Philanthropist,* May 31, 1843; see also Abdy, *op. cit.,* II, 227; *Niles' Register,* XLI (1831), 130-131; Wesley, *op. cit.,* 70-71; Nordhoff, *op. cit.,* 19-21; *Anti-Slavery Bugle,* August 19, 1854.

Reprinted in the *Anti-Slavery Bugle,* May 10, 1856.

See "The Report of a Meeting of Workingmen in the City of Wheeling, Virginia" in John R. Common's *Labor Collection,* Wisconsin Historical Society Library.

Kathleen Bruce, *Virginia Iron Manufacture in the Slave Era* (New York, 1930), 224 ff.

Quoted in Richard B. Morris, "Labor Militancy in the Old South," *Labor and Nation,* May, 1948, 35.

July 1, 1847.

Rosser H. Taylor, *Ante-Bellum South Carolina,* XXV, No. 2, *James Sprunt Studies in History and Political Science* (Chapel Hill, 1942), 81; see also Ulrich B. Phillips, "The Central Theme of Southern History," *The American Historical Review,* October 1928, 32; F. L. Olmsted, *A Journey in the Back Country* (London, 1860), 180-181.

Guion Griffis Johnson, *Ante-Bellum North Carolina* (Chapel Hill, 1937), 174.

Olmsted, *Back Country, op. cit.,* 180n.

Anti-Slavery Bugle, Sept. 5, 1857; Arthur Raymond Pearce, *The Rise and Decline of Labor in New Orleans* (unpublished Thesis, Tulane Univ., 1938), 13.

63. The *Eagle of the South,* cited in the *Anti-Slavery Bugle,* August 1858.

64. Commons, *Documentary History, op. cit.,* II, 108, 367-368; Julia Flisch, "The Common People of the Old South," in *Annual Rep* of the American Historical Association for 1908 (Washington, 190 139-140; "Slaves on a Federal Project," *Bulletin of Business Histc* January, 1934, 32-33; Robert R. Russel, *Economic Aspects of South Sectionalism* (Urbana, 1923), 219-220; Theodore M. Whitfield, *Slav Agitation in Virginia, 1829-1832* (Baltimore, 1930), 119 ff; Johns *op. cit.,* 71-72.

65. Commons, *Documentary History, op. cit.,* II, 176-177.

66. Nordhoff, *op. cit.,* 6.

67. Arthur Charles Cole, *The Irrepressible Conflict,* Vol. VII, *A His of American Life,* ed. by A. M. Schlesinger and D. R. Fox (N York, 1934), 36-37.

68. Sterling D. Spero and Abram L. Harris, *The Black Worker* (N York, 1931), 10.

69. Wesley, *op. cit.,* 80-81; Whitfield, *op. cit.,* 127 ff.; Green, *op.* 160-161; U. B. Phillips, in *The South in the Building of the Na* (Richmond, 1909), X, 477-478; Russell, *op. cit.,* 54.

70. John G. Palfrey, *Papers on the Slave Power* (Boston, 1846), 59.

71. *Republican Scrap Book, op. cit.,* 27.

72. *The Free South,* September 3, 1858.

73. July 15, 1845; in Clay, *Writings, op. cit.,* 268-269.

74. New York *Evening Post,* quoted in *Publications* of the New Engl Loyal Publication Society (Boston, 1862-1868), III, 278; Olms *Seaboard Slave States, op. cit.,* 308, 357; Ingle, *op. cit.,* 326; *National Era,* Nov. 18, 1858; Cleveland *Leader,* Sept. 24. 1 Chauncey S. Boucher, *South Carolina and the South on the Ev Secession,* Vol. VI, *Washington Univ. Studies* (St. Louis, 1919), Henry Bibb, *Narrative of the Life and Adventures of Henry* (New York, 1849), 24-25; Frederick Douglass, *My Bondage and Freedom* (New York, 1855), 169-170; Helper, *op. cit.,* 375-376; A *op. cit.,* II, 218 ff.

75. *The North Star,* May 25, 1849, quoted in Philip S. Foner, *Histor the Labor Movement in the United States.* (New York, 1947), 263-

76. Foner, *Labor Movement,* 264; for the participation of white worke previous slave revolts, see James Hugo Johnston, "The Participatio White Men in Virginia Negro Insurrections," *The Journal of N History,* April, 1931, 158 ff.

pp. 120-121.

E.g., see Gilbert J. Beebe, *A Review and Refutation of Helper's "Impending Crisis"* (Middletown, 1860) and Samuel M. Wolfe, *Helper's Impending Crisis Dissected* (Philadelphia, 1860).

See Herbert Aptheker, *To Be Free* (New York, 1948), and Wesley, *op. cit.*, 21-22.

Cited in Olmsted, *Seaboard Slave States, op. cit.*, 589-590.

Anti-Slavery Bugle, December 8, 1855.

M. W. Cluskey, *The Political Text-Book* (Philadelphia, 1860, 14th ed.), 220-222.

Foner, *Labor Movement*, 264.

"Extract from an Address Delivered by Thomas R. Whitney, December 23, 1851," in Commons, *Labor Collection, op. cit.*

See Chapter V.

"Establishment of Manufactures at New Orleans," *DeBow's Review*, January, 1850, 25-26; see also Governor Hammond's Address before the South Carolina Institute in *ibid.*, June, 1850, 518-520.

Cited in Boucher, *op. cit.*, 255-256.

Quoted in the *Anti-Slavery Bugle*, Oct. 18, 1856; see also Kenneth M. Stampp, "The Fate of the Southern Anti-Slavery Movement," *The Journal of Negro History*, January, 1943, 18.

Charleston *Standard*, cited in Nordhoff, *op. cit.*, 12; Greeley said: "Every free laborer taken to the South is a fresh nail in the coffin of slavery." (New York *Tribune*, June 4, 1853.)

Ingle, *op. cit.*, 242; Olmsted, *The Cotton Kingdom, op. cit.*, 229-301; Lander, *op. cit.*, 64-66.

James S. Green in the House, Jan. 4, 1850, in *Congressional Globe*, 31C. 1S., App., 426; The Pendleton (S.C.) *Messenger*, quoted in the *Liberator*, Aug. 10, 1849; Martinsburg *Republic*, cited in Howard C. Perkins, ed., *Northern Editorials on Secession* (New York, 1942), 872; Bruce, *op. cit.*, 235.

J. D. B. DeBow, *The Interest in Slavery of the Southern Non-Slaveholder* (Charleston, 1860), 5-8; D. R. Hundley, *Social Relations in our Southern States* (New York, 1860), 125.

Ingle, *op. cit.*, 240-241, 246; Joseph Dorfman, *The Economic Mind in American Civilization, 1606-1865* (New York, 1946), II, 951.

Alexandria *Constitutional*, Jan. 5, 1861, quoted in Shugg, *op. cit.*, 29; "Abolition of Negro Slavery," *American Quarterly Review*, Sept. 1832, 253; Nye, *op. cit.*, 187; T. H. Bayly in the House, in the *Congressional*

Globe, 30C. 1S., App., 579; DeBow, *op. cit.,* 8-9; Henry C. Carey, *North and the South* (New York, 1854), 7.

95. Olmsted, *The Cotton Kingdom, op. cit.,* 54-55.

96. *A Chapter of American History* (Boston, 1852), 62; Eaton, *op. cit.,*

97. Quoted in George M. Weston, *The Poor Whites of the South* (W▮ ington, 1856); see also Lewis Tappan, *Address to the Non-Slavehol▮ of the South* (New York, 1843), 8-9; Morris, *op. cit.,* 34.

98. Douglass, *My Freedom and My Bondage, op. cit.,* 309.

99. Quoted in Edward McPherson, *The Political History of the Un▮ States of America During the Period of Reconstruction.* (3rd. Washington, 1880), 55-56.

100. See Eaton, *op. cit.,* and instances of repression cited above.

101. *Douglass' Monthly,* February, 1859.

Chapter III: NORTHERN LABOR CONSIDERS SLAVERY

1. James Birney to Charles Hammond, November 14, 1835, in Dw▮ L. Dumond, ed., *Letters of James Gillespie Birney* (New York, 1▮ I, 270-271.

2. Thomas Wentworth Higginson, *Cheerful Yesterdays* (Boston, 1▮ 115-117; see also Martin, *op. cit.,* 74; the *Liberator,* May 12, ▮ Samuel J. May, *Some Recollections of our Antislavery Conflict* (Bo▮ 1869), 141; Henry Middleton, *Economical Causes of Slavery in▮ United States* (London, 1857), 51-53; The Haverhill *Gazette,* cite▮ *The Philanthropist,* August 3, 1836.

3. Richard R. Wright, *The Negro in Pennsylvania* (Philadelphia, ▮ 19-20; see also Dorfman, *op. cit.,* I, 119.

4. In *Collections* of the Massachusetts Historical Society (Boston: Society, 1877), 5th ser., III, 402.

5. The *Liberator,* Dec. 20, 1834; see also "Proceedings of the ▮ sylvania Convention of the State Anti-Slavery Society," 183▮ Williston H. Lofton, "Abolition and Labor," *The Journal of N▮ History,* July, 1948, 253-254.

6. Calvin Colton, *The Rights of Labor* (New York, 1847), 6-7.

7. Article in a St. Louis Democratic paper, cited in the *Anti-Sl▮ Bugle,* February 27, 1858.

8. *Anti-Slavery Bugle,* March 26, 1847, August 7, 1846, Sept. 18, ▮ July 16, 1853; Philadelphia *Daily Record,* cited in *Anti-Slavery l▮* Dec. 15, 1848; *Phil. Daily Republic,* cited in Foner, *op. cit.,* 281; R▮

National Enquirer, May 7, 1837.

E.g., see the issues of June 11, 1840, April 27, 1843, and July 3, 1845; see also *The Philanthropist,* September 18, 1838; the *National Enquirer,* January 3, 1838; the *Liberator,* May 8, 1846; *The Plaindealer,* in Sedgwick, *Writings of William Leggett, op. cit.,* II, 216; *The National Era,* December 23, 1847.

New York State Mechanic, April 9, 1842.

The *Liberator,* February 20, 1846.

Ibid., May 26, 1848.

Trenton *Daily State Gazette,* Dec. 6, 1851, cited in Foner, *Labor Movement, op. cit.,* 279.

Niles' Register, October 3, 1835.

March 26, 1836, cited in Foner, *Labor Movement,* 267.

The Man, July 10 to July 14, 1834.

Fall River *Weekly News,* August 28, 1845; see also the Boston *Weekly Reformer,* December 15, 1837, and the *Working Man's Advocate,* October 31, 1835.

"Address to the Free Laborers of the United States," in the *Emancipator,* cited in *The Philanthropist,* January 15, 1836; see also the issues of January 1, 1836, March 4, 1836, June 16, 1837, December 11, 1838, August 6, 1839, and November 4, 1840; S. B. Treadwell, *American Liberties and American Slavery* (New York, 1838), 162-163; the *National Anti-Slavery Standard,* April 27, 1843; The *Anti-Slavery Record,* September, 1836; The Boston *Weekly Reformer,* March 17, 1837; The *Liberator,* September 28, 1838; Russel B. Nye, "The Slave Power Conspiracy," *Science and Society,* Summer, 1946, 262 ff.

The Voice of Industry, February 13, 1846.

Lofton, *op. cit.,* 262-263.

Issue of September 11, 1830, in Commons, *Labor Collection, op. cit.*

July 17, 1845, cited in Norman Ware, *The Industrial Worker, 1840-1860* (Boston, 1924), 214.

Fall River *Mechanic,* November 2, 1844; *Working Man's Advocate,* March 16, 1844.

Vera Shlakman, *Economic History of a Factory Town* (Northampton, 1935), 133-134.

Northampton Democrat, cited in the *National Anti-Slavery Standard,* August 5, 1847.

The Lynn *Awl,* October 9, 1844.

New England Artisan and Laboring Man's Repository, October 4, 1832.

56. Issue of September 11, 1830, in Commons, *Labor Collection*, op

57. *Congressional Globe*, 33C. 1S., 1854, App., 1224. The labor press o
period is filled with discussions of this subject. In addition to
above, see especially *America's Own and Fireman's Journal*, Apri
1851, May 10, 1851, June 21, 1851, and February 12, 1853; the 1
of Industry, October 9, 1846; *Working Man's Advocate*, June 22, 1
The Harbinger, June 21, 1845 and July 5, 1845; *The Slavery of Po.*
(New York: Society for the Abolition of ALL Slavery, 1842), 1;
Boston *Laborer*, October 26, 1844; *New England Artisan*, Octob
1833; The Lynn *True Workingman*, October 22, 1845; and
Monthly Jubilee (Philadelphia), May, 1854.

Some labor spokesmen denied that the wages system was
parable to slavery, but this was almost invariably in rebutta
attacks on them by pro-slavery apologists—a case of "I can s.
about myself, but you can't say it." See, e.g., The *Weekly Tri*
November 29, 1845, in Commons, *Labor Collection, op. cit.;*
New York *Tribune*, November 21, 1845; The *National Enq*
January 10, 1830; The Fall River *Weekly News*, September 25,

As for the Negro workers, there was little question in their n
or any one else's that there was little to choose between their c
tions and those of the slaves. See *The Colored American*, Nove
25, 1837.

58. This contradiction was noted by the Northampton *Democrat*, cit
the *National Anti-Slavery Standard*, August 5, 1847, and by
Slavery of Poverty, op. cit., 4.

59. Dorfman, *op. cit.*, II, 687.

60. Simpson, *op. cit.*, 85-86.

61. Published in Cincinnati, 1847, by Thomas Varney.

62. See pp. 3-4.

63. *Ibid.*, 33-34.

64. *Ibid.*, 43-44.

65. Issue of February 12, 1853.

66. Foner, *Writings of Frederick Douglass, op. cit.*, I, 249. Walsh
published a paper entitled *The Subterranean*.

67. Lofton, *op. cit.*, 263.

68. Those historians who state that labor was against emancipation
this is common among those who mention the role of labor a
have been misled by several errors: first, they have identifie
anti-slavery movement with the abolitionist organizations, alth
the latter were at all times a minor element among the forces

brought about the overthrow of slavery; second, they have confused the policy of the workers, which was in favor of emancipation, with their tactics, which required the subordination of the slavery question to the labor question; third, they have failed to take into account the change in labor's position during the 1850's; and finally, they have too often based their judgment on a few spectacular events, like the draft riots in New York, rather than on a careful study of all the evidence.

Issue of August 15, 1833.

Ibid, Nov. 1, 1832. See also the Lynn *Awl*, September 4, 1844; Boston *Weekly Reformer*, January 20, 1837 and May 5, 1837.

The Workingman's Advocate, January 25, 1845.

Andreas Dorpalen, "The German Element and the Issues of the Civil War," *The Mississippi Valley Historical Review*, XXIX, 55 ff.

There is no adequate biography of Evans, nor of any of the important ante-bellum labor leaders.

Working Man's Advocate, July 6, 1844.

Ibid, June 1, 1844.

Young America, January 23, 1848.

William West to the editor of the *Liberator*, August 28, 1846.

Pickering, *op. cit.*, 68-69. For other material on the land reformers and slavery, see the *Monthly Jubilee*, August, 1854; The *Voice of Industry*, Jan. 22, 1847 and Aug. 13, 1847; The *Liberator*, July 4, 1845; *The Slavery of Poverty, op. cit.*, 4, 15.

Albert Brisbane, *Social Destiny of Man* (Philadelphia, 1840).

See pp. 97-112.

The Phalanx, November 4, 1843, cited in Commons, *Documentary History, op. cit.*, VII, 207-210.

Cited in *ibid.*, VII, 211-213. See also his explanation of this letter in the *Tribune*, June 20, 1845, and his second letter, printed in the *Voice of Industry*, August 21, 1845; *The Phalanx*, Dec. 5, 1843; *The Harbinger*, June 21, 1845 and July 5, 1845; Robert Owen's address in The *Liberator*, June 6, 1845.

The New Harmony Gazette, October 1, 1825; A. J. G. Perkins and Theresa Wolfson, *Frances Wright, Free Enquirer* (New York, 1939), 123 ff., 255, 329.

New Harmony Gazette, October 1, 1825 and succeeding numbers.

Elinor Pancoast and Anne E. Lincoln, *The Incorrigible Idealist* (Bloomington, 1940), 47-49, 57-58.

86. *Boston Quarterly Review,* October, 1838, 499-500, and July, 1 368 ff.; Boston *Weekly Reformer,* July 21, 1837, April 4, 1838.

87. The *Liberator,* December 24, 1841; see also the issue of Nover 19, 1836; the *Anti-Slavery Bugle,* Nov. 6, 1846, and Jan. 6, 1855; *Philanthropist,* February 26, 1836; *The National Era,* March 16, 1 April 20, 1848, April 27, 1848; *The National Enquirer,* March 1839; *America's Misfortune* (Buffalo, 1856), 38; *Third Annual Re* American Anti-Slavery Society (New York, 1836), 28; Olm *Seaboard Slave States, op. cit.,* 700 ff.

88. Korngold, *op. cit.,* 155-157.

89. The *Liberator,* January 1, 1831.

90. *Ibid.,* January 29, 1831.

91. *Ibid.,* January 1, 1841.

92. *Ibid.,* July 9, 1847; *The Harbinger,* July 17, 1847; George E. McN ed., *The Labor Movement* (Boston, 1887), 113.

93. Clay, *Writings, op. cit.,* 348-352.

94. *The Voice of Industry,* November 6, 1846.

95. *Voice of Industry,* February 19, 1847, in Commons, *Labor Collec op. cit.*; Ware, *op. cit.,* 221; Shlakman, *op. cit.,* 111-112. See also *Liberator,* March 19, 1847, February 4, 1837, and April 22, 1853; the *Anti-Slavery Standard,* October 14, 1847.

96. *Liberator,* January 7, 1837; The *Emancipator,* October 28, 1 Foner, *Writings of Frederick Douglass, op. cit.,* II, 168-169; *Nat. Anti-Slavery Standard,* August 5, 1847.

97. Issue of May 8, 1846.

98. Cited in Madeleine Hooke Rice, *American Catholic Opinion in Slavery Controversy* (New York, 1944), 103.

99. *Workingmen's National Advocate* (Washington), April 30, 1853; *Working Man's Advocate,* October 5, 1833; The *Irish-American,* 17, 1851, and June 28, 1851; Fall River *Weekly News,* August 1845 and September 4, 1845; Shlakman, *op. cit.,* 134; Foner, *L Movement,* 271.

100. May 14, 1846.

101. *The Radical,* March, 1841.

102. Quoted in Shlakman, *op. cit.,* 61; also see *The Harbinger,* Septer 6, 1845; Fall River *Mechanic,* May 18, 1844; John Campbell, *N. Mania* (Philadelphia, 1851), 469-470; *New Era,* August 3, 1839; *People's Paper,* September 9, 1843, in Commons, *Labor Collec op. cit.*

103. Wesley, *op. cit.,* 78-79.

Cited in Lofton, *op. cit.*, 276.

The Slavery of Poverty, op. cit., 8.

The *Voice of Industry,* August 21, 1845, in Commons, *Labor Collection, op. cit.;* Boston *Protective Union,* March 30, 1850; *Liberator,* September 5, 1845.

Liberator, March 20, 1846.

National Anti-Slavery Standard, June 20, 1850; *National Enquirer,* May 13, 1837; *Liberator,* January 9, 1836.

National Anti-Slavery Standard, December 28, 1848, June 20, 1850, October 25, 1856.

Congressional Globe, 24C. 1S., 1837, App., 288.

"Letter on Slavery," in *DeBow's Review,* March, 1850, 257-258.

E.g., see Harper's "Memoir on Slavery" in *DeBow's Review,* April, 1850; *The Southern Quarterly Review,* July, 1851, 118 ff.; Solon Robinson, "Negro Slavery at the South," *DeBow's Review,* Sept., 1849, 222 ff.; Lucien B. Chase, *English Serfdom and American Slavery* (New York, 1854), vii.

Elwood Fisher, "The North and the South," *DeBow's Review,* October, 1849, 308-309.

Congressional Globe, 31C. 1S., 1851, 500; *ibid.,* Appendix, 175; Columbia (South Carolina) *Times,* cited in the *Anti-Slavery Bugle,* Jan. 20, 1855; Washington *Cotton Plant,* cited in *ibid.,* October 8, 1853; Fisher, *op. cit.; The Church Review and Ecclesiastical Register,* VII, 431 ff.; Olmsted, *Seaboard Slave States, op. cit.,* 701-702.

Cleveland *Leader,* January 22, 1855.

Harper's "Memoir on Slavery," *DeBow's Review,* November, 1850, 503-504; see also J. K. Paulding, *Slavery in the United States* (New York, 1836), 266 ff.; George Fitzhugh, *Sociology for the South* (Richmond, 1854), 27-28; Fitzhugh, *Cannibals All!* (Richmond, 1857), 25-26.

Charleston, 1856.

See pp. 21-22.

See pp. 43-44.

See pp. 49 ff.

Congressional Globe, 35C. 1S., 1858, 962; my emphasis—B.M.

Calhoun, "Report on the Circulation of Abolition Petitions," in *The Works of John C. Calhoun* (New York, 1855), 207-208; Harper, "Slavery in the Light of Social Ethics," in E. N. Elliott, ed., *Cotton is King* (Augusta, 1860), 590-592; Edmund Ruffin, *Slavery and Free Labor Described and Compared* (n.p., n.d.), 1-2.

123. Fitzhugh, *Cannibals All!, op. cit.,* 27 ff.; see also *The South Quarterly Review,* 1856, 62 ff., and January, 1851, 221 ff.

124. Fitzhugh, *Cannibals All!, op. cit.,* 46; *The Southern Quar. Review,* January, 1851, 223; *DeBow's Review,* October, 1849, 295- McDuffie, *op. cit.*

125. J. H. Hammond, in Elliott, *op. cit.,* 638-639; Hammond to Clark in *DeBow's Review,* October, 1849, 295-296; McDuffie, *op. cit.*; Pick in the *Congressional Globe,* 24C. 1S., 1836, Appendix, 290.

126. Matthew Estes, *A Defense of Negro Slavery* (Montgomery, 1846)

127. *The Southern Quarterly Review,* January, 1851, 220-221; *Sout. Literary Messenger,* 1851, 260; Henry Hughes, *Treatise on Socic* (Philadelphia, 1854), 187 ff.; Estes, *op. cit.,* 168-172; Thomas R Cobb, *An Inquiry into the Laws of Negro Slavery* (Philadel 1858), ccxiv.

128. Grayson, *op. cit.,* 45.

129. See Thomas D. Jarrett, "Ideas in William J. Grayson's *The Hire and the Slave . . .* " (Unpublished Thesis, Univ. of Chicago, 1947)

130. See Chauncey S. Boucher, ed., *Correspondence Addressed to Joh Calhoun,* 1837-1849, in *Annual Report* of the American Historica sociation for the Year 1929, 328-329; *Congressional Globe,* 31C. 1850, Appendix, 394; The *Political Reformer* (Richmond), quote *The Philanthropist,* July 7, 1840; *The Washington Globe,* Sept. Sept. 9, 1838; The New Orleans *Delta,* quoted in The *National . Slavery Standard,* November 8, 1856.

131. Arthur M. Schlesinger, Jr., *The Age of Jackson* (Boston, 1947), Richard Hofstadter, *The American Political Tradition* (New Y 1948), 88.

132. *The Harbinger,* October 25, 1845.

133. *The Boston Quarterly Review,* January, 1841, 86 ff.

134. *Congressional Globe,* 24C. 2S., 1837, 82, 106; 25C. 3S., 1839, 2 Appendix, 237-241.

135. *Ibid.,* 33C. 1S., 1854, Appendix, 1220; see also *The Slavery of Por op. cit.,* 16.

136. Quoted in Charles A. and Mary R. Beard, *The Rise of Amer Civilization* (New York, 1930), I, 693.

137. *Congressional Globe,* 30C. 1S., 1848, App. 579.

138. *Register of Debates in Congress,* 25C. 1S., 1837, 1393-1395.

139. *Congressional Globe,* 25C. 2S., 1838, App., 62.

140. Cited in *National Anti-Slavery Standard,* April 27, 1843.

Quoted in The *Liberator,* April 30, 1841.

Quoted in Schlesinger, *op. cit.,* 246.

Cannibals All!, op. cit., 127 ff., 368; see also Fitzhugh, *Sociology for the South, op. cit.,* 71; Calhoun, *Works, op. cit.,* 207-208; *Congressional Globe,* 31C. 1S., 1850, Appendix, 381; New York *Herald,* February 28, 1860, cited in Philip S. Foner, *Business and Slavery* (Chapel Hill: Univ. of North Carolina, 1941), 193; Wilfred Carsel, "The Slaveholders' Indictment of Northern Wage Slavery," *The Journal of Southern History,* 1940, 518-519.

Washington *Globe,* December 25, 1834.

The Southern Review, August, 1830, 1 ff.; Fitzhugh, *Cannibals All!, op. cit.,* 127 ff.

Congressional Globe, 31C. 1S., 1850, Appendix, 242.

E.g., see *The Union, Past and Future* . . . (Washington: The Southern Rights Association, 1850), 30 ff.

Register of Debates in Congress, 25 C. 1S., 1837, 1393-1395; *Congressional Globe,* 35 C. 1S., 1858, 962; see also *ibid.,* Appendix, 394.

See Foner, *Business and Slavery, op. cit.,* and *A Chapter of American History, op. cit.*

The Plaindealer (New York), May 13, 1837. See also the *Congressional Globe,* 25C. 1S., 1837, Appendix, 255.

Reminiscences of Levi Coffin (Cincinnati, 1880), 525; *The Philanthropist,* Sept. 23, 1836, Dec. 5, 1837; Boston *Weekly Reformer,* Dec. 9, 1836; The *Liberator,* Nov. 7, 1835; Boston *Times,* cited in *ibid.,* Aug. 20, 1841; May, *op. cit.,* 153 ff.; *Letters of Lydia Maria Child* (Boston: Houghton, Mifflin and Co., 1883), 17-18; William Birney, *James G. Birney and His Times* (New York: D. Appleton and Co., 1890), 240 ff.; Nye, *op. cit.,* 156-157; Foner, *Business and Slavery, op. cit.,* 28-29; *The National Era,* Dec. 23, 1847; *Working Man's Advocate* (Phil.), Oct. 3, 1835.

Congressional Globe, 25C. 3S., 1839, App., 168; see also *The Philanthropist,* March 17, 1837.

Chapter IV: The Slave-Power and the Mudsills

Powderly, *op. cit.,* 44.

September 1, 1837.

The *Liberator,* November 8, 1844.

4. Cited in Foner, *Labor Movement*, 277.

5. Issue of October 25, 1845.

6. *Congressional Globe*, 28C. 2S., 1845, 111.

7. *Working Man's Advocate*, April 20, 1844; New York *Tribune*, Aug 15, 1850; *America's Own and Firemen's Journal*, December 15, 18

8. Foner, *Labor Movement*, 277-278.

9. *Ibid.;* Lofton, *op. cit.,* 281.

10. Quoted in *The Harbinger*, June 20, 1846.

11. *Congressional Globe*, 29C. 2S., 1847, 114.

12. *Ibid.,* especially 29C. 2S., 1847, Appendix, 202-203, 357, 442; 30C. 1848, Appendix, 1200; 30 C. 2S., 1849, Appendix, 100-101; 34C. 1856, Appendix, 949 ff.; 35C. 1S., 1858, 220.

13. David Wilmot, *ibid.,* 30C. 1S., 1848, Appendix, 1079-1080.

14. David Wilmot, *ibid.,* 34C. 1S., 1856, Appendix, 1218.

15. T. H. Averett, Va., *ibid.,* 29C. 2S., 1847, App., 87, and 31C. 1S., 18 App., 394; H. Bedinger, Va., 30C. 2S., 1849, App., 112.

16. New York *Tribune*, June 13, 1850.

17. *Monthly Jubilee*, September, 1852 and October, 1853.

18. New York *Weekly Tribune*, October 26, 1850, in Commons, *Do mentary History, op. cit.,* VIII, 329.

19. Issue of September, 1852.

20. New York *Tribune*, February 20, 1854.

21. *Ibid.,* February 4, 14 and 15, March 15 and 23, 1854, and July 3, 18

22. *Monthly Jubilee*, August, 1854; this action produced a split in Congress, the minority withdrawing in protest against the depart from the policy of confining their efforts to labor and land reform

23. Schluter, *op. cit.,* 75-77.

24. *Congressional Globe*, 33C. 1S., 1854, 1230-1232.

25. William Goodell, *A Full Statement of the Reasons . . .* (Boston, 183 27-30. See also *Proceedings* of the Rhode Island Anti-Slavery Conv tion (Providence, 1836), 37.

26. Issue of March 31, 1837.

27. Russel B. Nye, *Fettered Freedom* (E. Lansing, 1949), 166-167.

28. William H. Seward, *Works* (George E. Baker, ed.; Boston, 188 IV, 250.

29. Carl Schurz, "Speech at St. Louis, August 1, 1860," in Emerson Fite, *The Presidential Campaign of 1860* (New York, 1911), 253-2

30. New York *Tribune*, April 1, 1857; see also *The Free South*, Octo 29, 1858 and November 12, 1858; James Harlan, "Shall the Territo

be Africanized?" (New York, 1860; pamphlet reprint of speech in the Senate, January 4, 1860).

Charles Sumner, "The Slave Oligarchy and Its Ursurpations" (Boston, 1855), 9.

Arthur C. Cole, *Lincoln's "House Divided" Speech* (Chicago, 1923), 32-33.

Cleveland *Morning Leader*, April 6, 1855; William H. Seward, "Immigrant White Free Labor . . ." (Speech at Oswego, November 3, 1856).

Seward, speech at Rochester, October 25, 1858, in *Works, op. cit.*, 292.

Anti-Slavery Bugle, August 30, 1856.

For example, see the Cleveland *Leader*, June 15, 1854 and August 13, 1855; *Congressional Globe*, 35C. 1S., 1858, 1002 ff., 1025; Charles Mackay, *Life and Liberty in America* (New York, 1859), 248 ff.; Seward, *Works, op. cit.*, 289; *Anti-Slavery Bugle*, November 21, 1857; Henry L. Dawes, "The New Dogma of the South," pamphlet reprint of speech in Congress, April 12, 1860.

Quoted by F. P. Blair in the *Anti-Slavery Bugle*, October 11, 1856; by Representative Tappan, in the *Congressional Globe*, 34C. 1S., 1856, Appendix, 949 ff.; and throughout the anti-slavery press.

When the editor of the Charleston *Mercury* held up slavery as the natural and best condition of labor, he was burned in effigy by the mechanics of the city. See Cole, *Lincoln's "House Divided" Speech, op. cit.*, 31.

E.g., see George M. Weston, *Who Are and Who May Be Slaves* (n.p., n.d.); *American Jubilee*, March, 1854 and April, 1855; *Anti-Slavery Bugle*, October 18, 1856.

William Goodell, *The American Slave Code* . . . (2nd ed.; New York, 1853), 282 ff.; *Anti-Slavery Bugle*, August 30, 1856; *Frederick Douglass' Paper*, September 21, 1855; Cleveland *Daily True Democrat*, October 16, 1850 and August 3, 1853.

The Free South, January 7, 1859.

Cincinnati *Commercial*, cited in the *Anti-Slavery Bugle*, September 20, 1856; Buckmaster, *op. cit.*, 251.

James Russell Lowell, *The Biglow Papers* (Boston, 1891), 65-68.

Frederick Douglass' Paper, Dec. 9, 1853 and April 13, 1855, cited in Foner, *Writings of Frederick Douglass, op. cit.*, II, 58-59, 360-361.

Ibid., 460.

46. "The Address of the Southern and Western Liberty Convention the People of the United States" (Cincinnati, 1845).

47. William Goodell, "Address of the Macedon Convention" (Alb. 1847).

48. The *Voice of Industry*, July 9, 1847; Ware, *op. cit.*, 224-225. The erty party was split into three factions after 1848, but all three gre maintained the principle of unity between labor reform and aboli and one group advocated, in addition to abolition, free public for actual settlers, women's political rights, the ten-hour day, and right of workers to organize. See *Frederick Douglass' Paper*, Sep ber 25, 1851; *Anti-Slavery Bugle*, February 11, 1854.

49. Boston *Semi-Weekly Reporter*, September 9, 1848, quoted in Sch inger, *op. cit.*, 468n.; "Address by the Barnburners of the New Y Legislature," cited in *ibid.*, 462-463; Cleveland *Daily True Demo* quoted in *The Annals of Cleveland*, XXXII, 135.

50. Cited in Ware, *op. cit.*, 225.

51. *The New Era*, July 27, 1848, cited in *ibid.*, 225.

52. David M. Ludlum, *Social Ferment in Vermont, 1791-1850* (T York, 1939), 269; Helene Sara Zahler, *Eastern Workingmen National Land Policy* (New York, 1941), 98-99; W. G. Bean, "P Transformations in Massachusetts" (Thesis, Harvard University

53. *Memoirs of Prince Metternich*, ed. by Prince Richard Metternich translated by Mrs. Alexander Napier (New York, 1880-1882), 473-474.

54. Issue of April 17, 1851.

55. October 7, 1852.

56. Edward L. Pierce, *Memoir and Letters of Charles Sumner* (Bos 1894), III, 187; see also *Congressional Globe* 31C. 1S., 1850, Appe 268; *The Anti-Slavery Papers of James Russell Lowell* (Boston, 19 I, 9-10.

57. Russel B. Nye, "The Slave Power Conspiracy: 1830-1860," *Sci and Society*, Summer, 1946, 264.

58. The Free Soil party did not advocate abolition either, but its spo men did not attempt to conceal their hostility to slavery.

59. Cleveland *Leader*, October 28, 1856, cited in *The Annals of Clevel* XXXIX, 324.

60. Cited in *Republican Scrap Book*, *op. cit.*, 19.

61. Seward, *Works*, *op. cit.*, IV, 245-246; see also The Cleveland *Lea* June 28, 1856; *Republican Scrap Book*, *op. cit.*, 34-36.

April 16, 1856; see also the New York *Tribune,* March 10, 1856.

The *Radical Abolitionist,* August, 1856.

Ibid., June, 1856; see also the Cleveland *Leader,* April 16, 1856; *Anti-Slavery Bugle,* May 16, 1857.

For example, see Weston, *The Poor Whites of the South, op. cit.*

George M. Weston, *Southern Slavery Reduces Northern Wages* (Washington, 1856).

The Republican Campaign Songster (New York, 1856), 49-50; see p. 7 also.

Anti-Slavery Bugle, October 18, 1856.

May 14, 1856; see also *Republican Scrap Book, op. cit.,* 9.

The Republican Campaign Songster, op. cit., 67-68; also pp. 53-54, 81-82.

January 18, 1856; see also The Cleveland *Leader,* July 3, 1856, October 1, 1856, October 14, 1856; The *National Anti-Slavery Standard,* October 11, 1856; *Anti-Slavery Bugle,* October 18, 1856; *Republican Scrap Book, op. cit.*

See *The Irish-American,* July 12, 1856, July 19, 1856; Birnbaum, *op. cit.,* 22; *The Tribune Almanac,* 1857; The Cleveland *Leader,* October 15, 1856.

Richard T. Ely, *The Labor Movement in America* (New York, 1905), 221-222; F. I. Herriott, "The Conference in the Deutsches Haus . . ." in *Transactions* of the Illinois State Historical Society (Springfield, 1928), 108.

Autobiography, cited in Foner, *Labor Movement,* 279n.

New York *Tribune,* October 31, 1856.

Even among the businessmen who remained in the Democratic ranks, there was a split, the Douglas wing representing those who desired to challenge the domination of the slaveholders in the party and the Union, while at the same time they were willing to conciliate them in order to preserve the Union, their political ascendancy, and their business ties.

Philadelphia *Public Ledger,* March 13, 1860, cited in Foner, *Labor Movement,* 285.

See Hofstadter, *op. cit.,* 106 ff.

Abraham Lincoln, *Complete Works* (John G. Nicolay and John Hay, eds.; New York, 1894), I, 307.

Ibid., 580-582.

Ibid., 179.

82. *Ibid.,* 615-616.

83. *Ibid.,* 625.

84. See his interesting letter to his stepbrother, cited in Hofstadter, *op.* 103-104.

85. Lincoln, *op. cit.,* II, 104-106.

86. Albert J. Beveridge, *Abraham Lincoln* (Boston, 1928), II, 31, 437

87. "Lincoln's Lost Speech" (Bloomington, May 29, 1856), as repc by H. C. Whitney (n.p., 1896).

88. Lincoln, *op. cit.,* I, 240 ff.

89. *Ibid.,* 614, 629.

90. New York *Tribune,* October 30, 1860.

91. Cited in Osborn H. Oldroyd, *Lincoln's Campaign* (Chicago, 1896 see also p. 87, and New York *Tribune,* September 30, 1860.

92. Beveridge, *op. cit.,* II, 678.

93. Quoted in Birnbaum, *op. cit.,* 27.

94. Seward, *Works, op. cit.,* 372.

95. Boston *Daily Bee,* cited in Birnbaum, *op. cit.,* 28, 31.

96. See Dawes, *op. cit.,* Harlan, *op. cit.,* John Hickman, "Democra The Old and the New" (Washington, 1860), Schurz, *op. cit.*

97. Wittke, *We Who Built America, op. cit.,* 246-247.

98. William Windom, "The Homestead Bill—Its Friends and Its F (Washington, 1860), 2.

99. *The Free South,* February 11 and 18, 1859; *The National* September 30, 1852; *Lands for the Landless* (Washington, 1859), published in German; Seward, *Works, op. cit.,* 426-427; New *Tribune,* October 12, 1860.

100. In Perkins, *op. cit.,* I, 62-63.

101. Birnbaum, *op. cit.,* 24, 37.

102. Perkins, *op. cit.,* 66-68.

103. *Ibid.,* 71-72; see also the New York *Herald,* October 10 and 26, cited in Birnbaum, *op. cit.,* 30.

104. New York *Tribune,* October 29 to November 7, 1860.

105. *The Irish-American,* 1860, *passim; The Tribune Almanac,* 1 Gibson, *op. cit.,* 89 ff.; *Douglass' Monthly,* August, 1859.

106. Carl Wittke, *Against the Current: The Life of Karl Heinzen* (Chic 1945), 171 ff.

107. Schluter, *op. cit.,* 72-73.

108. Carl Wittke, *The Utopian Communist* (Baton Rouge, 1950), 159

109. Schluter, *op. cit.,* 77 ff.

110. *Ibid.,* 77; Herriott, *op. cit.,* 133-134.

Karl Obermann, *Joseph Weydemeyer* (New York, 1947), 85 ff., 103-104.

Foner, *Labor Movement, op. cit.,* 289.

Herriott, *op. cit., passim.*

New York *Herald,* October 31 and November 1, 1860; Obermann, *op. cit.,* 109 ff.

Birnbaum, *op. cit.,* 32 ff.

Chapter V: "THE UPRISING OF A GREAT PEOPLE"

Title of a book by Count Agenor de Gasparin (tr. by Mary L. Booth; New York, 1861).

Carey, *op. cit.*

Ruffin, *op. cit.,* 126-127, 141-145, 285 ff., 327. When Lee surrendered, Ruffin wrapped himself in a Confederate flag and committed suicide.

Gibson, *op. cit.,* 104-105.

Birnbaum, *op. cit.,* 49 ff.

Cleveland *Daily Plain Dealer,* January 12, 1861.

Birnbaum, *op. cit.,* 89; Gibson, *op. cit.,* 116-117.

November 14, 1860.

Powderly, *op. cit.,* 44-45; Saul Schindler, *Northern Labor and the American Civil War* (Thesis, Brooklyn College, 1941), 35.

The Irish-American, November, 1860 to March, 1861.

Carl Sandburg, *Abraham Lincoln: The War Years* (New York, 1939), I, 42-43.

Arthur C. Cole, *The Whig Party in the South* (Washington, 1913), 148n.

See *The Kentucky Statesman,* October 5, 1860, in Dwight L. Dumond, *Southern Editorials on Secession* (New York, 1931), 175.

Cincinnati *Commercial,* cited in Birnbaum, *op. cit.,* 101-103.

Ibid., 62-67.

But another speaker at the same meeting was cheered when he suggested that the politicians should fight their own battles and leave the laboring men in peace. See *ibid.,* 63-65; Schindler, *op. cit.,* 27 ff.

"New-York Workingmen's Executive Committee. Report of Committee on Resolutions, adopted February 4, 1861," broadside in the Library of Congress.

Frank T. Carlton, *Organized Labor in American History* (New York,

1920), 150-152; Kenneth M. Stampp, *And the War Came* (B.
Rougue, 1950), 126; Birnbaum, *op. cit.*, 67-68.

19. "Mass Meeting of the Workingmen of Massachusetts," February
1861, broadside in the Library of Congress; "Working Men's M
Meeting in Faneuil Hall," broadside in the Bostonian Society Libr
Boston *Daily Evening Transcript,* February 21, 1861; Boston
Directory, 1861.

20. Edgar Barclay Cale, *The Organization of Labor in Philadelf
1850-1870* (Thesis, University of Pennsylvania, 1940), 42 ff.; Birnba
op. cit., 71-73; Foner, *Labor Movement,* 300.

21. James C. Sylvis, *The Life, Speeches, Labors and Essays of William
Sylvis* (Philadelphia, 1872), 44-45.

22. The Philadelphia *Press,* February 22, 1861; Jonathan Grossr
William Sylvis (New York, 1945), 47; Cale, *op. cit.*, 42 ff.

23. The Philadelphia *Press,* February 23, 1861.

24. *Ibid.,* February 25, 1861; Birnbaum, *op. cit.*, 78 ff.

25. McNeill, *op. cit.*, 124; Schindler, *op. cit.*, 3-4; Benjamin A. Go
Investigations in the . . . Statistics of American Soldiers (New Y
U.S. Sanitary Commission, 1869), 210 ff.

26. *Fincher's Trades' Review,* January 14, 1865.

27. Cited in Herbert Aptheker, *The Negro in the Civil War* (New Y
1938), 37.

28. Lincoln, *Complete Works, op. cit.,* II, 562, 564, 576; see Aptheker,
Negro in the Civil War, op. cit., 8-10, 34-40.

29. Cited in Foner, *Labor Movement,* 310.

30. Cleveland *Leader,* May 6, 1863.

31. Cited in Foner, *Labor Movement,* 334.

32. See Foner, *Labor Movement,* 325 ff., 352-355.

33. Cited in Leonard Newman, "Opposition to Lincoln in the Elect
of 1864," *Science and Society,* Fall, 1944, 317-318.

34. In Perkins, *op. cit.,* I, 444-445; see also examples from the Irish p
cited in Gibson, *op. cit.,* 125-126.

35. *The Liberator,* August 8, 1862; see also *ibid.,* August 5, 1862; I
York Copperhead, May 30, 1863; Williston H. Lofton, "Nortl
Labor and the Negro during the Civil War," *The Journal of N
History,* July, 1949, 253-255; *The Irish-American,* November 8, 1
Senator Cox, in the *Congressional Globe,* 37C. 2S., 1862, Apper
248.

36. Stanton Ling Davis, *Pennsylvania Politics, 1860-1863* (Thesis, Wes
Reserve University, 1935), 246-247.

Cleveland *Plain Dealer,* September 18, 1865; Lofton, "Northern Labor and the Negro," *op. cit.,* 255-256; Wood Gray, *The Hidden Civil War* (New York, 1942), 90.

This order was countermanded by Lincoln.

Publications of the New England Loyal Publication Society, *op. cit.,* I, d.

Lincoln, *Complete Works, op. cit.,* II, 274-275; Lincoln repeated his advocacy of colonization in this address, stating that this would still further protect white labor against competition from free Negroes. See also The New York *Tribune,* July 11, 1862 and August 8, 1863; "Catechism for Free Working Men," (Cincinnati, n.d.; No. 3), 4; Cleveland *Leader,* August 6, 1862; *Harper's Weekly,* August 23, 1862; Charles C. Burleigh, "Slavery and the North," *Anti-Slavery Tract* No. 10 (New York, n. d.), 9-10.

Issue of June 13, 1863.

Lofton, "Northern Labor and the Negro," *op. cit.,* 257 ff.; Cleveland *Leader,* July 17 and 19, August 8, 1862.

The *Liberator,* December 5, 1862.

Gray, *op. cit.,* 99-100.

See the New York *Tribune,* August 5, 1862; Frederick Merk, "The Labor Movement in Wisconsin During the Civil War," *Proceedings* of the State Historical Society (Madison, 1915), 168 ff.; *The Liberator,* October 24, 1862; *Three Years among the Working-Classes in the United States during the War* (London, 1865), xiv.

Emerson D. Fite, *Social and Industrial Conditions in the North During the Civil War* (New York, 1910), 189-190.

Sylvis, *op. cit.,* 229.

Fincher's Trades' Review, June 6 and 18, 1863; see also "A Working-man's Idea of Conscription," reprinted from *ibid.* in *The Magazine of History* (1918), 103-107.

Quoted in the *National Anti-Slavery Standard,* July 25, 1863.

See the New York *Herald* and the New York *Tribune,* July 14 to July 19, 1863.

Fincher's Trades' Review, July 18, 1863.

Ibid., July 25, 1863.

"Don't Unchain the Tiger." By a Democratic Workingman. New York, July 24, 1863. (Library of Congress.) Also printed in German: "Entfesselt den Tiger nicht!" (Boston Public Library).

"To the Laboring Men of New York." By a Democratic Workingman.

New York, July 18, 1863. (Library of Congress.) See also *The Platform*, June, 1864.

55. McNeill, *op. cit.*, 126.

56. *Fincher's Trades' Review*, October 24, 1863, February 1, 1864.

57. Cited in Albert B. Moore, *Conscription and Conflict in the federacy* (New York, 1924), 71-72.

58. *Ibid.*, 129-131, 151-152, 221, 240.

59. Aptheker, *The Negro in the Civil War*, *op. cit.*, 10 ff., 41-43.

60. Sylvis, *op. cit.*, 232-233; Sylvis had a brief term of service in the a

61. Gibson, *op. cit.*, 127-130.

62. Horace Greeley, *The American Conflict* (Hartford, 1864-1866) 244-245.

63. *Speeches, Correspondence and Public Papers of Carl Schurz*, ed Frederic Bancroft (New York, 1913), 185 ff.

64. *Die Presse* (Vienna), January 5, 1862 and February 2, 1862, cite Karl Marx and Frederick Engels, *The Civil War in the United S.* ed. by Richard Enmale (New York, 1937), 131-133, 141-142.

65. Schluter, *op. cit.*, 158-159.

66. "The Working Men of Manchester and President Lincoln," *U and Emancipation Tracts*, No. 2 (Manchester, 1863), 1.

67. "The Manchester Workmen and Emancipation" (Broadside, Lik of Congress).

68. Lincoln, *Complete Works*, *op. cit.*, II, 301-302, 308-309.

69. *Publications* of the New England Loyal Publication Society, I, 60 53.

70. *National Anti-Slavery Standard*, May 30, 1863.

71. London *Bee-Hive*, January 7, 1865, quoted in Marx and Engels, *op* 279-283.

72. See, for example, Charles Nordhoff, *America for Free Working* (New York, 1865); *Southern Hatred of the American Govern* . . . (Boston, 1862); *The Spirit of the South Towards Nort. Freemen and Soldiers* (Boston, 1861).

73. *Publications* of the New England L. P. S., I, 88, II, 143, 169.

74. See Loyal Publication Society, *Pamphlets* (New York, 1864); *P cations* of the New England L. P. S., *op. cit.*, I-III, *passim*.

75. Foner, *Labor Movement*, 312.

76. "A Challenge!" (August 25, 1863); "White Slaves" (September 1863); "An Abolition Traitor" (August 29, 1863), all in the Lib of Congress.

"Daniel O'Connell on Democracy" (New York, October 13, 1863), in the Library of Congress.

"A Traitor's Peace" (New York, October 30, 1863), in the Library of Congress; see also "What Traitors say of Northern Democrats," in the Massachusetts Historical Society Library.

Catechism for Free Working Men, op. cit., 1-4.

Chapter VI: FRATERNITY IN FREEDOM

Sylvis, *op. cit.,* 31, 82.

Fincher's Trades' Review, October 10, 1863.

Sylvis, *op. cit.,* 140-141.

Wendell Phillips, *Speeches, Lectures, and Letters* (Boston, 1892), I, 139.

Boston *Daily Evening Voice,* November 3, 1865.

Ibid., December 5, 10, 12, 13 and 20, 1864.

Sylvis, *op. cit.,* 82; also see page 129.

Foner, *Labor Movement,* 397 ff.

Spero and Harris, *op. cit.,* 27 ff; Commons, *History of Labour, op. cit.,* 136-137; Wesley, *op. cit.,* 168 ff.; W. E. B. DuBois, *Black Reconstruction* (New York, 1935), 361 ff.

Birnbaum, *op. cit.,* 63-64, 78 ff.

Sylvis, *op. cit.,* 45-46.

Foner, *Labor Movement,* 335.

Publications of the New England L. P. S., II, 250.

Lincoln, *Complete Works, op. cit.,* II, 501-503; "A Workingman's Reasons for the Re-election of Abraham Lincoln," (Broadside in the Library of Congress); "The Workingman," (New York, 1864), 1; Obermann, *op. cit.,* 125-126.

"The Workingman," *op. cit.,* 3.

Fincher's Trades' Review, 1864, *passim.*

The Workingman's Advocate (Chicago), March 25, 1865.

Sylvis, *op. cit.,* 67; Commons, *Documentary History, op. cit.,* IX, 134-136; Foner, *Labor Movement, op. cit.,* 423 ff.

Sylvis, *op. cit.,* 186-187.

Foner, *Labor Movement,* 409 ff.

Commons, *Documentary History, op. cit.,* IX, 338-340.

Issue of December 2, 1864.

Sylvis, *op. cit.,* 232 ff.

24. Commons, *Documentary History, op. cit.,* IX, 157 ff.

25. Sylvis, *op. cit.,* 295.

26. Commons, *History of Labour, op. cit.,* II, 134-136; Wesley, *op.* 156 ff.; Sylvis, *op. cit.,* 295, 337.

27. *The Workingman's Advocate* (Chicago), September 4 and 11, cited in Foner, *Labor Movement,* 399.

28. Quoted in DuBois, *Black Reconstruction, op. cit.,* 364.

ACKNOWLEDGMENTS

is book could obviously not have been written without reliance on
many scholars whose work is cited in the footnotes. Its accomplish-
was likewise dependent on the innumerable persons who have con-
ted to the collection of source materials in libraries, universities, and
ical societies, and on the never-failing cooperation and skill of the
of those institutions. In particular I wish to record the assistance
h was given by the libraries of Western Reserve University, Columbia
ersity, and the University of Wisconsin; the public libraries of Cleve-
New York, Boston, and Lynn; the Library of Congress; The Western
ve, Massachusetts, New York, and Wisconsin Historical Societies;
American Antiquarian Society in Worcester; the Oberlin College
ry; the Bostonian Society and the New York Society; and the
rous libraries which furnished material through interlibrary loans.
ly, I am indebted to Dean Carl Wittke and Professors Harvey Wish
C. H. Cramer of Western Reserve University, who read the manu-
: with great care and called my attention to many errors of fact and
od. Of course, I am solely responsible for all deficiencies and interpre-
s in the final product.

knowledgment is gratefully given to the editors of Smith College
es in History for permission to quote from Vera Shlakman's *Economic
ry of a Factory Town* (1935); to Harcourt, Brace and Company for
. B. DuBois' *Black Reconstruction* (1935); to Richard B. Morris for
rticle, "Labor Militancy in the Old South," in *Labor and Nation*
-June, 1948); to Appleton-Century-Crofts, Inc., for Howard C.
ns' *Northern Editorials on Secession* (1942); to the Board of Pub-
on of Washington University for Chauncey S. Boucher's *South
'ina and the South on the Eve of Secession* (1919); to International
shers for Philip S. Foner's *History of the Labor Movement in the
d States* (1947); to *The Negro History Bulletin* for permission to
nt the substance of two articles by me in the issues of December, 1953,
February, 1954; and to *Science and Society* for permission to reprint
ubstance of an article by me in the issue of Summer, 1954.

                                                    Bernard Mandel

land, Ohio
mber, 1954

Index

Abolitionists, 25-26, 61-62, 147-148, 186; Southern, 50-55; say free Negroes will not go North, 68; appeal to Irish laborers, 68-70; attacks on their rights, 74-76, 109, 124-126; inconsistency, 79-80; attitude toward labor movement, 89-93; attitude of labor toward, 93-95; division, 135-138; *National Anti-Slavery Standard,* 47, 73, ci., 95; *Anti-Slavery Bugle,* 128, ci., 32, 36, 39, 40, 43, 47-48, 63, 64, 128; *National Enquirer,* 72. See Anti-slavery movement, Bailey, Clay, C.M., Douglass, Free Soil party, Garrison, Greeley, Helper, Higginson, Hunt, Lowell, Loyal Publication Society, Phillips, Rogers, Smith, Whittier.

Adams, Charles Francis, and English labor, 197-198.

Adams, John, on abolition in Massachusetts, 63; on slavery of working class, 77.

Agrarians. See Land Reformers.

American and Foreign Anti-Slavery Society, 136, 137.

American Anti-Slavery Society, 136.

Anti-Slavery movement, 22-27; in South, 43-55; workers in, 153. See Abolitionists, Free Soil party, Emancipation, Liberty party, Republican party.

Associationists, urge unity of reformers, 95; supported by Milne, 143. See Brisbane, Fourier, Greeley.

Bailey, William S., Southern abolitionist, 50; *The Free South,* 219, ci., 35, 50, 131-132, 164.

Barnburners, oppose extensi[on] slavery, 113; join Free Soil [move]ment, 143; return to Demo[cratic] party, 146.

Birney, James, abolitionist, c[i.] *The Philanthropist,* 109, 12[ ] 43.

Bledsoe, Moses, on unequal [ ] in South, 42.

Bray, John Francis, *Labor's W[rongs]* and *Labor's Remedy,* 80.

Bright, John, views on Civil [War,] 197.

Brisbane, Albert, on abolition [ ]

Brownson, Orestes A., on abo[lition,] 88-89; favors alliance of [labor] and slaveholders, 104.

Buchanan, James, hostility to [labor,] 151-152; vetoes Homestead [bill,] 163-164; criticized by *Irish-A[mer]ican,* 173-174.

Burritt, Elihu, Liberty candida[te for] Vice-President, 139.

Businessmen, opposition to [labor's] power, 24-26; Southern, o[pposi]tion to slavery, 30; alleged [sin]cerity of anti-slavery adv[ocates,] 67; conflict with planters, [ ] relation to slaveholders and [work]ers, 103-107; slaveholders a[ppeal] to against abolition, 107-11[0; al]liance with slaveholders, 114[-115;] and Free Soil party, 142-143[;] and Republican party, 148, [ ] 155, 165, 168-169; fear upr[ising] in case of war, 172; gains d[uring] Civil War, 183, 202-203; [and] labor and anti-Negro pra[ctices,] 187, 205.

t, Etienne, Utopian socialist,

oun, John, 123, 143, 152; on mocracy, 40; defines slavery,); on alliance of slaveholders d laborers, 105-106; positive od doctrine, 130; on free labor, 4.

eron, Andrew C., urges labor rty, 210; represents National bor Union at First Interna- nal, 211; urges cooperation of ite and Negro labor, 213; orkingman's Advocate, 210, ».

al, capitalists. See Business- n.

Lewis, candidate for President, ».

olics, and slavery, 69; attacked Helper, 163; and emancipa- n, 195.

liberties, of abolitionists, 74- 109, 124-126; of Negroes, 207.

War, 24; efforts to avoid, 173-); labor's participation, 180- l; opposition, 183-186.

Cassius M., on effect of slavery workers, 28-29; on slave com- ition with labor, 31; on op- ssion of Southern labor, 51; ported by German-American ialists, 54; press destroyed, 75; unions, 92; The True Amer- n, 50, ci., 38.

Henry, suggests anti-abolition ct, 67-68.

ett, William, compares labor- and slaves, 79.

1, Levi, abolitionist, ci., 109.

n, Calvin, urged to write anti- lition tract, 67-68; ci., 63.

munists. See Socialists.

promise of 1850, 118, 119, 143, -147.

Confederacy, 193, 195-196, 199, 200.

Conscription, law, 189; labor's atti- tude, 189-194; draft riots, 190-193; in South, 193.

Considerant, Victor, Utopian social- ist, 20.

Copperheads, 183-184, 190, 200, 201.

Crittenden plan, 177, 178, 179.

Davis, Jefferson, 193.

DeBow, J. D. B., ci., 57.

Democracy, in South, 40-41, 60; slavery a menace to, 70-76; slave- holders' attitude to, see Slave- holders.

Democratic party, 22, 121, 135, 148, 184, 191; and Irish labor, 68-69, 151; instrument of alliance be- tween slaveholders and workers, 103-104; becomes party of slave- holders, 143, 162-163; dissension over slavery question, 143-145, 147; and free labor, 151-152; and German-American workers, 153; rejects businessmen's program, 154; opposes Homestead law and tariff, 163-164; in secession crisis, 172-173, 176, 180; Peace Demo- crats, 184; election of 1862, 185. See Barnburners, Buchanan, Cal- houn, Cass, Douglas, Johnson, Milne, Van Buren, Walsh.

Douai, Adolph, Southern socialist and abolitionist, 54; in election of 1860, 168.

Douglas, Stephen A., 165, 166.

Douglass, Frederick, hires out his labor, 32; on race prejudice, 59; on discrimination, 65-66; on Walsh, 82; resented by Garrison, 135; on passive resistance, 136; The North Star, ci., 52.

Draft. See Conscription.

Dred Scott decision, 127, 134, 154; condemned, 127.

Emancipation, 185, 187, 190, 194, 204; labor and, 194-201; English labor and, 195-198.

English workers, appeal to American workers against slavery, 70-71; attitude toward Civil War and emancipation, 195-198; relations with American labor, 211-212.

Estes, Matthew, *A Defense of Negro Slavery,* ci., 102.

Evans, George Henry, land reformer, 21, 138; urges abolition, 71; defends rights of abolitionists, 75; on abolition, 84-85; on abolitionists, 94; *Working Man's Advocate,* 67, 84, ci., 115.

Expansion of slavery, 115-121, 127-128. See Manifest destiny, Mexican War, Slavepower "conspiracy," Territories, Texas.

Farmers, and slavery, 26; and Free Soil party, 146; and Republican party, 148.

Fincher, Jonathan, leader of machinists' union, 178; fears competition of freed slaves, 187; on conscription, 189-190, 191, 192; urges support of Union, 200; change in philosophy, 203; urges labor party, 210.

Fincher's Trades' Review, ci., 193. See Fincher.

Fitzhugh, George, attack on free society, 100-101, 160; attack on abolitionists, 107; ci., 101.

Fourier, 86, 99. See Associationists, Brisbane, Greeley.

Free Soil party, 149; and land reformers, 21; organized, 140-141; supported by dissident Democrats, 143-145; role in party realignments, 146-147; and free labor, 147, 148.

Fremont, John, Republican ca date for President, 147, 148, 1

Fugitive Slave Law, 118, 119, 131, 145.

Garrison, William Lloyd, 93, 144, 147; denies wage sla 90-91; attitude toward 1 movement, 91-92; narrow 136-137, 139-140; *Liberator,* ci., 63, 90, 93. See Abolition

German-American workers, ployment in South, 34; oppos to slavery in South, 53-54; position to slavery and v slavery, 84; on Kansas-Nebr Act, 121; in Republican p 153, 165; and slavery, 166 in secession crisis, 174; in (War, 180.

Goodell, William, abolitionist, 125, 131.

Grayson, William, *The Hire and the Slave,* pro-slavery po 97-99, 102.

Greeley, Horace, on wages, 1 and Fourierism, 20; and a tion, 86-87; and emancipa 195; on free labor and aboli 223; N.Y. *Tribune,* 20, 151, 190, ci., 36.

Gregg, William, criticized for moting industry, 56; on cap labor relations in South, 59.

Gunn, Lewis, anti-slavery la leader, 71.

Hammond, James H., defe slavery, 96, 99-100; threaten stir up insurrection, 108; ci., 102.

Harper, Chancellor, 73, 204; education, 41; defines slav 100; on alliance of slavehol and Northern democracy, 1 on superiority of slavery, 97.

zen, Karl, reform and anti-
ery activity, 54, 166.

er, Hinton R., on effect of
ery on labor, 38; *The Im-
ding Crisis of the South,* 52-
163, 219, ci., 38.

ert, Philip, kills Irish waiter,
.

nson, Thomas W., on aboli-
 movement, 62.

estead movement, 143, 147,
, 174, 176, 210; endorsed by
ublicans, 163-164; Homestead
, 183; in South, 208.

, Ebenezer, abolitionist, 93.

er, Gen. D. H., frees slaves,
.

grants, considered menace to
ery, 56; alleged victims of
e-power "conspiracy," 132,
; in election of 1856, 153; and
mestead bill, 163; contract
r, 183, 187, 210. See German-
erican laborers, Irish-Ameri-
laborers, Nativism.

trial Reformers, oppose Fugi-
Slave Law, 119.

try, development in U.S., 11
in South, 33-35; desirability
n South, 55-57; growth feared
slaveholders, 95-96.

ational Workingmen's Asso-
ion, congratulates Lincoln,
; relations with American
r, 211-212.

American laborers, employ-
it in South, 34; attacks on
gro workers, 66-67, 188; aboli-
ists appeal to, 68-70; alleged
nocratic hostility, 151; in
tion of 1856, 153; — of 1860,
; urged to sabotage Union,
172; in Civil War, 180, 200.

Johnson, Herschel, Democratic candidate for Vice-President, 163.

Kansas-Nebraska Act, 120-122, 127,
143, 147, 153, 161.
King, Preston, opposes slavery in
territories, 116.
Know-Nothing party, 148, 153. See
Nativism.
Kriege, Hermann, opposes aboli-
tion, 166.

Labor, size and composition of
labor force, 13-17; in South, 28;
conditions, 17-19, 77-81, 96-101;
and slavery, 26-27; Southern, effect of slavery on, 28-43; role in
Southern society, 40-43; opposition to slavery in South, 43-60;
Northern, effect of slavery on,
61-65, 150; Northern, competition with free Negroes, 65-70,
164-165, 184-189, 213; compared
with slavery by labor reformers,
77-81; — by Southerners, 96-101;
alliance with slaveholders, 103-
107; and annexation of Texas,
113-115; and Mexican War, 115;
and slavery extension, 115-122;
and Dred Scott decision, 127;
and Republican party, 148-154;
alleged Democratic hostility, 151-
152; and election of 1860, 166-
169; and secession crisis, 173-
180; and Civil War, 180-201; and
draft, 189-194; Southern, in Civil
War, 193; and emancipation,
194-201. See German-American
laborers, Irish-American laborers,
Labor movement.
Labor movement, 10-22; organization of unions, 18-19; concept of
"wage slavery," 77-81; and abolition, 82-89; attitude of abolitionists toward, 89-93; attitude

toward abolitionists, 93-95; in anti-slavery movement, 153; and depression of 1857, 155; and Republican party, 155-156; effect of Civil War on, 173, 202; during Reconstruction, 202-216; *Fall River Mechanic,* 64; *New York State Mechanic,* 73; *Mechanics' Free Press,* 77, 79; *America's Own,* 81; Lynn *Awl,* ci., 79; Manchester *Operative,* 114; *The New Era,* ci., 141; *The Iron Platform,* 199, 209, 212; *Daily Evening Voice,* 205, 212; *American Workingman,* 216; *Voice of Industry,* 67, 76, 77, 93, 141, ci., 27; *National Laborer,* 19, 75, ci., 71; *Workingmen's Advocate,* 19; *Workingmen's National Advocate,* ci., 94. See Associationists, Bray, Cameron, Fincher, Gunn, English workers, International Workingmen's Association, Labor, Labor party, Land reformers, Labor Reform League, Luther, Moore, National Colored Labor Union, National Industrial Congress, National Labor Union, National Labor Party, New England Association of Mechanics, New England Labor Reform League, New England Workingmen's Association, Sedgwick, Simpson, Socialists, Strikes, Sylvis, Touchstone, Wood.

Labor party, urged, 179, 203, 208-210, 214.

Labor Reform League of New England, 93.

Land reformers, 20-21; on abolition, 84-85, 134; on annexation of Texas, 115; on slavery extension and Fugitive Slave Law, 118-119; on Kansas-Nebraska Act, 121; support Free Soil party, 141;

Monthly Jubilee, 119, ci., 119 Evans, Homesteads, Indu Reformers, National Indu Congress, Pickering, West.

Las Casas, "A Plea for Slav 81.

Leigh, B. Watkins, 73; on pol role of labor, 40.

Liberty party, 138-140, 149.

Lincoln, Abraham, 148, 155, attitude to slavery, 156; philosophy, 156-162; election 1860, 165-169; and Ger Americans, 174; on Negro Civil War, 181-182; on eman tion, 186, 241; and English l 196-198; election of 1864, 20!

Lowell, James Russell, anti-sla poetry, 132-133.

Loyal Publication Society, 199.

Luther, Seth, on danger to r of labor, 19.

Lyell, Charles, ci., 35.

Manifest destiny, 111. See Ex sion.

Marshall, Thomas, on slavery, 30.

Marx, Karl, 80; congratulates coln, 198; appeals for unity English and American labor, 212. See Socialists, Internati Workingmen's Association, lish workers.

Mason-Slidell incident, 196.

Mathew, Father, temperance former and abolitionist, 69.

McDuffie, George, 73, 152; alliance of abolitionists and cals, 107, 134, 139; ci., 40.

Memminger, C. C., on dange manufactures to South, 56.

Mexican War, 127, 144; labor tests, 115; Liberty party dema end, 138.

, John C., leaves Democratic
ty over slavery question, 143-
.

e, Ely, favors alliance of labor
I slaveholders, 104.

is, Thomas, effect of slavery
labor, 64; on alliance of slave-
ver and money power, 109-
.

s, Isaac, Negro delegate to
ional Labor Union, 215.

nal Colored Labor Union, 207,
.

nal Industrial Congress, con-
ns slavery, 118-119; opposes
praska Act and Fugitive Slave
v, 118-119; endorses Liberty
ty, 139.

nal Labor Party, 210.

nal Labor Union, on new
ks of labor, 205; and the First
rnational, 211-212; and Negro
or, 213-215.

ism, in Republican party, 153,
; repudiated by Republicans,
, 168; in Confederacy, 199.

German-American laborers,
h-American laborers, Immi-
nts.

es, free, competition with
thern white labor, 36-37;
us in South, 36-37; laws
inst in South, 48-49; in North,
anti-slavery activities, 53;
petition with Northern white
or, 65-70, 184-189; attitude of
ublican party, 149-150; in
il War, 181-182; in Reconstruc-
, 206-208; demands of freed-
, 206-207; and post-war la-
movement, 212-216. See
glass, Myers, National Col-
d Labor Union, Slavery,
es.

New England Association of Mechanics and Workingmen, on
abolition, 83; will not fight for
slavery, 74; urged to unite with
abolitionists, 95; opposes Mexican
War, 115; *New England Artisan,*
83, ci., 79.

New England Labor Reform
League, endorses Liberty party,
139.

Nicholson, James B., chairman of
Philadelphia labor conference,
178-179.

Nordhoff, Charles, anti-slavery
writer, ci., 32, 34, 49.

Oberkleine, Frederick, leader of
German Workingmen's Society,
174.

O'Connell, Daniel, Irish abolitionist, 69-70, 200.

Olmsted, Frederick Law, traveler
in South, 35; ci., 30, 35, 38, 47,
53, 58.

Owen, Robert, Utopian socialist, 20,
99.

Owen, Robert Dale, Utopian socialist, 87; on slavery and abolition,
88; on annexation of Texas, 115.

Palfrey, John G., anti-slavery writer,
50.

Phillips, Wendell, abolitionist, 70;
on labor question, 92, 204-205.

Pickens, F. W., on political role of
labor, 40, 152; on crisis of slavery,
96; on alliance of labor and slaveholders, 105; threatens to stir up
insurrection, 108; on free labor,
204.

Pickering, John, compares laborers
with slaves, 80-81; on abolition,
85.

Popular sovereignty, 145.

Pro-slavery, forces, 22; arguments, 57-60, 96-103, 130-131; position of labor spokesmen, 81-82; *Southern Quarterly Review*, ci., 102. See Calhoun, Estes, Fitzhugh, Grayson, Hammond, Harper, Las Casas, McDuffie, Pickens, Ruffin, Slaveholders, Toombs, Van Deren, Walsh.

Purcell, Edward, favors emancipation, 195.

Purcell, John B., favors emancipation, 195.

Randolph, John, on alliance of planters and laborers, 105.

Raymond, Daniel, political economist, ci., 28.

Rayner, Kenneth, on taxes in South, 42-43.

Republican party, and land reformers, 21; formation, 147-154; election of 1860, 154-169; pro-business policy, 183; appeals for labor's support of emancipation, 199; and Negroes, 208. See Emancipation, Fremont, Greeley, Lincoln, Schurz, Seward, Sumner.

Rogers, Nathaniel P., abolitionist editor, 73.

Ruffin, Edmund, opposes universal suffrage, 40; defines slavery, 100; on secession, 171.

Schools, public, in South, 41-42; demanded, 207.

Schurz, Carl, and nativism, 163; and emancipation, 195; ci., 126.

Secession, threatened, 108, 154, 164; crisis, 170-180.

Sedgwick, Theodore, political economist, on slavery and labor, 64.

Seward, William, on sectional balance, 112; on Fugitive Slave Law, 126; "irrepressible conflict," 128;

on conflict between slaveh[ ] and freemen, 149, 162.

Simpson, Stephen, compares [ ]ers with slaves, 80.

Slaveholders, on free society[ ] free labor, 38-40, 101-102, 106, 150-151, 160, 199-201; in South, 55-60; fear grow[ ] capitalism, 95-96; alliance [ ] Northern workers, 103-107[ ] peal to capitalists to oppose[ ] tion, 107-110; alliance with [ ]tal, 114, 138; and Demo[ ] party, 143; demand for co[ ]tion of their land, 207. See [ ] power, South.

Slave-power, 111 ff., 117, 118[ ] 143, 146, 149, 150, 155, 156[ ] 183, 191, 193, 194, 202, 204; spiracy," 122-133, 152-153, [ ] See Slaveholders, South.

Slavery, effect on Southern [ ] 28-43; effect on Northern [ ] 61-65, 150; menace to demo[ ] 70-76; compared with wage[ ] ery by labor reformers, 77-8[ ] Southerners, 96-101; Repu[ ] policy, 147-149; extension, s[ ] pansion, Territories, Slave-[ ] "conspiracy." See Anti-Sl[ ] movement, Abolitionists, E[ ] cipation, Pro-Slavery, Slav[ ]ers, Slaves.

Slaves, resistance to slavery, [ ] in Southern industry, 46-4[ ] in Civil War, 181-182, 19[ ] See Slavery.

Smith, Gerrit, land reforme[ ] abolitionist, 138, 147; L[ ] party candidate for Pres[ ] 139.

Socialists, Utopian, 20, 99; on [ ]tion, 86-88; on annexatio[ ] Texas, 114; *The Harbinge[ ]* 114; *The Phalanx*, ci., 8[ ]

, *The New Harmony Ga-
e,* ci., 88; Marxian, 21; oppo-
n to slavery in the South,
in North, 74, 167; support
ublicans, 153, 167-168; *San
onio Zeitung,* 54. See Asso-
onists, Brisbane, Considerant,
ai, Fourier, Greeley, Hein-
International Working-
's Association, Owen, Weit-
, Weydemeyer, Wright.

slavery and workers, 28-43;
lic schools, 41-42; taxation,
3; anti-slavery movement, 43-
emigration of workers, 43-
laws against free Negroes,
9; abolitionists, 50-55; rule of
:holders, 55-60; industrializa-
, 55-57; and Homestead bill,
164; disaffection during Civil
, 193-194. See Confederacy,
ssion, Slavery.

L. W., on laws against Ne-
mechanics, 48.

d, Ira, on labor's demands,
205.

, repression in South, 38; at
legar iron works, 46-47; Lin-
's views, 158-159; during
War, 183, 185, 189, 191,
by Negroes in South, 206.

r, Charles, on nationaliza-
of slavery, 127; supported by
e, 145; on slave-power, 146.

William, president of mold-
union, 178; on labor's loy-
180-181; on conscription,
on emancipation, 194;
ge in philosophy, 203; on
e-breaking, 204; on tasks of
r, 205-206; on labor politics,
209; and First International,
212; urges cooperation with
ro labor, 212-214; ci., 211.

Tappan, brothers, support Liberty
party, 138; Lewis, on slavery in
territories, 117.

Taxation, in South, 42-43.

Taylor, John, on alliance of labor
and slaveholders, 107.

Territories, slavery in, 111-122, 144,
145, 147, 148, 163. See Expansion,
Kansas-Nebraska Act, Manifest
destiny, Mexican War, Popular
sovereignty, Republican party,
Texas, Wilmot.

Texas, annexation of, 112-115, 118,
134.

Tharin, Robert, tries to publish
labor paper, 49.

Toombs, Robert, racist views, 58.

Touchstone, James, anti-slavery
labor leader, 176, 179-180.

Trevellick, Richard, president of
National Labor Union, 214.

Trumbull, Lyman, Senator, 149-
150.

Tubman, Harriet, rescue of slaves,
24.

Union Leagues, 207.

Van Buren, Martin, 147; supported
by Harper, 106; attacked by
merchants, 109.

Van Deren, Dumas, pro-slavery
editor, 127.

Walsh, Michael, compares slaves
with laborers, 79; defends slavery, 81-82, 122; endorses pro-
slavery policies, 104-105.

Ware, N. A., political economist,
ci., 34.

Weitling, Wilhelm, Utopian socialist, 20; on abolition, 166.

West, William, land reformer, ci.,
85.

Weston, George, anti-slavery writer, ci., 59, 150.

Weydemeyer, Joseph, on Kansas-Nebraska Act, 121; on slavery, 166-168; and election of 1860, 168.

Whaley, J. C., president of National Labor Union convention, 213.

Whig party, 148; and businessmen, 103; demise, 143, 147; and Fugitive Slave Law, 145; "Conscience Whigs," 146.

Whittier, John G., "The Yankee Girl," anti-slavery poem, 72-73.

Wickliffe, Robert, ci., 42.

Wilmot, David, proviso a[g] slavery in territories, 116, 11[8] 145; on slavery, 117.

Wilson, Henry, Republican s[p] man, 162.

Windom, William, Republican gressman, 164.

Wood, A. H., on labor and [a] tion, 65.

Workers. See Labor, Labor r ment.

Wright, Frances, Utopian soc 20; on slavery and abolitio[n]